D0935982

Ireland before and after the Famine

CORMAC Ó GRÁDA

Ireland
before and after the Famine
Explorations in economic history, 1800–1925

Manchester University Press

Distributed exclusively in the USA and Canada by
St. Martin's Press, New York

Published by Manchester University Press
Oxford Road, Manchester M13 9PL, UK
Distributed exclusively in the USA and Canada
by St. Martin's Press, Inc.,
Room 400, 175 Fifth Avenue, New York, NY 10010, USA

British Library cataloguing in publication data
Ó Gráda, Cormac
    Ireland before and after the famine:
    explorations in economic history 1800-1925.
    1. Ireland—Economic conditions
    I. Title
    330.9415'081   HC260.5

Library of Congress cataloging in publication data applied for

ISBN 0-7190-1785-8 *hardback*

Printed in Great Britain
by Billing & Sons Limited, Worcester
Typesetting by H. Hems, Tower House, Queen Street, Gillingham, Dorset

CONTENTS

Preface   *page* vi

1   Poverty and progress: the pre-Famine economy   1

2   Agriculture before and after the Famine   46

3   The Famine: incidence and ideology   78

4   Of bullocks and men: agricultural change after the Famine   128

5   Inheritance, emigration and fertility   153

Index   177

PREFACE

This is not my attempt at writing *The* (or even *An*) Economic History of Nineteenth-Century Ireland. Despite the long gestation period of these pages, their focus is too narrow for that, seldom straying far from issues agricultural and demographic. Instead I offer a series of integrated studies, bearing on aspects of pre- and post-famine history that made Ireland special. The approach is interdisciplinary. I learned my history late, after regular schooling in economics. The book probably reflects this, but I have kept formal economic theorising to a minimum, and the embarrassingly large number of notes shows that I have learned something from the historians.

Cross-references from chapter to chapter are frequent. Still, each originally lived a life of its own for a while in draft form. An earlier version of chapter 5 was presented to the Conference of Irish and French Historians on Peasants, held in Paris in March 1983. Themes in chapter 1 were prompted by my participation in a small way in the on-going *New History of Ireland*, while some parts of chapters 2 and 4 have their origins in my Columbia doctoral thesis and in a presentation to the International Economic History Conference in Edinburgh in August 1978. Chapter 3 reflects work in progress for a monograph on the Great Famine. While none of the material here has appeared in print before, parts of chapters 1, 2 and 4 borrow from work of mine published in *The Journal of European Economic History, Hermathena, Studia Hibernica*, and *The New History of Ireland*, vol. 5. Besides, in chapters 1–3 I have used some of the results of joint work with Bob Allen, Phelim Boyle, and Joel Mokyr.

Those interested in Irish economic history tend to be a sociable band, and I value highly that camaraderie. *Aithníonn ciaróg ciaróg eile* (One beetle recognises another). It is a pleasure to thank those who have helped in various ways. I have probably learned most from Bob Allen, Austin Bourke, Louis Cullen, David Dickson, David Fitzpatrick, Liam Kennedy, John McManus, Joel Mokyr and Peter Solar. The last two especially have been an inspiration over the past decade or so, and have purged me of many errors and foolish notions. I must also thank Phelim Boyle, Mary Daly, Fergus D'Arcy, Michael Edelstein, Paddy Geary, Tim Guinnane, Patrick Honohan, Michael Laffan, Joseph Lee, Moore McDowell, Tim O'Neill, John Sheehan, Brendan Walsh, Sarah Ward-Perkins and Ron Weir for comments, clues and suggestions at various stages. Ed Buckmaster drew the map describing prefamine population change.

I am grateful to the Bank of Ireland and Allied Irish Banks for access to their nineteenth-century records, and to the Dublin and Belfast Public Record Offices, the Department of Irish Folklore, University College, Dublin, and the National Library for permission to quote from material in their possession.

And so *'mo bheannacht leat, a scríbhinn.'*

Dublin, March 1987

Do mo mhuintir

CHAPTER 1

Poverty and progress:
the pre-Famine economy

The comforts of the upper and middle classes have improved . . . The
state of society is better . . . The lowest class of all, the mere labourer,
is the only one whose advancement is ot evident. [Jonathan Pim,
1848[1]]

Mo mhíle slán do na fataí bána,
  Ba subhach an áit a bheith in aice leo,
Ba fáilí soineannta iad ag tíocht chun láithreach,
  Agus iad ag gáirí linn ar cheann an bhoird.
                                    [Peatsaí Ó Callanáin[2]]

Pre-Famine Ireland has become the classic 'Malthusian country'.
Odd, then, that as a source of insights on population and
economics Thomas Malthus himself dwelt little on the island next
door. Between 1798, when he became a celebrity, and his death in
1834 he never allowed it more than a few passing comments in
the different editions of the *Essay on Population* and the *Principles
of Political Economy*. It took substantial fees from the fledgling
Edinburgh Review to get him to produce—anonymously and at
speed—two review articles on Irish population in 1808–09. His
oral evidence on Ireland before the Emigration Commissioners of
1826 was reluctant, uninspired and laconic. Malthus, it seems, was
just not much interested in Ireland, and this may explain why his
only trip there in 1817 was a purely family affair.[3]

  Given Ireland's pre-eminent role in Malthusian exegesis, the
lack of attention from the man himself is curious. Still, why
Ireland was to become the classic 'Malthusian country' is no
mystery. The headlong population growth, the poverty and subdivision, the over-dependence on a single source of food, and the
culmination of all of these in the great Famine, would seem
ready-made ingredients for a classic Malthusian tale. Even if the
huge rise in population since the mid-eighteenth century was
spurred on by a 'gap in famines' for a few decades, surely the
series of mini-famines that struck from the turn of the new
century onwards sounded ample warning of impending doom?
This is one of the messages of the late Kenneth Connell's classic

monograph on Irish population, and it is hardly surprising to find it repeated in the recent outcrop of Malthusian reinterpretation. Pre-Famine Ireland has thus become 'a case study in Malthusian economics', a 'rabbit warren' where poverty and a 'vortex of sub-division' led to the 'ultimate Malthusian catastrophe' of 1846–50. The 'awful remedy', the Great Famine, cruelly 'dramatised the risks of improvident marriage' and marked Irish population trends for a century to come.[4]

1. Pre-Famine famines

A basic premise of this way of looking at pre-Famine Ireland is that the potato, staple fare of the impoverished masses, failed often and disastrously—one year in every two or three—before 1845, and that matters were growing steadily worse with time. The poor harvests of 1800–01, 1816–18, 1822 and 1831 particularly stand out, but partial potato scarcities in other years too seem to add support for this view. And so in June 1827 one reads of draper and schoolteacher Amhlaoimh Ó Súileabháin joining some of his middle-class friends in doling out maize to the poor of Callan in County Kilkenny. Three years later the same poor were again close to 'an gorta gorm' ('blue starvation'). Just a year later the starving poor of Erris in west Mayo were reportedly eating from the carcases of five porpoises, washed up on the beach. For part of the summer of 1836 islanders off the west coast of Donegal survived largely on periwinkles and seaweed. Again, in July 1842 the young William Thackeray saw women picking nettles and weeds for food near Naas, within twenty miles of Dublin.[5] Such examples are legion throughout the pre-Famine period. They prompt the question: how great was the excess mortality in bad years before 1845?

The calamitous famine of 1740–41 ranks as that century's worst by far. If recent attempts to calculate the ensuing excess mortality are worth anything, they imply that the loss then was proportionately greater than even during the Great Famine.[6] Other subsistence crises followed, notably in 1755, 1766 and 1782–83, but their demographic impact is elusive.[7] However, excess mortality from famine and starvation between 1800 and 1845 seems to have been of modest proportions. Precise calculations are impossible, but here are some clues. First, consider the answers of hundreds of witnesses—clergymen, magistrates and the like—from all over the country to the following question from the Irish Poor Inquiry Commissioners in 1835: 'Are any persons known to have died from actual destitution in your parish within the last three years?' Some replies, to be sure, speak of famine deaths. One such from a Mayo priest told of six persons dying of 'actual want' in his parish in 1831. A Kildare colleague had heard of 'one Kelly, a weaver in Clane, a diffident bashful creature, who is said to have died of starvation'. Several other replies referred to 'strangers' or 'travelling beggars' dying.[8] Yet a content analysis of the replies yields a different picture overall.

TABLE 1 Answers to Poor Inquiry questionnaire on starvation deaths, 1835/6 (% in parenthesis)

No, never, etc.	417 (85·1)	121 (76·1)	625 (95·0)	348 (83·3)
Indirectly only, hearsay evidence	62 (12·7)	27 (17·0)	29 (4·4)	57 (13·3)
Yes	11 (2·2)	3 (1·9)	3 (0·5)	9 (2·2)
Yes, but before 1832	0 (0·0)	8 (6·9)	1 (0·2)	4 (1·0)

In table 1 most of the references under the second heading are to what one witness called 'death inch by inch', deaths due more to enduring privation and hardship than literal starvation or starvation-induced disease at times of crop failure. The Connacht figures reflect the crisis of 1831.[9] Still, the impression overall is of individual deaths from destitution rather than general mortality crises at times of crop failure.

A second source is surgeon William Wilde's account of pre-famine famines in the 1851 census report. Indeed, this is the standard source on the subject, generating the longest running quotation in George O'Brien's hastily written but enduring *Economic History of Ireland from the Union to the Famine*.[10] Wilde's technique of producing a long and gruesome litany of earlier famines created an impression, which greatly influenced later accounts, of very few famine-free years after about 1700. Shortages and famine deaths there certainly were, but Wilde's account in the wake of *Phythophthora infestans* is worth comparing with his corresponding report for the 1841 census commissioners. His analysis of the hundreds of thousands of deaths retrospectively recorded in 1841 by the enumerators for the 1830s, with 'statistical nosology' and a 'special sanitary report on Dublin City', followed by over 200 pages of small-type cross-tabulations, was thorough and innovative.[11]

Under the heading of 'causes of death' Wilde's tabulations record 117 due to famine. The number is an underestimate, for three obvious reasons. First, few die of starvation in the literal sense during famines; diseases such as dysentry, relapsing fever and typhus do the damage, often when the worst of the food shortage is over. Yet Wilde paid no attention to famine-related causes in the earlier report either. Second, paupers who lived alone and died of hunger left no survivors to tell the tale to the enumerators. Third, one may well imagine some element of stigma in survivors ascribing a death in the family to famine, much as with suicide today. While his record of famine's toll during the 1830s therefore must not be taken literally, a comparison with the numbers attributed to some other given causes of death is still revealing. Against the 117 put down to starvation in the 1830s, there were 7,072 drownings, 197 were hanged, 3,508 murders, 1,239 deaths from alcoholic excess, 4,349 from burns. This seems consistent with our story of light pre-Famine *crises de subsistence*.

A third source is Francis Barker and John Cheyne's survey of the 1816–18 famine-related fever epidemics, the most complete contemporary account of early nineteenth-century famines. According to these eminent Dublin medical men, excess mortality in that crisis reached about 60,000.[12] This is no more than a careful, informed guess. For what they are worth, the numbers dying—mostly from fever rather than literal starvation—highlight Irish backwardness relative to the rest of the United Kingdom. They also indicate that this, one of the worst—if not the worst—of the earlier crises was trivial compared to 1846–50. More interestingly, perhaps, Barker and Cheyne's figure also implies that excess mortality was proportionately far less in Ireland during 1816–18 than in other parts of Europe. The 60,000 deaths were Ireland's share of what has been with some historic licence called the 'last great subsistence crisis of the Western world' by John Post.[13] Post's work records far higher mortality in those years in regions of Italy, Switzerland, Germany and Austria-Hungary. Barker and Cheyne's guess may also be compared with Thomas Newenham's estimate of 40,000 excess deaths—about 0·8 per cent of the population—during the 'two years of scarcity' of 1800–01.[14]

The famine of 1822 was confined to the west. For a few months it seemed to threaten hundreds of thousands, but in the end its toll was low: Barker, by then secretary to the General Board of Health, was at pains to stress that 'the mortality ha[d] been inconsiderable'. Professor Tim O'Neill, historian of this famine, concurs. Barker's officials kept statistics of distress and fever, and had mortality been high the data would surely have been published. The silence of the Board of Health, along with other evidence, leads O'Neill to conclude that 'it is certain that the figure was so small that it was not even mentioned'.[15] The winter and spring of 1831 also brought hard times, especially in Connacht.

Conditions were certainly not deteriorating over time in this sense, however. Though distress returned at different times—to Mayo in 1835, to Donegal in 1836–37, to the west generally in 1839—the stretch between 1832 and 1845 probably produced fewer deaths from hunger than any fourteen-year period since 1741. Ironically, had the potato famine of 1845 lasted just one year, it would probably have merited no more than a few paragraphs in the history books. Despite the destruction of almost half the potato crop, few deaths from hunger occurred; only in the wake of the even more serious failure of the summer of 1846 did casualties begin to mount. One likely reason for the improvement with time must not be forgotten: the increasing effectiveness of relief measures in the pre-Famine period. As O'Neill concludes in his study of pre-famine Erris, Ireland's Ultima Thule:[16]

> A common feature of all these [crises] was the ability of Erris to survive on the brink. Erris did have famine deaths before the Great Famine but these were rare. A complicated system of subsistence had evolved where local, national, and English charity combined with public works and food ships to get through in the difficult months whenever crop failure occurred.

In Erris as elsewhere, increasing population undoubtedly produced greater mass poverty. The link between such impoverishment and subsistence crises is not so clear cut, though. Malthus, of course, included famine in the armoury of positive checks to overpopulation:

> Famine seems to be the last, the most dreadful resource of nature. The vices of mankind are active and able ministers of depopulation. They are the precursors in the great army of destruction; and often finish the dreadful work themselves. But should they fail in this war of extermination, sickly seasons, epidemics, pestilence, and plague, advance in terrific array, and sweep off their thousands and ten thousands. Should success be still incomplete, gigantic inevitable famine stalks in the rear, and with one mighty blow, levels the population with the food of the world.

This extract from the First Essay could have been written with the Great Irish Famine in mind! Yet it is reassuring to find that, even in his small output on Ireland, Malthus himself leaves room for a different interpretation, which fits what seems to have happened before 1845 much better. In the first of his two anonymous contributions to the *Edinburgh Review* he produces quite a benign and hopeful prognosis of Ireland's struggle with overpopualtion, stressing the power of the preventive check, and explicitly ruling out a catastrophe such as the Great Famine: 'although it is quite certain', he wrote, 'that the population of Ireland cannot continue permanently to increase at its present rate, yet is as certain that it will not *suddenly* come to a stop'. Though a far higher population might be anticipated in time, in due course 'the habits necessary for an order of things in which the funds for the maintenance of labour are stationary' would ensure that supply would not outstrip the demand for labour.[17] The issue, then, is not so much 'Was Malthus right?' as *which* Malthus fits pre-Famine trends best? Between 1808, when those last-quoted words were written, and the mid-1840s Ireland's population was to rise another 50 per cent. Land hunger and structural unemployment were to intensify the hardships facing the poor. Yet economically and demographically the country was showing some signs too of the preventive check mechanism envisaged by Malthus. Comparing the 1821, 1831 and 1841 censuses fails to tell the full story, because taking the previous two or three pre-censal decades into account reveals a picture of continuous deceleration in population growth between Union and Famine.

Fig. 1 describes population growth by barony between 1821 and 1841. Clearly the pattern varied greatly across the island. In the area east of a line linking Waterford, Athenry and Derry the rate of growth was modest. Worryingly, however, population growth was most vigorous in what must have been the poorest areas, and where the famine was most murderous. Evidence of a perverse, explosive demographic response before 1845? While the island as a whole showed some signs of demographic adjustment,[18] one plausible reading of the map is that the adjustment was most radical where it was least needed. In this scenario, as explained by Joel Mokyr, 'population grew unrestrained, continuously exacerbating poverty, thus making the resolution of the problem by a catastrophe ultimately inevitable'.[19] This is not the full story, for the following reason. While population growth in the west and south-west was highest there in Ireland in 1821–41, it was also highest there before then. Moreover the drop in those areas seems to have been greater than average.

That is the implication of comparing county population growth rates after 1821 with the estimated growth in house numbers between 1791 and 1821.[20] The latter suggests headlong growth in much of the west before 1821, with annual rates above 2 per cent in several counties. But that pace did not persist. In the five fastest-growing counties in 1791–1821—Galway, Clare, Cavan, Kerry and Mayo—the increase in house numbers averaged an annual rate of 2·1 per cent. In 1821–41 that had given way to a

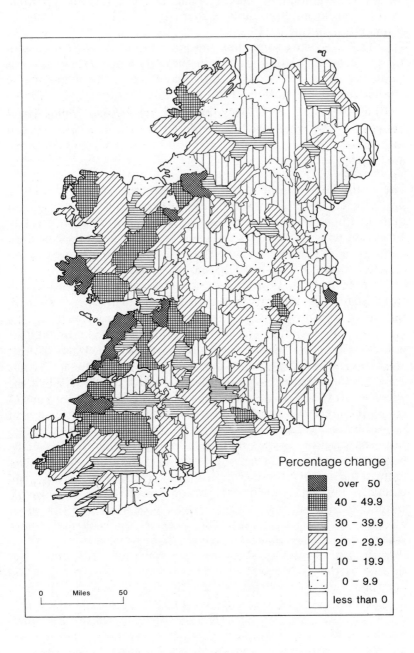

Percentage change

- over 50
- 40 – 49.9
- 30 – 39.9
- 20 – 29.9
- 10 – 19.9
- 0 – 9.9
- less than 0

0   Miles   50

Fig. 1 Population change, 1821–41

rate of population growth of 1·4 per cent. The implied adjustment would be magnified by making some allowance for the probable increase in mean household size before 1821, and for under-enumeration in the 1821 census.

True, it takes some imagination to consider a region with 1·5 per cent population growth in the early nineteenth century as 'adjusting' downwards. But in the conduct of its demographic affairs Ireland was nothing if not different. Presumably the adjustment would have continued in that might-have-been Ireland without the potato blight in the late 1840s.

2. The potato

The chronology of the potato's diffusion in Ireland cannot be precisely documented. From Cuzco in Peru it reached the dinner table of Philip II of Spain in 1565, and spread from Spain to Italy and elsewhere in Europe. In Ireland it was sometimes called *an spáinneach* in the early days, suggesting that to some Spaniard (and not to Sir Walter Raleigh) should go the credit for its introduction to Ireland. If indeed the potato reached Ireland directly from Spain, Galway rather than somewhere in the south may have been the point of entry. Potato diffusion continues to be a great topic of historical speculation, but at least we know that the new root crop was in use in Munster as a seasonal garden root crop, playing the part of cabbage or fresh carrots today, by the early seventeenth century. By about 1660 the fictional peasant alliance of the Rabelaisian classic *Pairlement Chloinne Tomáis* could threaten to boycott their exploiters, the millers, for a year 'acht bheith ag bruith phise, phonra, phutataoi agus mheacan; agus leis sin go gcuirfedis na muilteoiridhe don ghorta' ('and . . . boil peas, beans, potatoes and parsnips; and thus they would reduce the millers to starvation'). As keeping quality and yield gradually improved, the potato found favour with rich and poor alike. For the middle classes it was a delicacy, for the poor increasingly a substitute for dairy, cereal or bean-based foods. When did this process become 'over-specialisation'? Over-specialisation is part of standard pre-Famine historiography. Yet as long as the potato was just one element in the people's food portfolio it must have helped reduce the risks of famine.[21] Perhaps it was still so in the 1770s, when Arthur Young gave an enthusiastic account of it. As late as 1802 a Kilkenny gentleman might reminisce:[22]

> Before the introduction of a kind called the apple potatoe, the great portion of the sustenance of the poor here, consisted of oaten bread

and milk; from April to August barley bread was sometimes used, and in the hilly part of the parish [Fiddown] rye bread: but since the cultivation of apple potatoes has become general, the poor continue to eat them until the new potatoes come in. Before their introduction, the cottagers frequently sowed beans and esculent vegetables, and had little plots somewhat like a small kitchen garden, at the rere of their cabbins, but the apple potatoe has superceded everything of this sort.

Amhlaoimh Ó Súileabháin could also remember a time in Kilkenny 'when every capable tenant farmer had peas and beans, until potatoes made them old-fashioned'. In the 1820s, however, 'it [was] rare to see them planted other than by the gentry'. Again, in south Derry the switch to total reliance on the potato, this time from rye, came late enough for Sampson, the Dublin Society's reporter, to note it in 1802.[23] Presumably the potato's dominance in the south dates further back. In any case, potato acreage and dependence continued to increase right up to the Famine. By 1845 the crop's share in the tilled acreage was little short of one-third, and about three million people were almost exclusively dependent on it for food. Even if Austin Bourke's ingenious estimates of total consumption in a typical pre-Famine year exaggerate a little,[24] they nevertheless describe a reality that is difficult to properly absorb today.

In retrospect the dangers for both labourer and farmer are only too clear. Twenty-twenty hindsight vision may exaggerate their foolhardiness, however: if deaths from starvation were few and far between before 1845, then on the basis of information available to them their specialisation may have been sensible. Clearly the conditional probability of disaster, in the event of near-total potato harvest failure—not to speak of three-time failure—was high. Yet the real issue is the riskiness of the potato itself, compounded by non-storability and non-transportability, as highlighted by Oliver MacDonagh and by Joel Mokyr.[25] Unfortunately the basic data—year-by-year yields—are lacking. Mokyr has ingeniously attempted to get round the problem by appealing to contemporary French potato and grain yields, and found that potato yields fluctuated more. Perhaps this loads the dice somewhat against the potato, since pre-Famine Irish grain yields may also have been more variable than French.[26] Yet, whatever about the potato's vulnerability on this score, it was increased by higher transport and storage costs. That it cost more to store potatoes than grain is shown by the much greater seasonal trough-to-peak rise in potato prices (discussed in chapter 3). Mokyr argues from contemporary evidence that carrying potatoes over even short distances added appreciably to their price, thereby increasing the risk of famine. One is thus left with conflicting qualitative impressions and assertions. Against Charles Trevelyan, who claimed (after the event) that 'wise people' foresaw it all, there was the Irish economist Mountifort Longfield, who reminded a Trinity College audience just over a decade earlier:[27]

> Potatoes appear to be in bad repute among political economists. Some even hint that the poverty of Ireland is in great measure to be attributed to the use of this food. The strongest objection which is urged against the use of potatoes arises from the impossibility of storing them from one year to another. This is undoubtedly a disadvantage, which, however, I think is compensated by the utility of potatoes as food for cattle. This use, as it were, stores them up for succeeding years . . . Although potatoes cannot be easily hoarded or exported, yet pigs can; and potatoes may be considered as the raw materials of which pigs are manufactured. But whatever be the staple food of the people, if the nation is poor, a dearth will occasionally occur; and if we look at the history of England, or any country at a time when it was as poor as Ireland is now, we shall find that dearths and famines were more frequent there, and more tremendous in their effects than they have been in Ireland during the last thirty years.

Similarly positive claims for the potato were made by the novelist Maria Edgeworth and the Wexford agronomist, Martin Doyle. Also emphatic was the land agent Steuart Trench. 'There is no greater fallacy,' he wrote of the pre-Famine era, 'than to suppose that the potato at that time was an uncertain crop . . . My turnips were sometimes poor and thin in dry and parching weather; my wheat sometimes smutty, and did not turn out well under the flail; but, if I manured my land well, I was always certain of my potato crop.' But Doyle's namesake, the Catholic Bishop of Kildare and Leighlin, was less enthusiastic: he felt that, should a failure occur, 'famine and pestilence will set in together and rid us probably of a million'. The impressions gained from the literature before 1845 are thus conflicting, though it must be said that the discussion takes on a more sombre hue after about 1825.[28]

An advantage of the potato (compared to, say, the turnip) was that its flexibility as food for both man and beast probably led to some 'over-production' in average years. By May or June when the previous year's stocks began to spoil there was usually some buffer stock left over for pigs and hens. Mild crop failures would therefore make for thinner animals, not famine. By contrast, in underdeveloped countries today the bulk of the output of staple foods goes on human consumption or seed, with livestock typically accounting for 10 per cent or less: but half or less of

Irish potato production was destined for human consumption. Nor should the role of potato variety in spreading risk be overlooked. Varieties differed not only in taste, shape and colour but in use and in planting and growing time. Risk-spreading between varieties could substitute to some unknown extent for risk-spreading between crops. Take the following passage from one of the best of the Dublin Society's statistical surveys, that for county Kilkenny:[29]

> The varieties usually planted here are the *English reds*, the *apple*, and a few *white eyes* for early use: the first are ill-tasted, often wet, of a livid red without, and having a reddish circle within; they are cultivated because they produce good crops with little manure, and sometimes in fallow ground without any; they are rather early, and remarkable for producing no apples, though they blossom; they succeeded the *Turks* and *high-cauled caps*, which grow well in poor ground, and are still continued in some places: the *apple potatoes* were first introduced and planted in this country, between forty and fifty years ago, by the late Sir William Fownes; from whence they became general, and are invaluable to the poor, as they will keep longer than any other, by which means they will have potatoes all the year round; and they succeed better for being planted late, that is, in the latter end of May, and even in the first week of June; the *great apple* is a variety that some farmers possess: *Barber's wonders* are large, dry, and early, and fit for cattle; they are planted in many places; their disposition lately to the curl has been noticed: *Wicklow bangers* have the good qualities of the last sort, and have been raised by several persons: the *black potatoe* is not known much here . . . : a kind called *coppers* has been tried, and are said to grow too near the surface in a dry season: *pink-eyes* are long, dry, and early: many other early varieties are sown, one of the best is the *flat Spanish* . . .

Surely a conscious policy of adding and using varieties as insurance is indicated in this passage, written in 1801 or 1802. The point carries less force later, though. On the eve of the Famine one major variety, the lumper, bulked large in the diet of the poor, and the lumper and another variety, the cup, probably accounted for most of the acreage under potatoes. Ironically the lumper, which proved disastrous against blight after 1845, had been introduced at least in part for its resistance to a plant disease called 'curl'.

In the circumstances, was the shift to 'the' potato as fool-hardy as all that? At a minimum, the historian must guard against libelling the pre-Famine poor, against being over-critical after the event of the potato's record before 1845. Admittedly, then as now, there were people who argued sensibly that sole reliance on one kind of food is in principle unsound. Yet the potato's pre-blight history made something like the three-time shortfall of 1845–47 unprecedented and unimaginable. Even the worst medieval famines involved less. And if the 1820s and 1830s bore the hallmarks of overcommitment to the root, surely automatic, instantaneous adjustment is not to be expected. In retrospect we may well see the pre-Famine 'potato people' as living on a popula-tion bomb, yet they, on the basis of their experience before 1845, must have had no inkling of the dangers.

A striking aspect of the remarks about scarcity by Thackeray and others quoted earlier, and more in the same vein, is that they so often refer to the summer months. This is a reminder that seasonal shortages and the associated change in dietary regime—'July an chabáiste' ('July of the cabbage'), 'buidhemis brothallach biadh-ghann' ('sultry, food-scarce July'), 'the meal months'—must be distinguished from famine in the strict sense. At the same time there is no denying the problem of seasonal scarcity for the rural poor. Evidence presented to the Poor Inquiry suggested that 'the labourer never has any of his conacre potatoes remaining at the period when they become unfit for use; the greater number have used tham all at the beginning of April and scarcely one has a potato remaining at the 1st of May.'[30] This was so even though the durability of the potato seems to have increased over time. In the seventeenth century it was mainly a summer food, but the development of the famous apple marked a giant step forward. However, not even the apple could keep properly over a twelve-month, and neither the cup nor the lumper matched the apple's keeping quality.[31] The result was serious privation for a number of weeks, and sore stomachs for those who tried the new crop too soon.

A final boon of the potato should be remembered: thanks to its high nutritional content the pre-Famine Irish did not suffer much from common scourges of the hungry masses such as scurvy, pellagra and ophthalmia. All these diseases were rampant during the Great Famine. After the Famine living standards rose, but the nutritional content of the average diet seems to have fallen off.[32]

3. Irish poverty

For the Devon Commissioners who investigated Irish land tenure just before the Famine the 'sufferings . . . borne with exemplary patience' by Ireland's poor 'were greater than the people of any other country in Europe [had] to sustain'. What Wakefield saw as 'human nature degraded to the lowest state of misery' Henry

Inglis thought 'shocking for humanity to contemplate'.[33]
Individual examples of hardship are documented in profusion, in
the Poor Inquiry, in the annual reports of the Poor Law commissioners, and elsewhere.[34] A broader discussion of poverty
raises two immediate issues. First, who were the poor? By today's
standards nearly everybody would have qualified, but presumably
what is wanted is some kind of contemporary criterion of the
'poverty line'. Any definition referring to conditions on the eve
of the Famine would surely therefore encompass the 3 million
'potato people' (i.e. those almost totally dependent on the potato
for food), or the 2·4 million or so judged by the Poor Inquiry
commissioners in 1836 to be potential claimants on assistance.
This is also close to the number dependent on relief in one form
or another at the height of the Famine. These bottom two-fifths
of the population were the landless or semi-landless, the ragged
inhabitants of smoky 'fourth class' hovels, who rarely failed to
shock or impress travellers and observers.[35] Scarcely different
were many 'third class' householders, a diverse group accounting
for another two-fifths of the population in all.

Second, how poor? This depends somewhat on the measuring
rod. The pre-Famine poor seem poorer by some standards (for
example, tea and sugar consumption, housing) than others (for
example, life expectancy, literacy). As Sandberg[36] in a recent
essay on Gerschenkron's theoretical framework reminds us,
seeking an all-purpose invariable standard of poverty and backwardness may be futile. Contemporaries did not bother much with
the obvious candidates—income per head or real wage levels—nor
are they all that enlightening in the Irish case. The stock objection
against the first is that it overlooks income distribution, yet a
comparison of income estimates still usefully underlines Ireland's
backwardness.

According to Mokyr income per head in Ireland on the eve of
the Famine was £10 or so, in Britain about double that. By this
criterion alone Ireland was very poor indeed by European
standards.[37] Admittedly the comparison assumes purchasing
power parity, but it has been known at least since Ricardo's time
that the law of one price must be qualified when comparing
economies such as Ireland and Britain. Non-traded goods tend to
be dearer 'in countries where manufactures flourish'. Several
modern studies confirm that the law militates against poorer
countries. Measuring the real income gap between underdeveloped
and developed economies today by benchmarks other than the
official exchange rate—by US factor cost or some other weighting
device—nearly always reduces the gap between rich and poor. Thus

in a sample of fifteen underdeveloped countries analysed by Maddison, income per head rose from an average of 8·8 per cent of the US 1965 level to 12·6 per cent through such a correction. In ten countries studied by Kravis *et al.* for 1975 the rise was from 9·3 to 15·4 per cent. Nor is it just very poor countries that 'benefit' from such adjustment. In Maddison's survey French *per capita* income in 1965 rose after adjusting for factor cost from 53·1 to 62·7 per cent of US, German from 53·2 to 66·7, and British from 49·9 to 63·4. Unfortunately there is no way of knowing, given the state of nineteenth-century Irish national accounts, what correction would be appropriate there. All that can be said is that the direction of the adjustment seems clear, and that most of the gap would survive any adjustment.[38]

The main problem with the real wage levels is not that they apply only to a minority of the poor in pre-Famine Ireland: it is simply that the problems of adjusting available data for seasonality, regional variation and cost of living have not yet been sorted out. The wages of casual labour were subject to marked seasonal fluctuation, as may be seen from these extracts from Amhlaoimh Ó Súileabháin's Callan diary:[39]

> *16 August 1827.* Two shillings [a day] and a glass of whiskey, and meals for reapers; and one and four pence for women binders.

> *16 August 1828.* Nineteen pence and a glass for a reaper, and two shillings for some at day break. A reaper could not be had for love or money half an hour later.

> *27 July 1830.* . . . Men breaking stones at three pence a day.

> *31 August 1830.* Fifteen pence a day for sickle men, Saturday, yesterday, and today; though welcome, it is high time as far as the poor are concerned.

> *12 August 1831.* Sickle men have today only a shilling: the calmness of the weather is such that people can wait till the wheat is well ripe, so farmers are in no hurry.

> *16 August 1831.* Eighteen pence and a glass of whiskey for a reaper today.

Hence the wage data collected by Bowley from sources such as the Dublin Society statistical surveys, the Poor Inquiry and the Devon Commission are not easy to interpret. Real wages per hour, if available, would seem the best proxy for living standards. Even in a far from perfect labour market they would reflect the incomes of the self-sufficient and those paid in kind. However, measure of real wages per hour can give a distorted impression of economic well-being if individuals experience varying amounts of voluntary and involuntary unemployment. In our pre-Famine context this is a serious problem. In agriculture labourers were underemployed for half the year or more. There is little prospect of comprehensive wage data, appropriately corrected for unemployment, becoming available in the near future.[40]

By many of the other standard criteria the Irish poor were very poor indeed. At the most basic level, seasonal hunger has already been mentioned. Two-fifths of families were crowded into one-room cabins and tenements in 1841. Poor attendance at church and at school was sometimes explained away by the lack of presentable clothes. Straw often did service for beds and bedding, furniture and windows were rudimentary or lacking, overcrowding was severe. Tea (or coffee) and sugar, widely consumed by the poor elsewhere in western Europe, were rarities in the homes of the Irish poor. Begging was endemic everywhere.[41] What a Dublin medical man termed the 'extreme misery of a revolting character' soon struck most middle-class visitors to Ireland.[42]

However, if the Irish were abysmally poor by standard criteria, other evidence suggests that the picture of pre-Famine poverty based on such criteria alone is somewhat oversimplified. Not quote all was gloom and doom. For one thing, the pre-Famine Irish seem to have lived relatively long lives by the standards of the time. The evidence is indirect, since civil registration was not introduced until 1864, and pre-Famine parish registers typically provide few or none of the necessary details about deaths. However, by projecting the 1841 census population backward to 1821, suitably corrected and augmented by those who emigrated in the meantime, life expectancy may be inferred from the life table that provides the best fit with the 1821 census. The implied average life span on the eve of the Famine is thirty-seven to thirty-eight years. That may seem distressingly low by today's standards, but high infant mortality is largely to blame. Those who survived the first year of life could expect to live another fifty or so. This compares well with the norm elsewhere at the time. Ireland's high marital fertility and ensuing infant and child deaths make this longevity all the more impressive.[43]

A *caveat* is necessary here, though: the relative longevity may simply reflect the lower resource cost of healthy, monotonous food and fuel in Ireland. The easy-to-grow potatoes which reduced mortality below what it would have been on a diet of bread and tea could still have been associated with a lower standard of living.

Nor—to use a welfare criterion currently fashionable in the cliometric literature—did poverty prevent the Irish from growing as tall as their neighbours before 1845. The qualitative evidence on this is mixed. Arthur Young and Adam Smith had waxed lyrical in the 1770s about the strength and beauty of the Irish. On the eve of the Famine Robert Kane produced a few numbers which satisfied him that 'when at all well fed, there is no race more perfectly developed, as to physical conformation, than the inhabitants of Ireland'. The astute economist John Bicheno was more equivocal: 'we thought the common people small in stature, and coarse in their features; but as the children are remarkably pretty, the defects of the parents are probably to be attributed to smoke and hard living, and to their exposure to the inclemency of the weather'.[44]

Hard data are a better bet. Since height data, especially from military sources, are often available earlier than other more obvious economic indicators, and auxological research suggests a connection between a society's well-being and its average height, the temptations are clear.[45] If rather too much is sometimes being claimed for this approach, it can certainly complement more traditional measures, and seems worth trying in the Irish case. One source on the Irish is the continuous service records of the British Admiralty, which provide numbers compariable to those used elsewhere. Accounts of life on the lower deck suggest that the Admiralty data refer to the lower end of the socio-economic spectrum.[46] Moreover naval data are easier to handle than military in one respect: selection bias arising from the deliberate exclusion of smaller men is less of a problem, height being of no particular advantage aboard ship. Admittedly there is a problem as regards regional spread. Just as British naval recruits came disproportionately from maritime counties south of a line from Bristol to the Wash, the Irish tended to come from Munster, and especially from County Cork. The comparison is limited in this respect. Nevertheless the results of our look at the heights of over 6,000 sailors in service in 1853–54, including 700 Irish, are interesting enough. When heights are regressed on age and a nationality dummy, the Irish turn out to have been slightly taller.[47]

Mokyr and I found a similar gap in our analysis of a different sample of men, recruits from the United Kingdom (including Ireland) to the regiments of the East India Company during the Napoleonic wars. The conditions facing men in India were shocking, and the pay very low. Why so many took the step is something of a mystery: presumably John Company's forces were the refuge of the desperate and the gullible. (One is reminded of Frederick the Great's quip, 'If my soldiers began to think, not one would remain in the ranks.') The recruits' occupations are overwhelmingly working-class and their heights (if not their decision to enlist) must, like the sailors', tell us something about the nutritional status of the class whence they sprung. A comparison between the Irish and the British, correcting for under-representation of smaller men, gives the Irish a small advantage. This holds for sub-sets of our sample such as town-dwellers and former white-collar workers.[48]

These differences—less than half an inch—may seem trivial, but they count in this area. Indeed, a half-inch gap proves far too much, if taken strictly as a reflection on the condition of the poor in both islands. Needless to say, the point then is not to claim that the Irish were better-off than the British, simply that their poverty did not deny them adequate and more nutritious food when growing up. A comparison with data assembled by Roderick Floud for other European countries shows those born in pre-Famine Ireland to have been very near the top of the league. What is more, a preliminary analysis of our East India men suggests that in Ireland the trend was slightly upward between 1800 and 1845.

TABLE 2 *Estimates of the mean height of some western European populations (cm)*

Country	Date	Height	Age
Britain	1853–54	167·8	19–22
Ireland	1853–54	168·0	19–22
Belgium	1880–82	165·5	19–25
Denmark	1852–56	165·3	22
Bavaria	1875	164·6	Conscripts
Italy	1874–76	162·2	20
Netherlands	1865	165·0	19
Norway	1855	168·6	22
Sweden	1840	165·1	21

Source: For Britain and Ireland see text. For the rest, Roderick Floud, 'The heights of Europeans since 1750: a new source for European economic history', National Bureau of Economic Research Working Paper No. 1318, April 1984.

Our earlier discussion of pre-Famine famines may be linked to yet another index of poverty, that proposed by Joel Mokyr in *Why Ireland Starved* and elsewhere.[49] In order to capture both the level and the variability of income, Mokyr calls poverty 'the probability of a random individual at a random point in time dropping beneath subsistence'. One may quibble at the 'random individual': the very rich are not going to starve, come what may. But the wider appeal of such a definition should be noted: as historical demographic data become more plentiful, it will be useful for comparative history. Call $P(H)$ the probability of a harvest failure, and $P(D/H)$ the probability of a famine in the event of a harvest failure. Then $P(D \ U \ H) = P(D/H) \times P(H)$. Here 'harvest failure' is best interpreted as a serious shortfall, say one-third or half the staple food. Famines of that scale typically spelt disaster in early modern Europe: in a pre-blight world, surely this is the worst that even the most cautious Irishman could have expected. $P(D/H)$ rose with the decline in the poor's living standards, but it would have been a function also of relief policy, the degree of commercialisation of the rural economy, the availability of credit, and more generally what Amartya Sen has called 'exchange entitlements'.[50] To consider H a failure of potato blight dimensions would imply a $P(H)$ of zero and a very high $P(D/H)$. Our reading of pre-Famine trends suggests that $P(H)$ has been exaggerated in the past by historians, despite the theoretical dangers of increasing reliance on one or two varieties of potato. Probabilities were built on experience, and in the pre-blight setting the worst that could happen were once-off, often regional, failures that struck only some of the crop. The trend in $P(D/H)$ is a function of opposing forces; if the poor's command over marketed goods was falling, developments in government and communications to some extent compensated, by providing better insurance against disaster. But given the current state of knowledge I can only surmise that $P(D \ U \ H)$ was probably small before 1845, if rising somewhat over time.

Illiteracy is yet another common proxy for poverty and backwardness. The logic behind this is two-pronged: either a 'culture of poverty' reduces the demand for formal schooling, or the cost is beyond the reach of the masses. The former was hardly a problem in Ireland, since the eagerness of all for education was legendary: 'I do not know of any part of Ireland so wild that its inhabitants are not anxious, nay eagerly anxious for the education of their children.'[51] There was a widespread Ascendancy belief in pre-Famine Ireland that more schooling would be an effective way of civilising the poor, and a great deal of attention was devoted to how State help should be administered. Meanwhile private education, usually secular but sometimes supervised or partly subsidised by the local Catholic priest, was quite widely available, and had already achieved much in the east and north by 1800. The curriculum in these schools was hardly adventurous, but they did quite a good job of teaching the three Rs.

Pre-Famine literacy trends may be gauged from published official sources. The data come in two kinds, schooling attendance estimates, and the literacy survey in the 1841 census. The first two estimates, made in 1808 and 1821, are incomplete in their coverage. The 1808 figure is a grossed-up estimate based on returns from seventeen of twenty-two Established Church dioceses. The 1821 census returns refer to numbers 'on the books' rather than average attendance. The 1821 census has been harshly criticised for sloppiness by Lee:[52] what makes it useless for schooling comparisons is its patchy coverage. Two baronies in Kildare were completely omitted in 1821, while the numbers reported for many other areas are implausibly thin. In the County Derry barony of Tyrkeeran, for example, only 160 out of almost 8,000 children of schoolgoing age were reported to be at school. In Demifore, in Westmeath, the ratio was an utterly implausible twenty out of 3,644. Clearly, too, many schools in other baronies— Balrothery and Carlow, for example—were omitted. The 1824 returns, by contrast, were carefully constructed: again they refer to numbers 'on the books'. The same goes for 1834, but that year's estimate at least allows a guess at the average attendance rate. Thus the 1824, 1834 and 1841 data may be compared, and attendance per thousand population calculated. They indicate that attendance per thousand population rose from about 5·5 in 1824 to 5·6 in 1834 and 6·1 in 1841.

Literacy data from the census of 1841 (see table 3) would seem to buttress the schooling statistics. By comparing age cohorts we can infer trends in rough-and-ready fashion from 'snapshot' data.[53] In aggregate the numbers indicate quite· high literacy, at least in Leinster and Ulster, but unremarkable improvement between Union and Famine outside Leinster. This suggests that Ireland's early literacy spurt in the late eighteenth or very early nineteenth century was not sustained.

TABLE 3   Percentage illiterate, 1841

	66-75 years	26-35 years
Leinster	51·8	33·5
Munster	67·6	57·1
Ulster	41·4	33·6
Connacht	77·7	67·4

The crudeness of the numbers need not be laboured. The likelihood of an impressive rise is ruled out by data on teacher numbers—11,823 in 1824, 14,501 in 1841, an increase which marginally outstripped the rise in population. Yet those same numbers suggest a cross-section comparison of teacher density, and here Ireland scores quite well. Pre-Famine Ireland had seventeen teachers per 10,000 population; this compares with fourteen in Prussia and eleven in the Austrian Empire around the same time, while in 1860 the number was only eighteen in Holland and nineteen in France and Belgium.

While the numbers by no means confirm Wakefield's claim that education was 'universal', they show that, in Leinster and Ulster at least, the situation was not too different from across the water. The pity is that so few public resources were devoted to schooling in the west and south in the pre-Famine era.

TABLE 4   Children at school

Year	At school	Population (million)
1808	Over 200,000	5
1821	394,813	7·2
1824	568,964	
1834	633,946	7·9
1841	502,950	8·4

The regional dimension suggested by schooling data must not be forgotten. If illiteracy and poor housing are combined as a guide to regional contrasts, poverty was clearly greatest in the far west. Among the very poorest places would have been Kilnamanagh, in west Cork (which included the mining village of Allihies), with 91·5 per cent of families living in fourth-class housing, and 73·6 per cent of males illiterate, and Ballinakill, in west Galway, with percentages of 93·4 and 82·7 respectively. The parish of Newtownards in north County Down was probably one of the most prosperous in the whole country—with 21·1 per cent in one-room housing and only 16·8 per cent of males unable to either read or write. Places such as the Aran islands (24·1 and 79·3 per cent) and pre-Famine Gaoth Dobhair, in west Donegal (89·4 and 62·2 per cent)—immortalised for its backwardness by Lord George Hill—fit somewhere in the middle, with near-total illiteracy but far better housing than the very poorest parishes.

Turning to the census's occupational data, in 1841 Wicklow and Wexford, for example, supported about twice as many makers of boots and shoes and three times as many carpenters—producers, mainly, of output for local use—as Mayo or Kerry, and boasted literacy rates twice as high. The richest areas probably compared favourably with some of Britain. At the height of the great Famine Maurice Colles surveyed the Marques of Londonderry's estate in north County Down. He reported to his lordship:[54]

It is well known, indeed I will call it a national fact that the district in which your Lordships estate is situated was one of the few exceptions to the operation of relief works and soup kitchens during the last year, and received no eleemosynary aid from Government or public bodies; none in fact except was supplied through private and local charities. . . . During the number of years in which I have been occupied in making surveys . . . I can truly affirm that amongst the common run of farmers I never met, except on your Lordships estate, a tenant ready without preparation to produce a bit of cheese, with bread, butter and beer for an unexpected guest. This I met in almost every case where I was drawn into the homesteads of your Lordships tenants. An unwillingness, if they had it, to produce in other districts it is far from my intention to impute.

The district surveyed by the same Colles included the two small towns of Newtownards and Comber, and their rural hinterland. In the towns only thirty-nine of the 2,187 houses were thatched, while 463 out of 1,863 in the countryside were slated. On Colles's reckoning only six of the 567 houses on the estate had a valuation of less than £3, though such houses were 'prevalent through Ireland, and that even on some of the best circumstanced properties I have visited'. The prosperity was not founded on big farms—in that respect the Londonderry estate was little better-off than the (relatively poor) Grocers' estate in north County Derry, surveyed by Colles a few years earlier (see table 5). The difference

TABLE 5   *Some data from two surveys by Maurice Colles*

	Grocers' Co.	Londonderry estate
Farms	926	1,811
Horses	477	1,190
Cattle	2,097	4,165
Sheep	419	431
Pigs	690	1,674
Goats	74	209
% valuations under £3	52	53
% valuations under £20	88	83

is that domestic industry in north Down could coexist with or become factory industry, while after 1820 or so the tenants on the Grocers' estate were gradually made to rely wholly on the land. The case of Armagh is similar: it had the highest population density of all thirty-two counties, and holdings there (as throughout most of Ulster) were small, yet its prosperity could be seen 'even in the countenances of the dogs and cats'.[55]

What are the implications of this discussion of standard-of-living proxies and regional contrasts for social conditions in pre-Famine Ireland? There is no denying the abject poverty of the neglected masses, nor the likelihood of impoverishment for a high proportion, perhaps a majority, of the total population. To that extent traditional accounts relying on the impressions of travel writers like Kohl, Inglis, or Beaumont are correct. But poverty had strong regional and class components, and the island as a whole was less starvation-prone, less sickly and less illiterate than often depicted.

4. Trends in living standards

Whatever of comparisons across counties and countries, some reduction in the living standards of the poor over time seems likely. Data providing country-wide coverage are preferable to impressionistic quotes, and are available in the form of evidence to the Poor Inquiry. The subjective poverty index—*recte* impoverishment index, and so here called SII—devised by Mokyr[56] uses this evidence to the full. The index ranges from –2 (much deteriorated) to +2 (much improved). By province the story is as follows:

	No. of witnesses	SII
Ulster	499	–0·65
Munster	351	–0·22
Connacht	102	–0·62
Leinster	392	–0·27
Total	1,394	–0·43

Worst six		*Best six*	
Mayo	–1·02	Wexford	0·22
Sligo	–0·93	Wicklow	0·22
Louth	–0·91	Kerry	–0·03
Longford	–0·85	Queen's	–0·08
Tyrone	–0·85	Carlow	–0·11
Donegal	–0·83	Meath	–0·15

All provinces recorded a decline, but the provincial picture hides an even greater variation between counties. Can this variation be accounted for? Despite the well known lacunae and inconsistencies of pre-Famine data, they have provided a basis for useful econometric work in recent years.[57] Below I have regressed SII on census-derived county estimates of industrialisation and population pressure. The industrialisation proxy is extremely crude: the implied contraction in all provinces stems largely from the decline of spinning. The use of counties as units of analysis ignores some of the important intra-county differences highlighted by local historians. Yet the proxy presents a regionally consistent picture. Geographically the cottage textile areas of north Leinster, north Connacht and west Ulster were worst affected. And our results pack some explanatory punch (table 6).

TABLE 6   Explaining the variation in SII

	1	2	3	4
DIND	0·761	0·796	0·822	0·829
	(0·281)	(0·190)	(0·259)	(0·221)
DCRPP		0·190		
		(0·402)		
DCRPPA	0·00156			
	(0·00103)			
DLVR			0·405	
			(0·828)	
DLVRA				0·00348
				(0·0022)
Constant	−0·294	−0·181	−0·175	−0·287
RSQ	0·287	0·285	0·286	0·291
F	7·21	5·78	5·80	7·37

Note. DLVR is defined as (Population in 1841 – Population in 1821)/(Poor Law valuation), using half the total value for County Dublin. DCRPP is defined as (Population in 1841 – Population in 1821)/(Cropped area in 1851). DCRPPA and DLVRA use estimates of the agricultural labour force in the numerator. DIND is (Proportion of families mainly dependent on manufactures and trade in 1841 – Proportion of the total labour force in manufacture and trade in 1821).

Broadly speaking, the decline in SII was greatest where de-industrialisation was greatest, and not necessarily where suffering was greatest after 1845. The failure of our population pressure variables to affect SII much may come as a surprise. However, the population pressure variables to help explain the variation across counties in 1841 in such may come as a surprise. However, the population pressure variables to help explain the variation across counties in 1841 in such proxies for poverty as bad housing and illiteracy. The 1841 census provides the necessary data on those proxies. The result is shown in table 7. In these regressions the subjective impoverishment index does not help explain the picture across counties, and the sigh on the coefficients is 'wrong'. Our proxy for pressure on the land accounts for nearly half the variation in poverty, defined as above. The data underlying these tables are crude, and the single-equation specifications rough-and-ready. For what they are worth, they seem to imply that, while increasing population pressure is unhelpful in explaining the variation in impoverishment across counties before the mid-1830s, it does explain a good deal of the variation in poverty levels on

TABLE 7 *'Population pressure' and 'living standards'*

Explanatory variables	Dependent variable	
	Housing	Proportion illiterate
DCRPPA	0·00149	0·555
	(0·00029)	(0·136)
SII	−0·0605	−0·026
	(−0·0423)	(−0·56)
Constant	0·240	0·310
Rsq	0·483	0·376
F	13·53	8·74

Note. 'Housing' is the proportion of families living in fourth-class accommodation in 1841, 'Proportion illiterate' the proportion of the population over five who could neither read nor write. Standard errors are given in parentheses.

the eve of the Famine. In this sense Malthus ruled the land.

The analysis has focused on the regional spread of impoverishment. Note, however, that it deals with the poor only. Throughout pre-Famine Ireland others were doing well: 'the lowest class of all, the mere labourer, is the only one whose advancement is not evident'.[58]

This contrast in the fortunes of the poor—compare the 'bottom 40 per cent' singled out for attention by Lindert and Williamson in their study of British living standards during the industrial revolution[59]—and those of the rest is reflected in other data too. Though comprehensive Irish trade data were a casualty of the Act of Union, enough survive to chart trends in the imports of commodities such as tea, sugar and tobacco which tended not to be consumed by the very poor. Since they were not domestically produced to any worthwhile extent, the import statistics, if accurate, should track consumption. In fact the tobacco series is distorted by smuggling, but the others are considered reasonably accurate for the half-century or so before the Great Famine. Even in the case of tobacco, the most proletarian of these commodities, the data can be patched up to some extent.

Suppose that the quantity demanded of commodity i, Q_i, is captured by:

$$Q_i = Ae^{rt} P_i^{\alpha} Y^{\beta} P^{-\alpha-\beta}$$

where P_i is the price of i, Y is money income, P is the general price level and r a time-related shift variable. t refers to time and α and β are the price and income elasticities of demand. In terms of proportionate rates of change:

$$\dot{Q}_i = r + (\dot{P}_i/P) + (\dot{Y}/P)$$

Suppose that consumption and relative price change are known, and the price elasticity of demand guessed at. Then a residual consumption, attributable to some combination of income change and r, may be calculated. Applying this approach to Irish consumption of the goods listed during the pre-Famine decades in each case left a positive residual to be 'explained'. If a drastic change in taste is ruled out, the result is consistent with the trends in living standards and inequality outlined above.[60]

5. Economic change before the Famine

The culmination of half a century of misery and impoverishment for labourers and cottiers in the great Famine has naturally greatly influenced accounts of the pre-Famine economy. 'Predictors' of the Famine are sought in the pre-Famine setting, and structural weaknesses, institutional factors and, above all, overpopulation are stressed. This is understandable, but sometimes the story comes to mere Malthusian inference or nationalist rhetoric. This masks the considerable progress that occurred in many sectors of the economy, and the likelihood that a sizable minority of the population benefited from rising incomes between Union and Famine.

Some of the improvements—the diffusion of steam power, the mechanisation of spinning, the vast improvement of cross-channel shipping—were due to the industrial revolution across the water. The new Arkwright 'gadgets' caught on quickly in Ireland. Though the first spinning jennies were installed in Belfast—in the town workhouse in 1777—the new technology's impact was more spectacular in the south at first. A series of gigantic operations—including Robert Brooke's at Prosperous on the Bog of Allen (a capital of £40,000, 2,500 employees, mainly non-local), John Orr's at Stratford on Slaney (£30,000 and 500 imported employees), the Sadleir brothers' enterprise, spread over several locations near Cork (£40,000 and 4,000 employees)—attracted great publicity and enjoyed success for a time.[61]

Despite some sensational failures, including those of Brooke (1785) and Sadleir (1801), a hefty tariff prolonged the life of the new cotton industry in the south till the 1820s, by which time output was double its 1790 level. This modest southern success was based largely on coarse cottons and printing; in Ulster meanwhile output grew eightfold, founded instead on finer cloths and bleaching. While the industry was never important by British

standards—Irish output being about 5 to 7 per cent of British
c. 1800 and 3 per cent c. 1820—it deserves more than a footnote.
As late as 1810 or so the Irish cotton industry was producing
twice as much in volume terms as its more famous Flemish
counterpart.[62] Decline probably set in around then, and was
uninterrupted after 1825. It was gradual in the north, where
cotton gave way to linen, but headlong in the south. Weavers'
earnings tumbled. Around Carrickfergus the price commanded
by a length of calico dropped by almost three-quarters between
the 1790s and the 1820s. Worst hit of all, perhaps, was the town
of Bandon, which boasted many mills and over a thousand hand-
loom weavers at the peak, but where by 1837 'the mills were in
ruin and not more than 100 weavers employed'.[63]

The manufacture of woollen cloth—carpets, broadcloths,
friezes, blankets—also fell during the pre-Famine period, shrinking
to virtually nothing in such traditional strongholds as Kilkenny
and Carrick-on-Suir. Changing fashions, arising from the availability
of cheaper cotton substitutes, were part of the story, though it
was reported in 1837 that 'three-fourths of the frieze generally
worn by the peasantry throughout Ireland is now an article of
import'. Cottage industry suffered:[64]

> Is deas is is néata an ball éadaig í mo veistín liath,
> Ní cosmhail leis a' mbréid í do dheineadh an bhean ón tsliabh.

Factory employment in woollens fell too, however, from 1,231 in
1839 to 553 in 1850.

The success of linen was more enduring. Coarse linen had
been produced in Ireland since time immemorial, but around 1800
it was a major 'proto-industry' spanning the northern half of the
country and isolated parts of west Munster. Competition from
cotton and technical improvements in bleaching and spinning
gradually undermined the viability of household production after
1800. Cotton's impact was twofold. First, being a good substitute
for linen, it kept weavers' wages down. Second, the technical
improvements in cotton were gradually being adapted to linen.
Hand spinning in linen eventually succumbed in the late 1820s
and early 1830s, when wet spinning opened the way for fine-yarn
production by machine. Over a score of linen mills had been
established by 1835, nearly all of them in the greater Belfast
area, and mostly built by former linen bleachers or cotton manu-
facturers. Employment grew from 3,400 in 1835 to over 17,000
a decade later, but mechanisation did not bring vast increases in
the output of yarn. Factory yarn was sold in bulk to merchants
who hired out-working weavers on a piece-rate basis. Some inde-

pendent weavers stuck it out, but throughout most of the linen country the trend was against the independents, who could buy yarn only in small amounts, selling the finished product themselves.[65]

The localisation which was soon to mark the industry was hardly evident as late as 1820, at least within Ulster. Linen's rural base and water requirements made for dispersion, and the markets of Derry, Cootehill, Drogheda, Omagh and Nenagh—all outside the famour 'linen triangle' of Belfast–Lurgan–Dungannon—continued to count. All, with the exception of Drogheda, relied largely on their rural hinterland for supplies of cloth. Drogheda's weaving colony, specialising in unbleached 'market linen', thrived between 1780 and 1820: then the absence of bleaching facilities and the town's relative isolation brought crisis and decline.[66] Other areas suffered too, for the centripetal forces that concentrated the bulk of the English cotton industry into one-third of Lancashire and the American industry into Rhode Island and eastern Massachusetts were also at work in Ulster.[67]

The factors making for such specialisation are not yet fully understood. External economies of scale are often mentioned, though they remain something of a will-o'-the-wisp for the historian. Theory predicts that such economies are reaped where the industry, for whatever reason, has a headstart to begin with: ancillary activities locate there, producing a competitive advantage which ends up in centralisation. The cap seems to fit Belfast, which had been the principal textile port since the 1780s, and where there quickly developed the production of looms and shuttles and, later, of power machinery. Besides the usual printing, bleaching and dyeing work to be met in a textile centre there were 'various manufactories for machinery, iron-forges, and other chymical products . . . together employing about a thousand persons'.[68] The local foundries, moreover, soon began to invent and build machinery specifically geared to local conditions.[69]

The outcome was an industrialisation that was highly uneven regionally. Table 9 attempts to capture the trend across counties. The decline in the south coincided with an industrial revolution around Belfast quite as dramatic and thoroughgoing as anything happening in Preston or Middlesbrough. In the context Rodney Green's criticism of George O'Brien's analysis is worth recalling. Green called O'Brien's 'a highly unsatisfactory work . . . strongly southern and protectionist in tone, completely neglecting the problem of reconciling this with the industrial development in the north'.[70]

That 'the Union had proved disastrous' was, of course, the

main theme of George O'Brien's *Economic History*. To today's historian the argument seems far-fetched, since, given the massive secular drop in the prices of Britain's industrial staples, the protectionist wedge of 10 per cent or so provided by pre-Union tariffs would have mattered little. More substantial tariffs might have reduced unemployment and given Irish industry a respite—as they did a century later—but at a cost in redistribution (if not in efficiency) that was inconceivable in the nineteenth century. Because the final amalgamation of the currencies took place at a time of great economic hardship (1825–26) this other element in the Union settlement is also criticised. The argument has a modern ring to it: the ensuing appreciation of Irish money allegedly made exports less competitive and deflated the economy. In reality, since most trade was denominated in sterling in any case, the change made little difference, and prices and rents in Ireland quickly adapted to reflect what was in effect a revaluation of the Irish currency.[71]

There was progress too in traditional areas such as banking and inland communication which transformed those sectors out of all recognition. In the 1790s Ireland had to make do with an unstable currency and banking system, but by 1845 that state of affairs had given way to a wide network of secure joint-stock banks. Though the Bank of Ireland (created in 1783) sought to block progress by protesting ceaselessly at reductions in its mercantilist privileges, and made substantial monopoly profits for its shareholders decade after decade, it also usefully played the role of quasi-central bank. Besides holding the government's account and being the issuer of what amounted to the national currency—a power it abused without scruple during the Restriction (1797–1821)—it was also soon taking on the role of lender of last resort.[72] By December 1799 the bank was aiding Beresford's Bank in Dublin against a threatened run, a central banking function it was to perform several times, always showing the appropriate reluctance, in the following decades.

The new joint-stock banks, it is true, limited their lending to cash credits, overdrafts and short-term loans, and shunned the custom of small-scale depositors. Surviving records[73] show, for instance, that the average opening balance at the Provincial Bank's Birr (then Parsonstown) branch during its first year was £250 (£10,000 to £20,000 in today's money), while the humblest clients of the bank's Youghal branch were small traders and merchants. The earliest list of account holders at the Bank of Ireland's Sligo branch, founded in 1828, again includes professional people, farmers, agents and Catholic priests. A sample of those who signed the Dublin-based Hibernian Bank's account book up to 1846 reflects that bank's more Catholic, bourgeois clientele:

Merchants	220
Professional	46
Manufacturers, builders	49
Farmers, agents	17
Other	16

The new banks shunned even the lower middle classes; the success of the only bank to court them, Thomas Mooney's Agricultural & Commercial, proved ephemeral.[74] The structure of the pre-Famine banking system thus bespoke both commercialisation at one level and mass poverty at another.

To berate pre-Famine banks for failing to provide medium-term capital for industry is to misunderstand the role of banks generally in this era. Banks did not do so in Britain either; their lending was overwhelmingly short-term, and industry relied largely on retained profits for accumulation. Industry needed short-term capital too, though, and here the British banks came into their own. In Ireland too, if the banks were reluctant to provide investment finance, they nonetheless provided a useful service to business and professional interests. Thus in 1844 the Provincial's Birr branch sought accommodation from headquarters in London—standard Provincial practice—for graziers during the 'grass season', for a landed proprietor who had 'lately bought out a great many of his tenants', and for millers who 'because trade [was] dull at present . . . wish[ed] as few sales as possible'. The limits of the Provincial's facilities—and the ready availability of alternative outlets—are clearly shown by the Youghal branch's advice to a client 'whose engagements are likely to become permanent . . . to procure a loan from some private individual who could be satisfied to receive his interest regularly once or twice a year'. Indeed, the growth of the banking system itself relied largely on Irish capital. In the case of the National, substantial local backing was required before a branch could be set up. The creation of its Castlebar branch is a case in point; in 1836 over £25,000 was raised in Mayo to start the branch, merchants and publicans accounting for over half those investors whose professions could be identified.[75]

The removal of convertibility, inflation and wartime prosperity all contributed to the mushrooming of private banking after 1797. The number of concerns rose from eleven in 1797 to about forty by 1815; turnover was rapid. The total then dropped, gradually at first, until half the remainder were wiped out in 1820. It was during the next two decades that Ireland's modern banking system evolved. By 1845 the Bank of Ireland's monopoly had been whittled away, and private country banking was a thing of the past. Most towns of any size now had their own branch.[76]

Taking the long view, it makes as much sense to see the development of joint-stock banking as a symptom of commercialisation as its root cause. Nevertheless circumstances determined the timing of legislation. In the United Kingdom generally this was an epoch of banking legislation. In Ireland the severe crisis of spring 1820, which cleared Munster and Connacht of their banks, bespeaks the difficulties of restoring convertibility after two decades of inflation more than of the recklessness of the country's small provincial banks. That crisis produced symptoms never again to be witnessed in Ireland: people fainting in queues outside banks, fairs where nothing was bought or sold for want of a medium of exchange. Yet it was remarkably short-lived—by July the storm had died down. At the same time the crisis helped the argument of those seeking joint-stock banks—those mainly southern commercial interests who broke the Bank of the Ireland's monopoly and forced the legislation which allowed joint-stock banking after 1825. Meanwhile in Ulster the new system had been developing in embryo since the 1800s.[77]

The pre-Famine revolution in communications was quieter than that subsequently associated with the railways, but it produced changes just as impressive. Pre-Famine Ireland was not transformed by a canal revolution à l'anglaise, and few of the canals built proved a success. The ill conceived and disastrous Royal Canal went bankrupt in 1812; a new company, with government aid, extended the link to the Shannon, but the completed line was little used. To the great relief of directors the Royal was taken over by the new Midland Great Western Railway in 1845. Even in Ulster canals did not work out well; traffic on the Coalisland was disappointingly light, while the Ulster Canal, linking Lough Neagh and Lough Erne, proved an unmitigated disaster. The Grand saw some prosperity in the immediate pre-railway years, yet even then most of its traffic was in heavy and bulky items such as building materials and turf.[78] Competition from another mode was the reason for this:[79]

> The carrier trade on the Grand Canal is not very very extensive; country dealers in general finding it more convenient to have their goods conveyed by drays, which ply with great regularity on all leading roads, and on fares extremely moderate.

The same held for the busy Lagan valley, near Belfast, where road carriers vigorously competed with water for business.[80]

The railway made little impact in Ireland before the Famine either. True, rail ventures were mooted very early on; a Limerick and Waterford proposal received parliamentary assent as early as 1825, and Daniel O'Connell was one of those behind a more comprehensive scheme for a Munster and Leinster Railway in the same year. Still, only the Dublin–Kingstown and the Ulster were started in the 1830s, and the network had reached only sixty-five miles by the eve of the Famine.[81]

Yet this slow diffusion of the latest technology can hardly have counted for much. The pre-Famine half-century saw instead the blossoming of a comprehensive network of road passenger transport, which by 1845 had established a regular service between all towns of any size for about 1s 5d per mile. The huge concerns of Bianconi and Purcell were only the best known of many: in 1836 users of the network logged a total of over 30 million miles. Between 1800 and 1845 travel times on the main routes were cut by a third, frequency of service improved, and the risk of attack by highwaymen dwindled close to zero. The economic savings to the middle and lower middle-class travellers who were the mainstay of the coaches must have been substantial. The rise of coaching rested on improved roads, and grand juries and the Board of Works invested heavily in repair and construction in these years. The work of Richard Griffith in the south-west brought daily coach services to the Tralee–Cork and Killarney–Cork routes, and reduced the journey time on the latter by two-thirds. Freight traffic benefited too: carts became heavier and more frequent. A survey of freight movements on the Tralee road at Dromagh in 1838 counted 80,000 loaded carts passing, carrying farm produce, lime, culm, iron and groceries.[82]

One new technology which had an impact on travel was the steamship. Charles Wye Williams introduced steam for freight purposes in 1823. Finding the investing public sceptical, he and some business friends put £24,000 together to build the first two steamers to ply the Irish Sea for trading purposes. Others quickly followed, and intense competition reduced prices. Trades developed in fresh eggs, butter and slaughtered meat, and the live cattle trade was made much easier.[83]

Deindustrialisation was a key feature, but losses were not across-the-board (see appendix 1). Brewing, distilling and milling expanded, as did smaller trades such as confectioning and glassmaking. The 10,000 coopers and 4,000 millers recorded in 1841 attest to the progress registered in the food-processing industries. Nor were these industries necessarily technologically laggard; the largest flour mills in Ireland emulated Manchester. The main wheel of Alexander's Fairbairn-built mill near Carlow produced 140 h.p.:[84]

> In the two establishments producing flour and oatmeal, there are twenty-two pairs of millstones at constant work; thirteen of which with all the attendant machinery, are driven by one wheel. The concern is able to manufacture annually 60,000 sacks of flour—'without', as one of the workmen expressed it, 'lighting a candle' . . . Estimating flour at 60s. per sack, and the oatmeal at 30s., we have the concern yielding no less than £195,000 each year.

As explained in more detail in chapter 2, agricultural output rose substantially, and despite the huge rise in labour input after 1800 labour productivity seems to have kept its level or even improved slightly.

Ireland became a more open economy during these decades. As a result of the big expansion in agricultural exports and the steady rise in the trade in textiles and manufactured goods, the ratio of trade to GNP increased significantly between the Union and the Famine.[85] This growth in trade volume presumably increased living standards for textbook gains-from-trade reasons. Moreover, as productivity growth made the price of imported manufactures plummet, the terms of trade moved in Ireland's favour. That change alone probably added a few percentage points to the purchasing power of GNP. The same change probably reduced the living standard of workers, however. The loss to redundant weavers is clear-cut, but most unskilled landless workers suffered. An appeal to a standard trade model shows why. Assume the economy consisted of two sectors, agriculture and industry, both using labour, but land being specific to agriculture and capital to industry. In the left-hand panel of fig. 2 the demand for

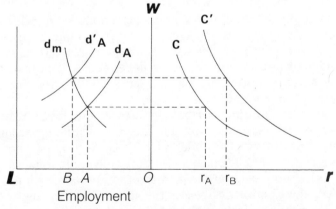

Fig. 2 w = *wage*, r = *rent per unit*

labour in industry is drawn in the standard way as a decreasing function of the real wage, while agriculture's is drawn from right to left. Initial equilibrium—in 1800, say—is at A, the intersection point of the two labour demand schedules.[86] The right-hand panel shows agriculture's unit-cost curve, with the levels of rent per unit of land consistent with a given wage and viability. Initially the equilibrium rent corresponding to A is at $r(A)$. A rise in the terms of trade, the product of the corn laws[87] and the industrial revolution, raises the unit-cost curve by the same amount. The effect on labour demand is to shift demand out to a new equilibrium at B. Wages thus rise, but by less than the cost of foodstuffs. The outcome for living standards depends on the consumption pattern of workers. Since before 1845 Irish workers spent a very high share—probably over two-thirds—of their income on food, a drop is likely. The implication of greater inequality between the minority with access to land and the landless masses follows.

Note that the mechanism producing the greater inequality is not that suggested by Simon Kuznets, who explains the association between economic development and increasing inequality in terms of sectoral differences in income distribution. For Kuznets the outcome was due to development typically causing the shrinkage of agriculture, a sector marked by low inequality, in favour of industry.[88] In pre-Famine Ireland, however, the mechanism seems to have been closer to that proposed by Hymer and Resnick for export-led growth in less developed countries in the twentieth century. Hymer and Resnick see international trade as a rather mixed blessing for the LDCs. The improvement in the barter terms of trade that it entails leads to the destruction of traditional cottage industries and pressure on the living standards of the poor.[89]

Other factors worked in the same direction. In the two decades or so before the Famine—to judge from the 1821 and 1841 censuses—the labour force in agriculture grew by about 50 per cent. In order to prevent wages from falling, productivity growth of something around 1 per cent annually would have been needed—a tall order not met even by contemporary Britain.[90,91]

The implication, again, is a dramatic increase in inequality.[92] Economic explanations like those suggested, which assume given resource allocations across classes, probably account for most of what was happening. The political dimension of inequality should not be overlooked, though. The poor in pre-Famine Ireland had no political voice of their own, nor were their interests well represented by politicians, who campaigned hardest on middle-class issues such as Catholic emancipation and repeal. Policies which would have increased the command of the very poor over resources—whether over land, education and skills, or just passage money—were pursued with reluctance or not at all. Who gained in agriculture, then? The common impression that landlords fared badly after 1815 is belied by landed estate accounts. In reality most estates saw their rentals rise during this period in money terms; the rise in terms of purchasing power was even greater. The scatter of results from surviving estate records given in table 8 is enough to make the point.[93]

TABLE 8   Some evidence on gross landlord income, 1815–45

Name	Period	Rent change (£)
Mohill	1816–28	2,300 to 3,200
Lismore	1821–38	29,454 to 31,452
Fitzwilliam	1815–26	11,525 to 11,491
Downshire	1815–44	55,000 to 72,500
Benn-Walsh	1829–47	3,439 to 5,317
Greville	1828–43	1,704 to 2,335
Garvagh	1831–45	1,950 to 2,750

The outcome is no more than what one would expect in theory: a rise in the terms of trade should increase the income of the export-oriented factor. However, the more dramatic rises here (notably on the Benn-Walsh estate) probably owed more to the easing out of middleman landlords than increases in the 'Ricardian' rent. The gauges of living standards discussed earlier suggest that farmers improved their lot too, but there is plenty room for research on the details.

6.   Conclusion

This chapter has set out to show that the pre-Famine economy, for all its problems and injustices, did not contain the seeds of its own inevitable destruction by famine. Far from being a 'lurking peril',[94] something as grotesque as *Phythophthora infestans* was beyond most people's worst nightmares before 1845. Of course, there were exceptions. Bishop Brinkley of Cloyne 'predicted the loss of the potato' and 'calculated mathematically the extent of ruin which was likely to follow', an exercise, he told a friend, which kept him awake all night![95] Yet the likelihood of mass starvation was, in the statistical sense, remote. Against this, there was the worrying reality of an expanding population virtually unsupported by industry, relying increasingly for subsistence on the worst variety of the cheapest food, often cultivated on wet bogs and barren hillsides. In the pre-Famine era the lot of these 'potato people' was helped neither by the O'Connellite campaign for repeal nor by the anti-interventionist politics still popular in Great Britain in the 1840s. Thus there is no room here for Dr Pangloss. The miserable and worsening lot of the bottom third of the population is enough to explain descriptions such as 'rural crisis' even in standard revisionist accounts.[96] Nor in a hypothetical non-blight Ireland after 1845 would the condition of the poor have improved without struggle, dislocation and emigration. This point is taken up again in chapter 3.

Still, would relief have come in due course without a holocaust of Great Famine dimensions? My own guess is that the plummeting cost of ocean transport after mid-century and the secularly rising demand for labour in Britain and North America would have eased Ireland's adjustment problems in the decades after 1850. Between mid-century and 1880 the United States alone absorbed about eight million emigrants from Europe, and other places many millions more. Another million Irish could have been handled with relative ease. Such migrants would most likely have been disproportionately drawn from the ranks of the poor, their departure posing no 'skill drain' threat to those who remained.[97] Politics in Ireland would also have increasingly reflected the aspirations of the poor over time. *Phythophthora infestans*'s ravages would thus have been far less deadly a generation later. Ireland was disastrously *unlucky* in the timing of the blight. Surely, then, there is no harm in having attempted to absolve those who relied on the potato before 1845 of suicidal irresponsibility, or in chronicling progress, however uneven, in some sectors of the pre-Famine era?

Appendix 1 'Deindustrialisation' by region

The occupational data in the nineteenth-century censuses offer one way of summarising the decline of industry across counties. Since the quality of reportage varied and the categories used varied from census to census, the story they convey must not be pushed too far. Still, I think the data in table 9 are helpful. The numbers are an attempt to capture the percentage of the labour force in 1821, 1841 and 1881 involved in what might loosely be considered industrial occupations. In 1821 this entailed including 'persons chiefly employed in trades, manufactures and handicrafts' and in 1841 'persons ministering to clothing and lodging, furniture, machinery, etc.'. For 1881 I used the percentage of the total in class V, the 'industrial' class.[98]

TABLE 9   *Percentage of the labour force in industry, 1821–81*

	1821	1841	1881
Ulster			
Antrim	57·2	48·7	43·2
Carrick	54·7	43·7	
Belfast	n.a.	57·0	68·2
Armagh	60·7	48·7	43·2
Cavan	45·8	37·4	15·3
Derry	60·1	47·3	34·2
Donegal	52·5	41·8	22·6
Down	57·0	51·2	45·3
Fermanagh	45·1	41·1	19·5
Monaghan	56·1	40·0	17·8
Tyrone	56·2	47·8	26·3
Total	55·3	45·9	37·1
Leinster			
Carlow	21·2	19·8	22·1
Dublin (city)	54·6	39·8	55·1
Dublin (county)	32·7	19·5	29·0
Kildare	23·4	18·5	22·2
Kilkenny (city)	60·3	37·7	
Kilkenny (county)	17·4	8·2	22·6
King's	26·8	19·8	21·2
Longford	42·5	29·4	18·0
Louth	46·8	28·3	31·5
Drogheda	63·1	48·9	
Meath	32·7	22·4	20·9
Queen's (Laois)	23·1	19·2	20·4
Westmeath	32·6	24·6	19·9
Wexford	22·9	24·2	22·5
Wicklow	48·7	20·0	22·0
Total	33·6	24·1	29·9
Munster			
Clare	24·2	23·5	19·1
Cork (city)	40·9	38·2	48·3
Cork (county)	19·4	19·0	22·2
Kerry	26·8	22·4	19·7
Limerick (city)	38·3	27·1	43·9
Limerick (county)	28·0	21·9	20·9
Tipperary	17·8	16·8	22·0
Waterford (city)	45·7	34·2	50·8
Waterford (county)	14·9	14·4	20·6
Total	23·7	20·8	24·3
Connacht			
Galway (county)	33·9	26·4	16·3
Galway (town)	30·6	35·0	
Leitrim	47·0	37·2	13·5
Mayo	48·8	28·2	13·3
Roscommon	40·4	23·9	15·2
Sligo	46·5	30·7	17·8
Total	42·9	28·4	15·2

Appendix 2 A note on child mortality before 1845

Some measure of Irish child mortality before the Famine would be useful, since child mortality is often considered another proxy for backwardness and poverty. Unfortunately there is very little to go on. Mokyr's pioneering census-based estimates of infant mortality require enough plausible but unsubstantiated assumptions to be considered tentative. Other potantial sources have either not been tried or produce ambiguous results. The latter is true of Rev. Thomas Willis's Dublin data[99] and the burial records quoted by William Wilde in the 1841 census.

At first glance the evidence of Willis, a north city clergyman, is impressive. He produces a great deal of statistical evidence on child mortality and other related questions. However, in his mortality-by-age tabulations he makes the kind of error for which the 1841 census is notorious: after providing mortality data in age-by-months for Dublin children up to eleven months, he jumps from the category 'eleventh month' to 'second year'. How did he allocate those children who died in the twelfth month? How important are omissions? Any estimate of infant mortality based on Willis's tantalising data depends on such imponderables.

The Dublin burial records provided by Wilde are another tempting source. They are an account of weekly burials by age between mid-1839 and mid-1841. The troble here is that evidently some dead children are 'missing'. Comparing an estimate of the number of children born in, say, 1835 or 1836 with the number of five or six-year-old survivors in 1841 implies a far higher number of burials than the cemeteries reported to Wilde. Again, how the missing deaths are allocated across ages determines our guess at infant mortality. To assume that those who went unrecorded were distributed like those included produces an infant mortality rate of about 250 per thousand. This is a good deal less than the 320 per thousand suggested by Mokyr.[100] Yet it might be plausibly countered that infants were more likely to go 'missing' in a source such as this.

This note presents an alternative approach to the problem. Its strategy is to focus on the age gap between children enumerated at some age j in the manuscript forms of the census of 1821 and brother or sister next in line. The data are available in sufficient numbers from Counties Fermanagh, Meath and Galway to be worth considering. Then, given some prior notion of the gap in births, a rough-and-ready guess at mortality follows.

Let us look at the question of births first. The pre-Famine birth rate was probably between thirty-five and forty per thousand.[101] Given that the number of married women aged seventeen to forty-five in 1841 was 858,442, a child per three women yearly would have given thirty-five per thousand; two children per five, forty-two per thousand.

An alternative handle on births is given by the 1841 'Tables on Marriage', which are an attempt to report the number of children born to women marrying between 1830 and 1840:

Children per marriage contracted, 1830–40

1830	3·87	1836	1·99
1831	3·63	1837	1·63
1832	3·32	1838	1·25
1833	3·03	1839	0·88
1834	2·70	1840	0·44
1835	2·35		

Here marriages contracted in 1830 are reported as producing 3·87 children by 1841. The implied fertility here is higher than reported above, but the result is based on a younger, more fecund set of women. Most women above thirty-five years would be excluded, having married before 1830.

What does this imply for the average gap between births? If all families were of the same size, a child per three marriages would mean a gap of 3·3 years between births, and so on. Childless and one-child marriages must reduce the gap, however. It seems reasonable to expect a gap of about 2·5 years, then, in the absence of child deaths.

Now the 1821 census data produce the following results on age gaps:

Age of child	Number	Average gap
7	487	2·920
8	440	2·968
9	453	3·124
10	509	3·145
11	336	3·208
12	447	3·436
13–14	786	3·215

Calculating gaps at younger and older ages would face the problems of more and more children 'missing' through emigration or under-emuneration. As they stand the numbers are 'contaminated' somewhat by the well known age-heaping phenomenon. Both the recorded number of ten and twelve-year olds and the 'low' age gap at age twelve are probably due to this factor. Nevertheless a gap of about three years is indicated, and in general the gaps rise with children's age as expected. What is the implication for child mortality? Against the birth interval suggested by fertility these age gaps seem small, implying rather low child mortality in the mainly rural areas supplying the 1821 data. Data such as those from the 1821 and 1841 census just analysed are weak reeds to build a case on, but they seem to argue tentatively in favour of 'light' child mortality.

Notes

1 Jonathan Pim, *The Condition and Prospects of Ireland* (Dublin, 1848), pp. 36–7.
2 Seán Ó Ceallaigh, *Filíocht na gCallanán* (Dublin, 1967), p. 67. The verse is a Galway balladeer's ode to the memory of the white potato in its heyday.
3 T. R. Malthus, 'Newenham and others on the state of Ireland', *Edinburgh Review*, July 1808; *id.*, 'Newenham on the state of Ireland', *Edinburgh Review*, April

1809; both essays are reprinted in B. Semmel (ed.), *Occasional Papers of T. R. Malthus on Ireland, Population, and Political Economy* (New York, 1963), pp. 32–71; Malthus to David Ricardo, 17 August 1817, in P. Sraffa (ed.), *The Works and Correspondence of David Ricardo*, VII (Cambridge, 1952), pp. 174–5; *Select Committee on Emigration*, [550] H.C. 1826–7, V, 311–27. Malthus's views are further discussed in C. Ó Gráda, 'Malthus and the pre-Famine economy', in A. E. Murphy (ed.), *Economists and the Irish Economy* (Dublin, 1984), pp. 75–95.

4 K. H. Connell, *The Population of Ireland, 1750–1845* (Oxford, 1951); *id., Irish Peasant Society* (Oxford, 1968); David Grigg, *Population Growth and Agrarian Change* (Cambridge, 1981), pp. 115–40; J. K. Galbraith, *The Age of Uncertainty* (New York, 1977), pp. 37–8; Nassau William Senior, *Journals, Essays and Conversations relating to Ireland*, II (London, 1868), pp. 2–3; Barbara L. Solow, *The Land Question and the Irish Economy* (Cambridge, Mass., 1971), p. 196.

5 Michael McGrath (ed.), *Cinnlae Amhlaoimh Uí Shúileabháin* (London, 1936), I, p. 78; II, p. 290; Timothy P. O'Neill, 'Poverty in Ireland, 1815–45', *Folklife*, XI (1974) 30; *id.*, 'Social History of Erris', paper presented at Eigse Riocaird Bairéad, Gaoth Sáile, Mayo, 18 June 1983; W. M. Thackeray, *Irish Sketch Book*, in *Collected Works*, vol. 18 (London, 1888), p. 27.

6 M. Drake, 'The Irish demographic crisis of 1740–1', *Historical Studies VI*, (ed.), T. W. Moody (London, 1968); S. Daultrey, D. Dickson and C. Ó Gráda, 'Eighteenth-century Irish population: new perspectives from old sources', *Journal of Economic History*, XLI (1981): 626–7.

7 The notion, associated with Connell and Drake, that the half-century or so after 1741 saw a 'gap in famines' has been questioned by David Dickson in 'Famine in Ireland, 1700–1775: a review', a paper presented to the Economic and Social History Society of Ireland conference, Derry, September 1981.

8 Poor Inquiry, Supplement to Appendix A, pp. 21, 64, 118, 359. Joel Mokyr, *Why Ireland Starved: A Quantitative and Analytical History of the Irish Economy, 1800–1845*, revised edition (London, 1985), has pioneered the use of the Poor Inquiry evidence along these lines: see his pp. 12, 25–8. For an assessment of the representativeness and reliability of these data see L. A. Clarkson and E. M. Crawford, 'Dietary directions: a topographical survey of Irish Diet, 1836', forthcoming in a volume edited by R. Mitchison and P. Roebuck.

9 The mainly Western character of this crisis is also well reflected in P.R.O. (London), H.O. 100/235/189–211.

10 George O'Brien, *The Economic History of Ireland from the Union to the Famine* (Dublin and London, 1921), pp. 224–32.

11 Wilde's reports are in the *Census of Ireland for the Year 1851*, Part V, *Tables of Deaths*, vol. 1, containing the report, tables of pestilences, and analysis of the tables of deaths, [2087-I] H.C. 1856, xxix, 261; *Report of the Commissioners appointed to take the Census of Ireland for the Year 1841*, [504] H.C. 1843, xxiv, 1.

12 F. Barker and J. Cheyne, *An Account of the Rise, Progress and Decline of the Fever late Epidemical in Ireland* (Dublin, 1821).

13 John D. Post, *The Last Great Subsistence Crisis in the Western World* (Baltimore, Md., 1977), pp. 108–22.

14 T. Newenham, *A Statistical and Historical Inquiry into the Progress and Magnitude of the Population of Ireland* (Dublin, 1805), pp. 131–2.

15 P.R.O. (London), Barker to Wellesley, Home Office 100/206, 26 September 1822; Timothy P. O'Neill, 'The Famine of 1822' (unpublished M.A. dissertation, National University of Ireland, 1966), 'Conclusion', p. 1.

16 Timothy P. O'Neill, 'Poverty and Administrative Reform in Ireland, 1815–1845', paper presented to the Irish Historical Society, 11 October 1983; *id.*, 'Erris'. I am very grateful to Dr O'Neill for giving me copies of these papers. See too Mrs E. Costello, *Amhráin Mhuighe Seola* (Dublin, 1923), pp. 23–5, for a song about famine relief in the 1820s. Also Stephen A. Royle, 'Irish famine relief in the early nineteenth century', *Irish Economic and Social History*, XI (1984), pp. 44–59, and Timothy P. O'Neill, 'The famine of 1822', on relief in

the remote west in 1822.

17 Malthus, *Essay on the Principle of Population* (London, 1798 (1965)), p. 141; *id.*, 'Newenham and others', p. 42. For references to the literature on Malthus and Ireland see Mokyr, *Why*, pp. 38-45; C. Ó Gráda, 'Malthus'.

18 Phelim P. Boyle and C. Ó Gráda, 'Fertility trends, excess mortality, and the great Irish Famine', *Demography*, 23 (1986), 542-62.

19 Mokyr, *Why*, p. 43.

20 D. Dickson, C. Ó Gráda and S. Daultrey, 'Hearth tax, household size and Irish population change, 1672-1821', *Proceedings of the Royal Irish Academy*, Section C, 82 (6) (192), 178; Joel Mokyr and C. Ó Gráda, 'New developments in Irish population history, 1700-1850', *Economic History Review*, ser. 2, XXVII (4) (1984), 473-88. The role of increasing nuptiality in accelerating population growth earlier is stressed by Thomas Newenham, *A Statistical Inquiry into the Progress and Magnitude of the Population of Ireland* (London, 1805).

21 Dr Austin Bourke, to whom I am very grateful for insight into this question, would like to see the fourth centenary of the potato's introduction celebrated in 1990 (private communication to author, 20 November 1986)! For more on the diffusion controversy see Redcliffe N. Salaman, *The Influence of the Potato on the Course of Irish History* (Dublin, 1943); *id.*, *The History and Social Influence of the Potato* (Cambridge, 1949), chapters 11-12; L. M. Cullen, 'Irish history without the potato', *Past and Present*, XI (July 1968), 72-83; Joel Mokyr, 'Irish history with the potato', *Irish Economic and Social History*, VIII (1981), 8-29. Also N. J. A. Williams (ed.), *Pairlement Chloinne Tomais* (Dublin, 1981), pp. 62-3, 115.

22 Elizabeth Hoffman and J. Mokyr, 'Peasants, poverty, and potatoes: transaction costs in prefamine Ireland', in Gary Saxonhouse and Gavin Wright (eds.), *Technique, Spirit and Form in the Making of the Modern Economy: Essays in Honor of William N. Parker* (Greenwich, Conn., 1983), pp. 115-45; Arthur Young, *Tour in Ireland* (Dublin, 1780); W. Tighe, *Statistical Survey of Kilkenny* (Dublin, 1802), pp. 479-80.

23 McGrath, *Cinnlae*, I, p. 276; George Vaughan Sampson, *Statistical Survey of the County of Londonderry* (Dublin, 1802), p. 135. Also Samuel Lewis, *Topographical Dictionary of Ireland* (London, 1837), entry on County Clare.

24 P. M. A. Bourke, 'The extent of the potato crop in Ireland at the time of the Famine', *Journal of the Statistical and Social Inquiry Society of Ireland*, XX, 3 (1959/60), 1-35; Mokyr, 'Irish history with the potato', *Irish Economic and Social History*, VIII (1980): 15-24. Mokyr puts his revised data to ingenious use in an attempt to explain the pattern of diffusion. But can cross-section 1840s data explain a temporal process spanning two centuries?

25 O. McDonagh, *The Nineteenth-century Novel* (Dublin, n.d.), p. 7; J. Mokyr, 'Uncertainty and prefamine Irish agriculture', in D. Dickson and T. Devine (eds.), *Ireland and Scotland, 1600-1850: Parallels and Contrasts in Economic and Social Development* (Edinburgh, 1983), pp. 89-94.

26 This was apparently not so later, though. For the 1871-1913 period the detrended coefficient of variation in oat yields was 0·091 in France and 0·085 in Ireland. For wheat the numbers were 0·133 and 0·100. The data are in Brian Mitchell, *European Historical Statistics* (London, 1975), pp. 203, 214, 240, 253, and Brian Mitchell and Phyllis Deane, *Abstract of British Historical Statistics* (Cambridge, 1962), pp. 92-3. Earlier calculations underlying claims in my 'Malthus', pp. 83-4, were incorrect.

27 C. Trevelyan, *The Irish Crisis* (London, 1848), p. 2; M. Longfield, *Lectures on Political Economy* (Dublin, 1834), pp. 249-52. Price seasonality is discussed in chapter 4; for transport costs see Hoffman and Mokyr, 'Peasants, poverty, and potatoes'. As regard Longfield's storage through pigs, it must be noted that this was a very costly form of storage; pigs conserve only one-fifth or so of the calories they consume.

28 P. Sraffa, (ed.), *Ricardo*, IX, pp. 232, 252-3; Robert McKay, *An Anthology of the Potato* (Dublin, 1961), p. 58; William Steuart Trench, *Realities of Irish Life*

(London, 1966), p. 47. For the statement by Dr Doyle and advice on the literature generally my thanks to Dr Austin Bourke.

29 Tighe, *Kilkenny*, pp. 234–5. A Canadian farmer who aims to preserve heritage seeds and in 1985 grew 110 potato varieties tells me, 'over the years I have noticed that some years a few varieties do well and in other years others do well. I realize that this is only anecdotal evidence but that I have been aware of this for several years'. Alex Caron, King City, Ontario, communication to author, 26 Fesbuary 1986. On the allocation of grain production in LDCs between man and beast see Raymond F. Hopkins and Donald J. Puchala (eds.), *The Global Political Economy of Food* (Madison, Wis., 1978), p. 277. On the lumper's neglected advantages, A. Howden, 'Reports on experiments on the comparative value of different varieties of potato', *Transactions of the Highland and Agricultural Society*, XI (1837).

30 Kevin Danaher, *The Year in Ireland* (Cork, 1972), pp. 163–6; McGrath, *Cinnlae*, I, p. 83; *Poor Inquiry*, Appendix E, Part I, p. 1.

31 This point is further discussed below in chapter 4.

32 E. Margaret Crawford, 'Dearth, diet, and disease in Ireland, 1850: a case study of nutritional deficiency', *Medical History*, 32 (1984): 151–61; *id.*, 'Indian meal and pellagra in nineteenth-century Ireland', in J. M. Goldstrom and L. A. Clarkson (eds.), *Irish Population, Economy and Society: Essays in Honour of the Late K. H. Connell* (Oxford, 1981), pp. 113–33. See also n. 46 below.

33 *Evidence taken before Her Majesty's Commissioners of Inquiry into the State of the Law and Practice in Respect of the Occupation of Land in Ireland* (Devon Commission), p. 1116; Wakefield, *An Account of Ireland, Statistical and Political* (London, 1812), vol. II, p. 730; H. D. Inglis, *A Tour of Ireland in the Year 1834* (London, 1835), p. 323. See also J. K. Trimmer, *A Brief Inquiry into the Present State of Agriculture in the South of Ireland* (London, 1809), p. 7.

34 See, e.g., *Poor Inquiry*, Appendix A, and the harrowing catalogue of 'Selection of Cases from Returns of Paupers relieved in the Three Months from 10th January to 9th April, 1844, in Unions in Ireland', in *Tenth Annual Report of the Poor Law Commissioners* (London, 1844), pp. 398–460.

35 P. M. A. Bourke, 'The use of the potato crop in pre-Famine Ireland', *Journal of the Statistical and Social Inquiry Society of Ireland*, XXI (6) (1968): 72–96; *Third Report of the Commissioners for Inquiring into the Condition of the Poorer Classes in Ireland*, [43] H.C. 1836, XXX, p. 5.

36 L. Sandberg, 'The case of the impoverished sophisticate: human capital and Swedish economic growth before World War I', *Journal of Economic History*, XXXIX (1979), 225–42.

37 J. Mokyr, *Why*, pp. 9–11; Paul Bairoch, 'Europe's gross national product, 1800–1975', *Journal of European Economic History*, 5 (2) (1976), p. 286.

38 R. Dornbusch, 'Purchasing power parity', in J. Eatwell *et al.* (eds.), *The New Palgrave Dictionary of Economics* (New York, 1986); A. Maddison, 'A comparison of levels of GDP *per capita* in developed and developing countries', *Journal of Economic History*, XLIII (1983), 31, 40.

39 McGrath, *Cinnlae*, I, pp. 113, 323; II, pp. 315, 335; III, pp. 63, 67.

40 A. L. Bowley, 'The statistics of wages in the United Kingdom over the last hundred years, III, Agricultural Wages, Ireland', *Royal Statisticsl Society Journal*, LXII (1899), 395–404. How prevalent was seasonal unemployment? Mokyr, *Why*, pp. 214–16, presents two sets of estimates, the first of which stems from his income data, the second from evidence collected by the Poor Inquiry. The substantial gap between them must be due in part to the computing error explained in the revised edition, p. xi. Very much in line with the Poor Inquiry evidence, a correspondent in the *Irish Farmers' Gazette*, 17 August 1822, suggests, 'The peasantry are generally employed in the spring about six weeks, in digging, planting, and sowing for the farmers and cutting his turf; after which they commence their own business of potato tillage, and turf cutting which occupies about three to four weeks more. In the autumn they may be employed about the same length of time, which leaves them about thirty-two or thirty-four weeks of idleness in

each year, out of which deduct seventy-four days for Sundays, holy days, and bad weather, and the remainder will leave them about 150 days that are idly and often profanely spent, but which under a better system, might be applied to useful and profitable labour.'

41 1841 census, p. 436; de Latocnaye, *A Walking Tour of Ireland* (Dublin, 1917), p. 17; Thackeray, *Sketchbook*, pp. 80, 106, 306.

42 Poor Inquiry, Appendix C, Part II.

43 Boyle and Ó Gráda, 'Fertility trends'. The point about fertility is Joek Mokyr's.

44 Adam Smith (R. H. Campbell, A. S. Skinner, W. B. Todd, (eds.), *An Inquiry into the Nature and Causes of the Wealth of Nations* (Oxford, 1976), p. 171; Robert Kane, *The Industrial Resources of Ireland* (Dublin, 1845), p. 400; J. Bicheno, *Ireland and its Economy* (London, 1830), p. 37. For a defence of heights as a proxy for health and welfare, see R. W. Fogel, 'Nutrition and the Decline of Mortality since 1700: some preliminary findings', NBER Working Paper Series, No. 1402.

45 R. Steckel, 'Height and *per capita* income', *Historical Methods*, XVI (1983).

46 Christopher Lloyd, *The British Seaman, 1300-1860: a Social Survey* (London, 1968), pp. 269-71; Eugene L. Rasor, *Reform in the Royal Navy: a Social Hisyory of the Lower Deck, 1850 to 1880* (Hamden, Conn., 1976), pp. 9, 17, 26-8.

47 J. Mokyr and C. Ó Gráda, 'From Poor to Poorer? Irish Living Standards before the Great Famine' (Centre for Economic Research, University College Dublin, 1984); C. Ó Gráda, 'Bochtaineacht, Bás, agus Beatha roimh an nGorta', forthcoming *Studia Hibernica*. The rest of this section builds on these papers.

48 Mokyr and Ó Gráda, 'Living Standards in Ireland and Britain, 1800-1815: the India Office Company Data', paper presented to the Social Science History conference, St Louis, October 1986. The data set of over twenty-three thousand men was collected at the India Office Library, London. Of related interest are the findings of the Army Medical Board on morbidity and mortality in the ranks in Ireland in the 1790s. Their comparison of men in the militia (Irish-born) and the Fencible regiments (British-born) showed the Irish to be far fitter. Age had something to do with it, but the Board stressed too the Irishmen's hardy peasant origins, 'inured by labour in the fields to every vicissitude of climate and season', by contrast with the Englishmen, many of whom were 'mechanics from unhealthy parts of Great Britain and from unwholesome sedentary trades'. 'Observations on the Diseases of the Militia and Fencible Regiments of the Irish Establishment . . . by the Army Medical Board, written in March 1796', quoted in Kenneth P. Ferguson, 'The Army in Ireland from the Restoration to the Act of Union' (unpublished Ph.D. dissertation, Trinity College, Dublin, 1983), p. 95.

49 J. Mokyr, *Why*, p. 15-16; *id.*, 'Industrialization and poverty in Ireland and the Netherlands: some notes towards a comparative case study', *Journal of Interdisciplinary History*, X (3) (1980), 429-59.

50 A. Sen, *Poverty and Famines* (Oxford, 1981). For instance, it seems a safe guess that $P(D/H)$ increased with the changes in relief policy associated with Sir John Russell's administration during the Famine (see chapter 3).

51 E. G. Wakefield, *An Account*, II, pp. 397-8.

52 Joseph J. Lee, 'On the accuracy of the pre-Famine Irish censuses', in J. M. Goldstrom and L. A. Clarkson (eds.), *Irish Population, Economy, and Society* (Oxford, 1981), pp. 37-56.

53 Mokyr and Ó Gráda, 'From Poor to Poorer?'.

54 P.R.O.N.I., T 1536/4.

55 P.R.O.N.I., T 1556/4; T 2204/2; Royal College of Physicians, Kirkpatrick Ms. 94 (Letter from Thomas Mills, M.D., to Michael Mills, Loughbrickland, County Down, August 1805).

56 Mokyr, *Why*, p. 12; see also Mokyr and Ó Gráda, 'From Poor to Poorer?'.

57 Mokyr, *Why*; Eric Almquist, 'Pre-Famine Ireland and the theory of European proto-industrialization: evidence from the 1841 census', *Journal of Economic History*, XXXIX (3) (1979), 699-718; Patrick McGregor, 'The impact of the blight upon the pre-Famine rural economy of Ireland', *Economic and Social*

Review, XV (1984), 289-304.

58 J. Pim, *The Condition*, pp. 38-9.

59 P. Lindert and J. G. Williamson, 'English workers' living standards during the industrial revolution: a new look', *Economic History Review*, XXXVI (1983), 1-25.

60 Mokyr and Ó Gráda, 'From Poor to Poorer?'.

61 J. J. Monaghan, 'The rise and fall of the Belfast cotton industry', *Irish Historical Studies*, 3 (1942-43); E. R. R. Green, *The Lagan Valley: a Local History of the Industrial Revolution* (London, 1949), pp. 95-111; David Dickson, 'Aspects of the Irish cotton industry', in Cullen and Smout (eds.), pp. 100-16.

62 Compare Dickson, *op. cit.*, pp. 105, 108, and Joel Mokyr, *Industrialization in the Low Countries, 1795-1850* (New Haven, Conn., 1976), pp. 28-36. Admittedly the Irish industry had a head start.

63 Samuel McSkimmin, *The History and Antiquities of Carrickfergus* (Belfast, 1909), pp. 358-9; Samuel Lewis, *Topographical Dictionary of Ireland* (London, 1837), I, p. 179.

64 George O'Brien, *Economic History*, pp. 297-308; Séamus Ó Duillearga (ed.), *Leabhar Sheáin Í Chonaill* (Dublin, 1977), p. 380. ('My grey waistcoat is neat and pretty, not like the tweed made by the woman from the mountain.')

65 Conrad Gill, *The Rise of the Irish Linen Industry* (Oxford, 1925); William H. Crawford, *Domestic Industry in Ireland* (Dublin, 1973); Green, *The Lagan Valley*; Eric L. Almquist, 'Mayo and Beyond: Land, Domestic Industry, and Rural Transformation in the Irish West, 1750-1900' (unpublished Ph.D. dissertation, Boston University, 1977), chapter 4.

66 John Fitzgerald, 'The Organization of the Drogheda Economy, 1780-1820' (unpublished M.A. dissertation, National University of Ireland, 1972).

67 D. A. Farnie, *The English Cotton Industry and the World Market, 1815-1896* (Oxford, 1979), pp. 45-77; J. S. Hekman, 'The product cycle and New England textiles', *Quarterly Journal of Economics*, 94 (1980): 697-717. For a relevant discussion of scale economies and 'insignificant historical events' see W. Brian Arthur, 'Competing technologies and economic prediction', *Options* (Vienna), April 1984, pp. 10-13, and *id.*, 'Industry Location Patterns and the Importance of History' (unpublished discussion paper, Stanford University, March 1986).

68 Lewis's *Topographical Dictionary*, I, pp. 194-5.

69 W. E. Coe, *The Engineering Industry of the North of Ireland* (Newton Abbot, 1969), chapters 1-5.

70 Green, *The Lagan Valley*, p. 176.

71 George O'Brien, 'The last Years of the Irish Currency', *Economic History* (supplement to *Economic Journal*), 2 (1927).

72 F. G. Hall, *The Bank of Ireland, 1783-1946* (Dublin and Oxford, 1949); Charles Munn, 'The emergence of central banking in Ireland: the Bank of Ireland, 1814-1845', *Irish Economic and Social History*, X (1983), 19-32; G. L. S. Barrow, *The Emergence of the Irish Banking System* (Dublin, 1973). Of the Restriction policy and the Bank of Ireland's monopoly Henry Parnell was the most brilliant critic. His *Observations of the State of the Currency* (Dublin and London, 1804) anticipates the best fruits of the bullionist controversy, while his later *Observations on Paper Money, Banking and Overtrading* (London, 1827) is one of the classics of the 'free banking' school.

73 This paragraph draws on the archives of the Bank of Ireland (Foster Place and Baggot Street, Dublin) and Allied Irish Banks (Foster Place, Dublin).

74 Barrow, *Emergence*, pp. 108-20; *id.*, 'Justice for Thomas Mooney', *Dublin Historical Record*, XXIV (1970), 173-88.

75 Allied Irish Banks archive, records of the Parsonstown (Birr) and Youghal branches of the Pronvincial Bank; Bank of Ireland archives (Foster Place), records of the Castlebar National Branch.

76 Barrow, *Emergence*, pp. 215-21.

77 *Dublin Evening Post, passim*, 1820; Barrow, *Emergence*, pp. 17-23; Eoin O'Kelly, *The old Private Banks of Munster* (Cork, 1959), pp. 23-9, 158-60.

78 W. A. McCutcheon, *The Canals of Northern Ireland* (Newton Abbot, 1965), pp. 62-85, 98-119; V. T. H. and D. R. Delany, *The Canals of the South of Ireland* (Newton Abbot, 1966); V. T. H. Delany, *The Grand Canal of Ireland* (Newton Abbot, 1973).

79 N.L.I. Ms. 10736.

80 Thomas G. Ferris, 'The Ulster Railway' (unpublished M.A. dissertation, Queen's University, Belfast 1979), p. 20.

81 P.R.O.N.I., D 207/27/39, Massarene Papers, D. L. Rosse to Lord Oriel, 28 January 1828 (quoted in Ferris, *op. cit.*, p. 24). More generally see J. Lee, 'An Economic History of early Irish Railways' (M.A. thesis, National University of Ireland, 1965). W. A. Thomas, *The Stock Exchanges of Ireland* (Liverpool, 1986), chapter 6, is useful on investment in the first railway ventures.

82 Drummond Commission, Second Report, pp. 40-1; Seán Ó Lúing, 'Richard Griffith and the roads to Kerry', *Journal of the Kerry Historical and Archaeological Society*, 8 (1975), 89-113, and 9 (1976), 92-124.

83 Select Committee on the State of the Poor in Ireland, evidence of Charles Wye Williams, q. 3110-81; David B. McNeill, *Irish Passenger Steamship Services* (Newton Abbot, 1969 and 1971), I, pp. 1-28, and II, pp. 11-19, 34-8; Samuel Lewis, *Topographical Dictionary of Ireland* (London, 1837), entry for Cork; *Gore's General Advertiser*, 'The cattle trade', 8 January 1829. I owe the last reference to Peter Solar.

84 Mr and Mrs S. C. Hall, *Ireland* (London, 1845), I, pp. 404-7. See too Lewis, *Topographical Dictionary*, entries for Cork, Ennis, Mallow, Navan, Enniscorthy, Gorey, even Cahirciveen.

85 According to Ralph Davis (*The Industrial Revolution and Overseas Trade*, Leicester, 1979, tables 38-64) the value of Irish exports to Britain rose from £3·5 million in 1794/6 to £9·4 million in 1824/6. The change in real terms was probably not too different. To assume that output grew in line with population implies increasing openness.

86 The model is outlined in R. W. Jones and J. P. Neary, 'The positive theory of international trade', in R. W. Jones and P. B. Kenen (eds.), *Handbook of International Economics*, I (Amsterdam, 1984), pp. 1-62.

87 This extract from a Roscommon farmer's plea highlights the contentious distributional aspects of the corn law: 'Humble as I am I beg you will add my name to those who feel indignant at this revolutionary measure intended and calculated to excite the passions of an ignorant and deluded populace and to produce further agitation to return in office ministers who have deranged the finances of the state . . . and who seek by the repeal of the corn laws to reduce this part of the Empire to utter distress . . . After leaving Ireland nothing but agriculture, they seek to excite the passions of the lower orders to England against our only and last resource.' N.L.I. Ms. 10127, 18 May 1841.

88 Simon Kuznets, 'Economic growth and income inequality', *American Economic Review*, 45 (1) (1955), 1-28.

89 Stephen Hymer and Stephen Resnick, 'A model of an agrarian economy with non-agrarian activities', *American Economic Review*, 59 (1969), 493-516.

90 Suppose $Q = AL^{\alpha}e^{\mu t}$, where Q is output, L labour input, t time, and A, μ and α are constants. Then for

$$\frac{\dot{Q}/L}{Q/L} = (\alpha - 1)\frac{\dot{L}}{L} + \mu$$

to exceed zero, where α and $\dot{L}/L$ both about 0·5, productivity growth of 25 per cent over the period would have been required.

91 N. F. R. Crafts, 'Income elasticities of demand and the release of labour by agriculture during the British industrial revolution', *Journal of European Economic History*, 9 (1980), 153-68.

92 The tendency towards greater economic inequality seems also to have been present in Great Britain during these years. See J. G. Williamson, 'Earnings inequality in nineteenth-century Britain', *Journal of Economic History*, XL (1980),

457-76.

93 James S. Donnelly, 'The journals of Sir John Benn Walsh', *Journal of the Cork Archaeological and Historical Society*, LXXXI (1975), 89; William A. Maguire, *The Downshire Estates* (Oxford, 1974), p. 39; Eric A. Almquist, 'Mayo and Beyond', pp. 126-38; National Library of Ireland, Mss. 6077-81 (Fitzwilliam estate), 6915, 6923, 6969 (Lismore estate); 1740 (O'Callaghan, Shanbally); 1756 (Trant, Tipperary); 12792-805 (Mohill, Leitrim); P.R.O.N.I., D 1606/7A/34, 48 (Gosford estate, Armagh); D 623/c/4/1, 10 (Abercorn papers, Strabane part); D 3531/12/2 (Shirley estate, Monaghan); Kevin O'Neill, *Family and Farm*, pp. 51-7 (Hodson and Garvagh estates, Cavan).

94 J. K. Galbraith, *The Age of Uncertainty* (New York, 1977), p. 37.

95 I owe this reference to Austin Bourke. See too L. M. Cullen, *Life in Ireland* (London, 1968), p. 142.

96 Cullen, *Life in Ireland*, chapter 6.

97 On the 'skill drain' see the discussion in Mokyr and Ó Gráda, 'Emigration and poverty in prefamine Ireland', *Explorations in Economic History*, 19 (1982), 360-84.

98 The data for 1821 and 1841 form the basis of maps in my *Éire Roimh an nGorta: an Saol Eacnamaíoch* (Dublin, 1985), pp. 46-7. The maps highlight how important non-agricultural work was in the northern half of the island in 1821, and the decline between 1821 and 1841 in south Ulster and north Connacht. It must be pointed out, though, that the decline in industrial occupations hit women more than men in these decades.

99 Thomas Willis, *Facts concerning the Social and Sanitary Condition of the Working Classes of Dublin* (Dublin, 1845).

100 Mokyr, *Why*, pp. 37-8.

101 Mokyr, *Why*, pp. 33-4; Boyle and Ó Gráda, 'Fertility trends'.

CHAPTER 2

Agriculture
before and after the Famine

If England had the five talents confided to her stewardship, let her not taunt Ireland, to whom none has been entrusted, that she has not made usurious interest. [J. E. Bicheno, 1830] [1]

For several decades after the great Famine farming accounted for more than half Ireland's occupied population, one-third or more of national output, and the bulk of merchandise exports. On the eve of the Famine agriculture's role was even more dominant. This is the logic behind George O'Brien's truism that 'the land and its industries occupied such a prominent place in Irish life that a history of Irish agriculture would be of necessity something not very far removed from an economic—and indeed a political—history of Ireland'.[2] Too often, though, research on nineteenth-century Irish agricultural history (not least O'Brien's) has been dominated by just one part of the story, the politics of land tenure. Even when the more economic and technical aspects of farming are considered, the discussion is still usually nested in some controversy about the land issue. Revisionist work has changed the verdict, not the main focus of attention. Landlords, whether 'rack-renting' or 'great', still claim more than their share of attention at the expense of those who managed and worked the fields. As a result the intricacies of the various Land Acts are far better understood than, say, the diffusion of certain possibly key process innovations on the farm.

Across the Irish Sea the story of eighteenth and nineteenth-century agriculture is told instead largely in terms of leading 'improvers' and technical and organisational change. This will hardly do in the Irish case, for although Ireland too had its own Youngs and Mechis and Laweses, and some of the contemporary trappings of the 'age of improvement'—a hundred local agricultural societies by 1845, for example, and a small agriculturess replete with examples from the Lothians of Scotland—their impact was less, and they have been largely forgotten. More to the point, the goals and achievements of the ordinary Irish farmer and farm worker have attracted little attention. Few, however, have had a good word for them. Outside observers tended to see them as a lazy and ignorant mass, and apologists as too oppressed to function effectively. But work on the humdrum details of farming practice and technique has been neglected. While the study of rent movements and outlays on improvements by particular landlords reaches the stage of diminishing returns, issues such as the change in yields and seed requirements, or the pattern of innovation diffusion, remain almost a blank.

A definitive account of efficiency and productivity change on the land, crucial aspects of the economic history of Irish agriculture, cannot be given at this stage, and attempts at comprehensiveness would therefore be premature. Yet Ireland is not alone in this. The authors of a recent American survey admit that 'much of American history is not ready for textbook treatment', and more disarmingly that 'much can never be unravelled from the extant materials'.[3] So consoled, let us explore some aspects of Irish farming before and after the Famine.

1. Pre-Famine productivity

How backward was nineteenth-century Irish agriculture? To contemporaries, for whom British agriculture was a convenient yardstick, pre-Famine backwardness was often defined in terms of one country's chronological yield over the other. Thus a Cork clergyman-farmer noted in 1837 that 'it is now a common saying that we are a century behind England'. Not too disappointing, perhaps, if one credits Arthur Young's throw-away remark of five decades earlier that Irish tillage was 500 years behind England's most advanced areas.[4] The search for further evidence along these lines leads only to confusion, however. In the 1820s, according to a French reporter, Irish farming implements were 300 years out of date, but to the English agriculturalist Henry Thompson Irish farming methods before the Famine had gone unchanged 'from the time of Conn of the Hundred Battles of Niall and his train of hostage kings'.[5] Later the comparison, again invariably unfavourable or damning, tended to be with Denmark.[6] Yet this definition of backwardness, besides being ambiguous, rests on claims that are rarely supported in detail. If backwardness is defined instead in terms of low productivity, how much is there to explain? How should performance on the farm between the 1840s and the 1920s be assessed? These are some of the issues discussed here and in chapter 5.

Ireland before the Famine was almost a 'statistical dark age' in most respects, agriculture included. Contemporary guides are few and often unreliable. Still, a rough-and-ready estimate of pre-Famine output can be pieced together, with the help of sources such as the 1841 census, the Poor Inquiry of 1935–36 and guesses at pre-Famine crop acreages. An earlier estimate of mine has been published elsewhere: it is reproduced with minor changes in table 10. The 1841 census provides the necessary estimates of livestock

TABLE 10 *Irish agricultural output at current prices, 1840-45 (£ million)*

Crops	
Wheat	4·9
Oats	8·1
Barley	1·8
Flax	1·3
Potatoes	8·8
Hay	0·6
Other	1·3
Subtotal	26·8
Livestock	
Cattle	4·7
Butter and Milk	4·8
Pigs	3·4
Sheep	0·8
Wool	0·5
Eggs	0·9
Other	0·8
Subtotal	15·9
Total	42·7

numbers, but my guesses at productivity in the livestock sector rely on a range of unrelated sources. Hopefully they are good guides, though the traps set by such sources need hardly be stressed. My estimates of tillage output rely heavily on the pioneering work of Austin Bourke, which imply a small drop in cereal output in the immediate wake of the Famine (table 11).[7] Note that while Bourke's estimates envisage a fall in aggregate acreage, they assume a *rise* in wheat acreage in the wake of the potato failure.

Now the hard quantitative evidence for this famine-induced shift does not exist, since official statistics begin only in 1847. But many qualitative accounts, particularly from the west, seem to bear it out. Thus in the Poor Law Unions of Ballinrobe, Westport and Castlebar, 'many fields and patches that might have been advantageously sown, [were] left bare' in 1847, while in neighbouring Ballina Union 'the extent of arable land which has been left has been left uncultivated and producing nothing but

TABLE 11 Estimated tillage output

Crop	Acreage ('000)		
	1845	1847	1849
Oats	2,500	2,201	2,061
Wheat	700	744	688
Barley	300	333	352
Potatoes	2,187*	284	719
Total	5,687	3,562	3,820

*Cf. Mokyr, 'Irish history with the potato', Irish Economic and Social History, VIII (1981), 12.

weeds, cannot fail but excite the attention of anybody who visits this country'. In the area around Clifden 'the non-cultivation of the land [was] plainly observable', and around Kilrush 'about 6,000 notices to quit have been served and all the lands under ejectment are literally bare of all stock or produce'. Meanwhile in west Wicklow 'half the country [was] left untilled', and in Sligo 'excepting among the landlords and strong farmers . . . the lands lie status quo, choked with weeds'. Among smaller farmers 'the animus is also wanting, for they calculate that a grain crop after the rates and rent have been paid, cannot maintain them'. Evidence to the contrary may be found too, however. In Wexford and parts of Waterford the acreage under wheat was reported to be up and, in general, tillage with horses was affected less than spade cultivation.[8] In September 1847 the Farmers' Gazette reported 'wheat crops never before so extensive in culture' and 'oats, never so extensively cultivated, except in the case of the small farmers, who have become as a class, all but extinct, whose holdings are, in many instances, lying waste'.[9] Yet, allowing for the eastern, strong-farmer perspective of the Gazette, some slight falling-off in the aggregate grain acreage is plausible.

Theory too seems to support something like Bourke's estimates. True, the blight-induced drop in potato cultivation must have caused many of those smallholders still in business to shift in desperation to turnips and cereals. Other forces worked in the opposite direction, though. First, death and emigration reduced the numbers in agriculture after 1845; hunger surely cut the productivity of those remaining. Second, most grain was grown not for smallholder consumption but for sale off the farm by both smaller and larger land-holders. As argued in more detail in chapter 4, the effect of the potato failure was to increase the wage that farmers had to pay in order to acquire productive workers. Thus men were 'ready and willing to work for their own sustenance and that of their families, for such moderate wages as shall enable them to live *at present prices*'. Before 1845 these were potato wages: now the minimum wage must reflect the higher 'sustenance' costs entailed by a grain-based diet. Since the increase in labour costs caused by the change in diet far exceeded the rise in grain prices, in principle farmers should have been inclined to grow less grain and hire fewer men. As the pamphleteer John Stanley predicted in a perceptive comment to the Lord Lieutenant in the early stages of the Famine:

> The great body of the rural population produce their own food. Now, affording employment other than as heretofore, must, in the ratio you afford it, increase wages. It is manifest that Irish farmers, from want of capital, could not pay a serious advance in wages, nor could they carry out production, with a high wages rate even by the system existing. Should any measure tend to considerably raise wages, I submit, there are good reasons to believe, that it would diminish production; and hence we are only at the beginning of a train of difficulties. Again money wages does [*sic*] not enter into the calculation of Irish farmers, commonly operating. If labourers should get money wages elsewhere they might prefer it, to the old system of payments, and the danger becomes visible of decreasing products . . . One shilling a day may not feed the people, yet it may deeply decrease production of food in Ireland![10]

The numbers in table 10 prompt a few comments. First, they raise a question about the pre-eminence of the potato, at least in terms of output share. The staple food of more than one-third of the population turns out to have accounted for only one-fifth of output. This is our earlier distinction between mean holding size and the proportion of land in farms above a certain size in another guise. While the outcome confirms the potato's importance relative to elsewhere, it is the massive role of tillage crops generally that is most striking. Admittedly the potato formed a higher proportion of gross agricultural production, since a higher proportion of the crop was absorbed as intermediate output.

Second, there is little scope in these numbers for the pre-Famine switch to pasture emphasised by some writers, notably Raymond Crotty.[11] Tillage items were still contributing over three-fifths of total output in the early 1840s. This marks a prodigious change from earlier centuries, for, although table 10 hides the fact, Irish agriculture had traditionally been largely pastoral. Late eighteenth-century population growth and parliamentary bounties had given a strong boost to corn, however. In the pre-Famine decades buoyant demand in Britain greatly increased the acreage under the plough and spade, and the decline

of domestic industry added to it. Scattered evidence of consolida-
tion and shifts to pasture before 1845, and of associated peasant
resistance, are not hard to find. Nevertheless tillage arguably
accounted for an increasing proportion of output from the 1780s
until very close to the Famine, so that table 10 is a snapshot of
what was the culmination of a very long-drawn-out process. A
corollary was a landscape very different from that of Ireland
today. 'The view presented by the country in the months of July
and August,' according to one account from the 1830s, 'is an
interwoven patchwork of potatoes, wheat, barley, and so little
intervention of meadow and pasture, that one is surprised how the
inhabitants contrive to maintain their cows, horses, and sheep . . .'
In his diary Amhlaoimh Ó Súileabháin wrote of the summer scene
around Callan being 'chomh glas le geabhar' ('as green as corn
grass').[12] Hyperbolic licence apart, contemporary micro-data tell
the same story.[13]

Third, the outcome suggests how highly commercialised Irish
agriculture had become on the eve of the Famine. Although
comprehensive Irish trade data were no longer kept after economic
union in 1825, it is safe to assume that the bulk of the livestock
and up to a quarter of all grain—and therefore a quarter of all
output—was being exported during the 1830s and early 1840s.
Two-fifths of even the oat crop were being marketed on the eve
of the Famine, and Bourke's calculations[14] imply that a quarter of
grain output was being exported. To assume in addition that half
of all livestock was being shipped out—hardly an extravagant
claim—would mean that exports accounted for a quarter of all
output.[15] The potato, mainstay of the poor smallholder, was the
subsistence crop *par excellence*, yet the better varieties and
qualities were sold in quantity in town and city markets throughout the year. Perhaps three-fifths of all agricultural output, then,
was being marketed. This squares rather poorly with the once
popular view of an insulated subsistence-bent agricultural sector in
the pre-Famine period.[16] Still, the degree of commercialisation
undoubtedly had a regional and social aspect, being lowest in the
west, where farms were smallest and dependence on the potato
was greatest, and among agricultural labourers, who had little use
for money, partly because they were poor, partly because they
paid their conacre rent mostly in labour. Yet the demand for these
workers' labour was market-derived.

Estimates of acreage and employment totals underly the
productivity calculations in table 12. The Irish census of 1841
reports 453,000 adult male farmers and 1,105,258 adult male
servants and labourers in agriculture. Ploughmen, gardeners,

graziers, herds, agents, etc., bring the total employed on the land to just below 1·6 million. Since some of these were part-timers, to assume an agricultural labour force of 1·6 million for 1840–45 surely takes care of an increase occurring over these years.[17] Agricultural land accounted for 15 million acres. When coupled with British data these numbers yield the figures in table 12.[18]

TABLE 12 Agricultural output and productivity in Ireland and Great Britain, c. 1845

1	Output (£ million)	40 – 43	120 – 130
2	Acreage (million)	15	30
3	Employment (million)	1·6	2·0
4	1/2	2·5 – 2·8	4·0 – 4·3
5	1/3	24 – 26	60 – 65

The 'backwardness' of pre-Famine agriculture is now seen in clearer focus. Allowing for the lower prices obtaining in Ireland, British superiority in terms of labour productivity was still more than two to one. This may be compared with a recent estimate putting Britain's advantage over France around this time at 1·8 to one.[19] Focusing on land productivity lessens the gap: Irish productivity per acre turns out to have been impressively high before 1845. In value terms the use of a common price level would remove much of the disparity between the two islands. Besides, in physical terms livestock yields in Britain and Ireland were also quite close.

As table 13 shows, in the 1840s Irish tillage output per acre was high by contemporary standards, being as high only in places long celebrated for 'improvement' and convertible husbandry. How Irish yields reached such levels is discussed below. Enough to mention here that high Irish yields were in part the product of a soil-cleansing root crop, the potato, and spade cultivation. Nitrogen requirements were assured by animal manures and grasses, as in Britain, and by large doses of seaweed and sea sand. Even street dung fetched a price: the 'sweeping of John Street' in Kilkenny city was worth £4 a year in 1802.[20] But these data are also a reminder that yields per acre in themselves are hardly an infallible index of prosperity.

The gap in labour productivity is a better measure of relative backwardness, and, clearly, had output per acre in Ireland and Britain been identical most of that gap would have remained. Table 13 prompts a check as to how the labour productivity gap before the Famine—£35 to £40—might be explained in terms of resource endowments. A list of factors accounting for Britain's

TABLE 13 *Nineteenth-century crop yields (cwt per acre)*

	Wheat	Barley	Oats
England, 1830–60	14·9	15·4	12·9
Ireland, 1845	12·5	18·0	13·0
Britain, 1884–87	16·6	15·9	13·1
Ireland, 1884–87	14·9	15·1	13·1
France, 1862	9·5	9·5	8·9
France, 1892	10·1	9·4	8·6
Italy, 1870–74	3·7 – 9·0		
Germany, c. 1800	9·2	8·8	4·0
N. Europe, c. 1800	7·2	6·0	4·4

Sources. England, 1830–60, Germany and Northern Europe *c.*
1800, and Italy, papers presented to the session on
agricultural productivity, seventh Economic History
Conference, Edinburgh, August 1978, by B. Holderness,
G. Chorley and G. Porisini respectively; France, 1862 and
1892, Patrick K. O'Brien, D. Heath and C. Keyder,
'Agriculture in Britain and France, 1815–1914', *Journal
of European Economic History*, 6 (1977), 365; Ireland,
1845, P. M. A. Bourke, 'The average yields of food crops
in Ireland on the eve of the great Famine', *Journal of the
Department of Agriculture and Fisheries*, 66 (1969), 3–16;
Ireland and Britain, 1884–87, B. R. Mitchell and P. Deane,
Abstract of British Historical Statistics (Cambridge, 1962),
pp. 90–3.

big lead might include the following:
1. Perhaps the most obvious point is that the Irish land–
labour ratio was only slightly more than half the British. On less
than heroic assumptions about the output elasticity of land, the
standard Cobb-Douglas production function implies that Britain's
output on the Irish land–labour ratio would have been considerably lower. Given a land output elasticity of 0·4, a halving of the
land-labour ratio would have cut English output by 24 per cent; an
elasticity of 0·3 would have reduced it by 19 per cent. Something
like one-third of the initial gap in output per man is thus
accounted for.
2. If the land–labour ratio in Ireland was clearly lower,
contemporary evidence is divided on the question of soil quality.
Among pre-Famine observers, Young and Wakefield rated Irish soil
fertility high, but Bicheno gave good reasons for a more pessimistic
view. The evidence of such observers, however careful, is almost
inevitably biased. They travelled the main roads, and therefore the
low-lying, more fertile areas. In the circumstances it is perhaps
better to rely on the evidence of modern soil maps. Since inherent
fertility is what is at stake, it is probably not too far-fetched that
the balance shown in table 14 will not have changed too drastically

in the interim.[21] Thus, for example, while 47 per cent of Britain's total area consists today of 'prime land suitable for intensive farming, horticulture', only 30 per cent of Irish land is considered capable of either high-yielding tillage or pasture.

If the comparison carries, it suggests that the value of output per acre of a given quality in Ireland could well have reached British levels on the eve of the Famine. But supposing that one-sixth more of Irish land was of first rather than third quality, how would output have been affected? The elasticity of output to soil quality in the 1840s is not known, but let us suppose that the output difference is captured by the difference between the rent on good tillage and low-grade rent—about 50p per acre. Output then would have been worth £14 x 0·17 x 0·50 million or £1·28 million more. So soil quality differences do not explain much: this would have come to only £0·7 more per worker.

TABLE 14 Soil quality in Ireland and
Great Britain

Class	Britain	Ireland
1	46·8	30·1
2	9·9	9·9
3	19·8	32·9
4	15·9	10·0
5	6·8	16·6
6	0·2	0·4

3. The difference in agricultural prices due to transport costs has already been mentioned. Output mixes differed too, giving rise to a potential index number problem. For instance, potatoes cost more than twice as much in Britain as in Ireland, and for that reason alone, presumably, Irish weights would give a bigger price gap than British. However, no satisfactory estimate of British agricultural output by category exists for this period. Deane and Cole's figure (and Thompson's proposed upward revision of it) are based on tax assessments, and McCulloch's 1846 estimate for England and Wales is based on too great a confusion between production and value added to be of much use. But the price data given in table 15 surely suggest that an adjustment of 10 per cent is in order.[22]

Supposing that British agriculture operated under the constraints just mentioned—less land per worker, poorer soils, lower prices—how much lower would output per man have been? The allowances in table 16 do not seem excessive.

Half the gap in table 12 is thus quickly accounted for. Several

TABLE 15 *Some agricultural prices in Ireland and Britain, c. 1840–45*

	Ireland	Britain
Wheat (s per cwt)	12·13	12·65
Oats (s per cwt)	6·8	7·8
Barley (s per cwt)	7·5	8·3
Potatoes (£ per ton)	1·33	3·3
Wool (d per lb)	13·1	15·9

TABLE 16 *'Accounting' for the productivity gap*

Constraint	Drop in output per worker
Lower prices	6
Lower land–labour ratio	10 to 13
Lower land quality	1
Total	17 to 20

other factors stand out, though no attempt is made to gauge their relative importance here. First, Ireland suffered from handicaps of poorer internal communications—despite the progress reported in chapter 1—and a poor supply of capital, physical and human. The parish of Gaoth Dobhair (Gweedore) in west Donegal, where, it was claimed in 1837, there was no wheeled car, no coach, no resident gentry, a single plough, thirty rakes and sixteen barrows, where the roads and bridges were 'few and barely passable', and where there was only one 'very primitive corn mill . . . and none superior to it within thirty miles', highlights all these disadvantages. Though typical of the island as a whole, Gaoth Dobhair could be matched almost anywhere in counties along the western seaboard, and even outside such areas isolation was a common excuse for backwardness. The marked regional specialisation which followed the spread of the railway system—more impressive than anything occurring across the water—suggests that poor internal communications were a greater constraint in Ireland.[23]

Next, turning to the labour force, Irish literacy and educational levels were lower than British, if (as we have seen) not sensationally so. However, lower human capital levels in turn may have reduced the input of complementary capital inputs. A further possible influence frequently mentioned in literary sources, if impossible to measure, is the impact of inadequate diet on the productivity of the labour force. Some of the force of this argument lies in the fact that the potato, though good food while it lasted, was often in short supply during the summer months when the demand for agricultural labour was keen. Reports from those parts of Britain employing seasonal Irish labour, and impressionistic remarks about the qualities of Irish and British workers in Britain, point in the same direction. The wage differential faced by Irish workers has been explained in this way also (though it is clearly far from the whole story), and even some decades after the Famine the beneficial effect of some months of British diet on returning workers has been noted. Yet our earlier verdict of 'not proven' must stand.[24]

Finally, the data leave some room too for those 'institutional' factors stressed by the traditional literature--insecurity of tenure and insecurity of property generally. Recent research, it is true, de-emphasises such factors, though quantitative assessment of their importance is not feasible at this stage. Perhaps, then, what our numbers indicate is that the lower Irish productivity can be accounted for in rather straightforward economic fashion without recourse to old psychological arguments about the 'habits of the Irish' and so forth? Our numbers support the reinterpretation of some peasant behavioural responses formerly often seen as the product of 'indolence' and incompetence, and prompt the rationalisation of others in economic terms. Examples include the lazy-bed and the spade: anachronistic to outside observers, they made sense because draught animals and heavy ploughs were a luxury not geared to small farms, small fields and soils that were often wet and rocky.[25] Marked regional variation in cultivation techniques and tillage implements is another example of methods which at first sight seem to reflect conservatism but (at least to some extent) may simply show a determination to get the most out of what capital there was to hand. Horatio Townsend's verdict on the average Irish cultivator may thus have been not far from the mark:

> A thorough knowledge of the Irish occupier's means, and an inspection of his domestic premises, would not only remove all feeling of surprise for the inferiority of his crops, but would procure for him great credit for the amount of valuable produce which under such circumstances he is able to elicit. The skilful British farmer will indeed see here much to condemn, and little to approve; yet all things considered, the wonder is not why our common farmers are not better but why they are not worse.

2. Pre-Famine productivity growth

Townsend's notion that Irish agriculture was poor not because it was inefficient but because of poor production possibilities should not be pushed too far, though, since neither land quality nor the land–labour ratio was exogenous in the long run. Our snapshot analysis has been unduly static. Dutch polders and Oklahoma or Sahel dustbowls merely highlight what man can do on occasion to what David Ricardo, one-time Member for Portarlington, called 'the original and indestructible powers of the soil'. In the Irish case soil erosion is hardly an issue, but if it is asserted that population pressure improves soil quality, modern soil surveys should tell against pre-Famine Ireland, the rural population having fallen relative to Britain in the interim. A more telling argument is that a low land–labour ratio may have been as much a result as a cause of 'backwardness'. Particularly in view of post-Famine demographic developments, it is tempting to hypothesise that much of pre-Famine Ireland found itself caught in what development economists call a 'low level equilibrium trap', with labour immobile and an inadequate surplus for accumulation being generated by or channelled into agricultural activity.[26] Progress in the pre-Famine era seems likely, however.

Data problems, as we have seen, are serious enough on the eve of the Famine: they rule out detailed calculations for an earlier date. Nevertheless, it can be shown that, despite persistent poverty and hardship, agriculture was far from stagnant before 1845. This, as already noted, follows from the considerable increase in output implied by population and trade data. Between the Union and the Famine the number of bellies to be fed in Ireland rose from 5 million to 8·5 million. Food exports (see table 17) rose too. While the most spectacular increase was in grain, meat exports rose impressively. The rise in livestock exports reported in table 17 far outmatched the decline in the provision

TABLE 17 *Some Irish agricultural export data*

(a) *Irish corn (grain and meal) exports to England, 1801–45 (quarters)*

1802	461,371
1815	821,192
1825	2,203,962
1835	2,679,438
1845	3,251,907

(b) *Irish livestock exports, 1790–1846*

	Swine	Sheep	Oxen
1790	5,185	–	19,457
1826	73,912	62,929	57,427
1832	145,917	90,622	92,000
1835	376,191	125,452	98,150
1846	480,827	259,257	186,483

trade: meat exports on the eve of the Famine were probably double their 1800 level.[27] By 1845 exports were providing enough food for over 2 million people. Unless Irish living standards dropped significantly after the Union—prompting a big decline in food intake—the crudest political arithmetic indicates close to a doubling of output in the interim. Admittedly this way of getting a fix on output change asks a lot of the reader's credulity. In its defence, it is a 'state of the art' gambit that, for the want of something better, has been tried by others in quest of a measure of past agricultural productivity change.[28] Moreover, if the doubling of agricultural output in the interim is considered ambitious, it may still be shown that more conservative assessments of output growth also suggest impressive productivity performance.

Suppose, first, that both labour force and output doubled: then, some combination of technical change and capital accumulation must have contributed significantly to prevent the law of diminishing returns from cutting output per worker. Even an 80 per cent rise in output would imply a productivity rise from non-labour sources of 20 to 40 per cent over the period. These results follow from the identity:

$$\Delta Q^*/Q^* = \Delta Q/Q - R - \Delta OI/OI.B = \Delta L/L.A$$

where $\Delta Q^*/Q^*$ = output growth with no accumulation, no technical change, $\Delta Q/Q$ = actual output growth, $\Delta L/L$ = posited change in labour input, $\Delta OI/OI$ = change in other inputs, A, B = factor shares, and R = 'unexplained' productivity change. Table 18 uses this identity. It assumes first that output doubled between

TABLE 18 'Guesses' at productivity change in Irish agriculture, 1800–45

ΔL	A	ΔQ^*	$R + B.\Delta OI$
50	0·6	30	70
50	0·7	35	65
80	0·6	48	52
80	0·7	56	44
100	0·6	60	40
100	0·5	50	50
50	0·6	30	50
50	0·7	35	45
80	0·6	48	32
80	0·7	56	24

the Union and the Famine. The range assumed for A is surely not too low: if too high, a larger part of output growth would be unaccounted for. An example will explain the rest. Suppose that output doubled: then the first row states that $[100 - (50)(0·6)]$ or 70 per cent of the rise was due to $[R + B\Delta OI/OI]$, implying an annual rate of productivity growth due to 'other factors' of about 1 per cent between 1800 and 1845. *Ceteris paribus*, a doubling of labour input would still have left 40 per cent for 'other factors' to explain, or 0·8 per cent annually. That these numbers must not be taken literally need hardly be stressed. Still, they may be compared with the (admittedly controversial) 0·62, 0·42 and 1·27 per cent rates recently calculated for British agriculture in 1700–60, 1760–1800 and 1820–40 by Nicholas Crafts.[29] The second part of table 18 assumes an 80 per cent increase in output, and there is still substantial productivity growth to account for.

Both contemporaries and historians—implicitly or explicitly— often take the rise in exports to Britain as a proxy for the rise in tillage or in output.[30] Perhaps, though, some of the rise in exports was at the expense of domestic consumption? To assume that agricultural output doubled between Union and Famine entails more or less constant food consumption *per capita* in the interim. If that seems too high, a 60 per cent rise in output implies—using estimated population in 1800 as numeraire—a drastic drop of $[(5/5 - 6/8·5)/(5/5)]$ or about 30 per cent in average consumption. That follows from two-thirds of the extra output being absorbed by exports by 1845. Now some fall in the living standards of the poor—a group with a high income elasticity of demand for foodstuffs—is plausible, but surely the case for such a drop in *average* living standards is less cogent. On the contrary, there is evidence of an improvement in the lot of those further up the socioeconomic scale, and though their income elasticity of demand for food was lower, their *share* in total food consumption was significant.[31] The 10 per cent drop in average food consumption implied by an 80 per cent rise in output is thus more plausible. Hard evidence on the trend in the composition of output is elusive. While, particularly from the 1830s, there is much mention of larger farmers laying land down to grass, claims that both the acreage and the productivity of land under grain were expanding are plentiful.[32] In the circumstances an output increase of 80 to 100 per cent between 1800 and 1845 seems reasonable.

When the focus of attention is switched from travellers' accounts of potato patches to farm and estate accounts and printed discussions of farming, such an outcome becomes less puzzling. Alongside the continuing squalor and poverty of cottier agriculture, signs of progress are evident. One good example is the county summaries in Samuel Lewis's *Topographical Dictionary*.

Though laced with 'improving' jargon, the *Dictionary* reflects what was happening on the ground as regards farming technique and equipment. Relevant extracts from each county in Ireland are given in appendix 4. While the reports are certainly not unanimous, their overall gist is hardly stasis. Such reports are supported by evidence in the county surveys commissioned by the Dublin Society, and reports in the *Quarterly Journal of Agriculture* during the 1820s and 1830s. These sources repeatedly highlight improvements in livestock and crop *quality*, and in farm equipment.[33]

Comparing the evidence on crop yields provided by Arthur Young (1776–78), the Dublin Society county surveys (1801–26) and Wakefield (1809–10) with the earliest official data also rules out the likelihood of agricultural stagnation in the interim.[34] More than a generation ago Slicher van Bath noticed that the yield data reported by Young from virtually all over the country in his *Tour in Ireland* were high enough to place Irish agriculture in the 'advanced' category.[35] But how reliable are Young's data? Reliable enough, probably, since in Ireland as elsewhere he seems to have taken great pains to report the outcome of average rather than best-practice husbandry. From his very first informant, the steward at Lutrellstown, he sought details on 'the general state of husbandry in the county of Dublin'. On his journey north, at Slane 'Mr. Jebb gave [him] . . . particulars of the common husbandry, which, upon reading over to several intelligent farmers, they found little reason to correct'. And so it continued: even when prevailed upon to note the achievements of some improving farmer, Young almost invariably also sought information on the typical practices of the district.[36]

On his English tours Young has been accused of exaggerating somewhat by highlighting the achievements of the 'improvers' who entertained him. Even there the criticism is unfair: he draws a clear distinction between his elaborate (and sometimes tedious) accounts of the feats of experimenting farmers, and his assessments of the common-or-garden kind. His yield data typically refer to the latter. Such bias seems even less of a problem in the Irish case, where Young's focus in not on individual farms but on whole districts. True, in his day Ireland's grain acreage was still low, and thus to be found on the better land with good access to fertilizer. To some extent, then, a comparison of yields flatters Irish farming relative to English in the 1770s. However, any bias in this sense would simply mean a greater true rise in yield per acre, adjusting for land quality, between the 1770s and the 1840s.[37]

Like Young's, the Dublin Society and Wakefield data are

impressionistic and probably sometimes unrepresentative. They should not be rejected out of hand for that reason. The best of the Dublin Society surveys—which are usually also those which report yield per acre—easily match in quality the contemporary reports of the British Board of Agriculture. And if Wakefield seems occasionally to have confused weights and measures, and included a few suspiciously high yields, overall he took good care to report representative evidence. The results are reported in tables 19 and 20.

TABLE 19 Estimates of Irish grain yields, 1776-1845 (bushels per statute acre)

Source	Wheat	Barley	Oats
Young	21·0	34·7	34·6
Dublin Society	22·1	35·4	37·3
Wakefield	23·4	39·7	43·0
Agricultural Statistics	26·2	42·0	39·3

Note. The estimates are fully explained in Allen and Ó Gráda, 'Ireland, England and France'.

TABLE 20 Crop ratios in England and Ireland: Arthur Young v. Edward Wakefield

Young:			
Southern	10·3	9·0	7·8
Northern	9·9	9·2	8·0
Eastern	9·2	9·1	8·9
Wakefield	9·9	12·4	8·6

Why the high and rising yields? Mostly owing to greater efficiency, I suspect. Admittedly there is an identification problem here. Labour being much cheaper in Ireland, the difference *could* have been due to a more intensive form of tillage. There is undoubtedly something to this argument. Better weeding, deeper digging, more spadework, higher seeding rates—all could have led to higher output per acre. The objection applies not just to the present context but anywhere else historians have used crop yields as a proxy for agricultural progress.

The issue is thus an important one. But does inferring progress from land yields alone not assume a Leontief technology in agriculture? It does, but only as an approximation, and only in a rather limited sense. Something close to fixed coefficients might be defended as follows. More workers, *ceteris paribus*, will certainly shift the output mix from pasture to tillage and thus increase aggregate output. Within tillage, though, the law of diminishing returns may assert itself much more firmly. Thus the leap in grain acreage before the Famine could have been due in large part to cheap labour, and the simultaneously high and rising grain yields to the diffusion of new knowledge and better farm management. This approach finds explicit precedent in the classic work of Parker and Klein on nineteenth-century American grain yields, where it is taken as axiomatic that 'at a given level of mechanical techniques . . . the operations of the soil—plowing, sowing and harrowing—use labor in a relatively fixed proportion to the area under cultivation'.[38] It is also implicit in Peter Solar's impressive comparative assessment of Scottish and Irish farming around mid-century. Following Patrick Chorley, Solar argues:

> Labour intensity is one explanation of these high returns, but recent work by Chorley suggests another. First, it is necessary to recognise that Irish yields, like English and Scottish, were high by European standards. Midd-century Irish yields were 10-40 per cent higher than the figures Chorley gives for north-western Europe around 1880, and two to three times higher than his estimates of European yields c. 1800. Chorley argues quite persuasively that the increase in northern European yields, and by implication the earlier increase in British yields, was due primarily to improved nitrogen supplies resulting from the generalisation of leguminous crops. Labour does enter the story, for cultivation of root crops cleaned and prepared the soil, and liming and marling prevented valuable nutrients from being leached away. However, the major change was apparently managerial.[39]

The approach finds some support in the literature of development economics. There it is shown that the well known relationship between farm size and the value of output per acre does not generally translate into one between farm size and physical crop yields, and the labour output elasticities in production function studies are typically quite small.[40] Thus the 'high' Irish yields both in the 1770s and in the 1840s can hardly be accounted for by different labour intensities. However, the rise over time may in part be due to this factor.

A little simulation can add some insight here. Suppose that labour input in tillage farming rose by 60–100 per cent and land under tillage and other inputs by 40–50 per cent. The occupational shift implied by the upper bound is, as noted earlier, too massive to be plausible. The lower bound allows for occupational shift, but reflects the likely growth of population from 1810 or so, when Wakefield was doing his rounds and the Dublin Society was in full stride. Given such ball-park estimates, how sensitive are output and yield per acre to assumptions about the elasticity of substitution (δ) and factor share (α)? The Cobb-Douglas ($\delta = 1$) and constant-elasticity-of-substitution (CES; for $\alpha = 0.5$ and 0.25) production functions produce the outcome reported in table 21 for initial values of 100 for L (labour), R (other inputs), and O (output). Constant returns to scale and zero technical change are assumed.

TABLE 21 *Cobb-Douglas and constant-elasticity-of-substitution production functions*

	Assumed rise in inputs		Increase in output	
δ	L	R	$\alpha = 0.5$	$\alpha = 0.4$
1	100	100	15·5	12·2
1	80	50	9·5	7·6
1	100	40	19·5	15·3
1	60	40	6·9	5·5
0·5	100	50	14·3	11·1
0·5	80	50	9·1	7·1
0·5	100	40	17·6	13·6
0·5	60	40	6·7	5·3
0·25	100	50	12·2	9·2
0·25	80	50	8·2	6·3
0·25	100	40	14·2	10·7
0·25	80	40	6·2	4·8

Even on low values of δ a doubling of labour inputs (taken alone) would have increased yields considerably. For example, with $\delta = 0.25$ and $\alpha = 0.4$, doubling L would have increased yields by over 15 per cent. Any increase in land under crops would have reduced them, and table 21 captures the net effect. If a δ of unity described the aggregate farm sector, in grain production δ was presumably less. The low income of farm labour indicates a low value of α: applying an income of, say, £12 to the 1·6 million male labourers and their dependants in agriculture in the early 1840s accounts for less than half of agricultural income. Factor input increase on such assumptions accounted for perhaps a third to half the record rise in yields.

The history of post-Famine yields would seem at first sight to negate this claim. Indeed, Bourke has attributed the decline in yields per acre recorded by the official statistics after 1847 to the fall in labour input.[41] This worked indirectly: the switch out of labour-intensive potatoes meant that the soil was less well prepared for grain crops. While Bourke's mechanism is plausible, it is not a clean test of the effect of labour inputs on yields, since the decline in potato acreage was in large part due to the blight. Had the blight not struck, surely grain cultivation in the early 1850s would have been more potato-intensive. A fairer test, then, would compare yields in two later periods. I present below the result of comparing oat yields across counties in 1857–59 and 1870–72. The choice of period was dictated by census dates: the 1861 and 1871 censuses contain comparable occupational data. I opted for 1857–59 yield data to avoid the dampening effect of the agricultural crisis of 1859–64: 1870–72 were unexceptionable years. Between these dates the average yield across counties (unweighted) rose by slightly over 3 per cent, while land input dropped by over 18 per cent and labour input by almost 12 per cent. An ordinary least-squares regression across counties gives:

$$Y = 0.0576 + 0.0199 \text{ labour} + 0.12242 \text{ land}$$

$$R^2 \text{ (adjusted)} = -0.044$$

Arthur Young also provides data on French grain yields. Comparing the Irish with the English and French record suggests that Irish yields were already 'high' in Young's time, and continued to grow, while French yields stagnated. The irony is that while both Young and Wakefield were scathing in their comments about Irish farming methods, their numbers belie their criticisms. Unlike Young, Wakefield provides national estimates of yield ratios, and these are reported along with Young's English averages in table 20. Wakefield's is near ten-to-one for wheat, it exceeds it for barley and the figure for oats is 8·6 to one. Like the acreable yield data, these numbers are all very respectable by contemporary standards.[42] Moreover Wakefield also provides the raw material for a check on one of Young's most basic accusations, that in Ireland 'all is under the old system, exploded by good farmers in England, of sowing wheat upon a fallow, and succeeding it with as many crops of spring corn as the soil will bear'. The rotations suggested by Wakefield's data are 'modern'. Wheat and barley almost routinely followed potatoes, while oats were sown after a variety of other crops. By Wakefield's time at least, the role of the fallow in Ireland was secondary.[43]

Pre-Famine farmers were receptive to livestock and grain seed and potato varieties. They were 'stubborn' or laggard when it came to turnips and artificial grasses, as the propagandists of improvement repeatedly pointed out. However, the impressive yield performance suggests that the Irish had every right to spurn these hallmarks of improvement à l'anglaise. The key is that Irish climate and soil produced a great deal of grass naturally, increasing the marginal cost of the artificial version. Pomponius Mela had noted Ireland's advantage in this respect in classical times and Boate in 1652 noted the 'natural aptness for grass, the which, in most places, it produceth very good and plentiful of itself, or with very little help'.[44] Even Arthur Young noticed 'the great quantity of spontaneous white clover (*trifolium repens*) in almost all the fields, which much exceeds anything we know in England'.[45] The Dublin Society surveys provide ample evidence too, albeit sometimes reluctantly, for this claim. John Dubourdieu's account of County Down, after noting that 'the propensity of the soil to grass is so great that any field left to itself in heart, from manure and judicious tillage, immediately produces grass of the best kind', continued:

> While we are celebrating the fertility of our isle, let us not ungratefully pass by the white clover (trifolium repens), the never failing attendant on good farming, and which, in spite of the very worst of management, often clothes, in winter, our fields with green, or in summer enamels them with its fragrant flowers.

In his survey of County Galway Hely Dutton makes the same point:[46]

> The natural grasses are the same in general produced in every part of Ireland, in similar soils and situations. A bountiful Providence provides the seeds, and the constant feeding keeps it good, otherwise it might be anything else; the grazier takes no pains; he neither drains, sows hay seed, nor destroys weeds.

In his able survey of Wicklow Robert Fraser listed sixteen natural grasses, noting that he gathered specimens 'of these and many other grasses and plants . . . in this summer, too numerous to be inserted'. Hard data would be better, but surely such evidence as there is suggests that artificial grasses would have been no pot of gold.[47]

If the Irish were slow to sow grass seeds, their enthusiasm for the potato knew no parallels in Europe. The potato caught on more in Ireland probably because it grew so easily there relative to substitutes. Climate, temperature, daylight and soil were well geared to good potato crops. In France potato yields before the blight were only slightly more than half the Irish norm: they averaged 3·1 tons per acre in 1839-44.[48] 'In regard to the introduction of turnips,' admitted the energetic Ulster land agent William Blacker, 'the opinion of even experienced farmers is much divided'. Many of his own tenants preferred the potato, and Blacker did not insist on turnips but left it to the tenants 'to follow their own inclinations after making trial of each'.[49] But when the blight struck, desperate farmers even in the remotest areas needed no prompting to grow turnips. In 1847 in the backward and starving Union of Castlebar there were 803 acres under potatoes and 2,071 under turnips, 'sown . . . in despair, as the food of man, not cattle'.[50]

Other signs of pre-Famine progress in farming exist. The vogue for market house building bespeaks greater commercialisation and competition. Over seventy market houses were built in the province of Ulster alone between 1800 and 1845.[51] There was also a great deal of landlord surveying, and county agricultural societies sprang up all over the island. Of dubious worth, perhaps, as far as increasing productivity was concerned, such developments nevertheless reflect a wider dynamism.[52] Finally, backwardness has always been associated with potato conacre; yet at least in part this was an adaptation which blossomed with the shift towards corn-growing during the Revolutionary and Napoleonic wars, and faded away with the Famine.[53]

It is time to take stock. First, our productivity calculations and the yield estimates, together with a fair amount of qualitative evidence, seem to rule out stagnation in the pre-Famine half-century. Yet much of the evidence is flimsy and inferential. Further research, focusing on farm accounts, output quality shifts and consumption patterns might lead us back towards a more traditional assessment which highlighted stagnation more. Nor does our estimate of pre-Famine output deny the image of a 'ramshackle, ill-balanced agricultural system'[54] in the sense that the huge grain output was dependent on the corn laws and low-cost labour, and therefore ultimately on the potato. It also suggests that the outcome of agricultural change after the Union was highly inegalitarian. The conacre labourers who spent perhaps fifty or sixty days of the year cultivating and harvesting their potato ground spent the rest of the year (when not without work) contributing to Ireland's peculiar agricultural revolution by doing some farmer's hard work for a pittance.[55] This kind of agricultural progress, in its implications for income shares, was uneven development with a vengeance. On the eve of the Famine the distribution of land holdings must have looked something like table 22. This table represents a compromise between the flawed data prepared by the Census commissioners in 1841 and the information collected for Poor Law purposes about the same time.[56] By implication access to land was highly unequal, and inequality in pre-Famine

TABLE 22 The distribution of farmland, c. 1845

	Number	Mean acreage
Wealthy farmers	50,000	80
'Strong' farmers	100,000	50
Family farmers	200,000	20
Poor farmers	250,000	5
Cottiers, labourers	1,000,000	1

Irish agriculture matched that found in many underdeveloped countries today.

However, as I argued in chapter 1, the potato-based system may have been the logical answer from the vantage point of the 1820s or 1830s, since the great Famine could not reasonably have been predicted from trends and fluctuations in farm output. Before 1845, largely unaided by government agency, the potato sustained an economy in the throes of economic and demographic adjustment.[57] It is thus important not to overlook the real achievements of the system, and see its fragility in perspective. In its last years the system bore the burden of a declining cottage industry, and by the 1830s—as was widely recognised at the time—further long and painful adjustment was in prospect.

The juxtaposition of agricultural backwardness and the massive mortality of the great Famine, as if the potato blight were just a catalyst occasioning a catastrophe inevitable in any case, was a cornerstone of the dogmatic version of political economy articulated and popularised by Nassau Senior, Charles Trevelyan and Harriet Martineau (see chapter 3). By and large, historians have succumbed to their version of events. Without wishing to forget the injustices and problems besetting Irish agriculture, I would argue instead that the blight probably made agriculture before the Famine seem more vulnerable and unhealthy than might have been plausibly judged *a priori.*

3. Agricultural productivity and the Famine

Recent work confirms the traditional view that excess Famine mortality was about one million.[58] The immediate impact on aggregate output may be gauged from the Marquess of Landsdowne's claim that the failure of the 1846 harvest alone had been 'equivalent to the absolute destruction of 1,500,000 acres' of produce worth £15 million. Worse was to come in 1847 and 1848. The acreage under potatoes, which was over 2 million in 1845, dropped to just over 1 million in 1846, 0·3 million in 1847 and 0·7 million in 1848. Tillage recovered during the next few years but was never again to reach anything like its pre-Famine norm.[59]

From 1847 on, data on livestock, crop acreages and yields, and the numbers of holdings were collected annually by the Irish Registrar General. These data form the basis for the estimate of output in 1854 given in table 23. That year was chosen for comparison for three reasons. Output was on trend, data were most plentiful than in the early 1850s, and 1854 was late enough to have allowed production to recover from the ravages of the crisis itself. Some prices, it is true, were inflated by the onset of the Crimean war, but this is corrected for in our volume comparisons. That in 1854 the enumeration took place later in the summer than in 1841 is another irritant, which, however, does not much affect the outcome. Compared with table 10, perhaps the most striking

TABLE 23 *Irish agricultural output at current prices, 1854 (£ million)*

Crops	
Wheat	4·1
Oats	5·7
Barley	1·6
Flax	2·3
Potatoes	6·7
Hay	0·4
Other	1·1
Subtotal	21·9
Livestock	
Cattle	7·9
Butter and Milk	8·4
Pigs	3·9
Sheep	2·0
Wool	0·9
Eggs	1·1
Other	1·3
Subtotal	25·5
Total	47·4

feature is the shift in the proportion of output due to tillage from a pre-Famine level of two-thirds to half. The numbers also imply that in constant terms the value of output dropped by about 17 per cent between the early 1840s and 1854. Since the male agricultural labour force fell by slightly more—from about 1·6 million to less than 1·2 million[60]—the data belie the notion that 'a removal of 25 per cent of the labor on the land in poor countries will not reduce agricultural production'.[61] Admittedly the Great

Famine is not a 'clean' test of this claim, since the blight reduced the labour supply *and* the land endowment. Farmers could no longer rely on the potato crop in the same way, so they grew fewer, despite higher prices. But for the deterioration in quality to explain all the decline in output would have required an implausibly large reduction in land 'efficiency units'. The data are thus consistent with the view that the pre-Famine labour force was fully occupied at least part of the year, though productivity at the margin may have been very low. Further evidence along these lines is the marked seasonal variation in rural wage levels before the Famine, and the tendency towards labour shortages during the harvest period.[62]

Labour productivity rose and land productivity dropped slightly in the wake of the Famine. The data also confirm the common view that non-landlord incomes rose impressively in money terms. What of total factor productivity change? A familiar approach to its measurement is to begin with the assumption of constant returns to scale, and to take output, 'measurable' inputs and factor shares: the residual emerging when output grows faster than the weighted sum of inputs is then equated with productivity change. Productivity change can also be gauged from product and input price information, since, if the price of output rose more slowly than the price of land, labour and other inputs used up in producing it, the same growth in productivity must have occurred. The residual is equated with productivity change, though, strictly speaking, it absorbs misspecification of inputs (the omission of human capital, for instance), outputs (failure to adjust for product quality changes or external economies) and the production function (neglect of scale economies and organisatonal technique). Still, the smaller the residual the less scope left for such factors, so that a sizable residual may therefore be considered a 'plus' in a loose sense.

Assuming away the problem of capital on the basis that changes in its share are unlikely to have made much difference, and imputing land's share from an estimate of aggregate rent, our data allow estimation of the productivity growth equation:

$$A = \dot{P}/P + B.\dot{W}/W + C.\dot{T}/T + D.\dot{I}/I$$

where $\dot{P}/P$ = output change, $\dot{W}/W$ = change in the wage rate, $\dot{T}/T$ = change in rent, $\dot{I}/I$ = change in the return on capital, B, C, D = factor shares, and A = productivity change. $\dot{W}/W$ is inferred from dividing residual income by labour force estimates for 1840–45 (1·6 million) and 1854 (1·2 million). Values of 0·06 and 0·0 are assumed for D and $\dot{I}/I$, while rent is allowed to fall from £12 million to £10 million over the period. The numbers imply a rise of 64 per cent in residual income per head. The use of end-year weights in calculating productivity growth to some extent finesses a problem mentioned earlier: an index based on 1854 prices reflects the unwillingness of farmers in the wake of the blight to grow as many potatoes as they would have done earlier, given the higher prices. The outcome is an average annual productivity growth of about 0·5–0·6 per cent over the period. In relative terms this is not too bad (see chapter 5), though it certainly belies the most sanguine hopes of some hard-line Malthusian commentators.[63]

Appendix 3 A note on the output calculations

Historians of pre-Famine agriculture owe a great deal to Austin Bourke. However, his pioneering estimates of pre-Famine potato and cereal acreages have recently come in for some criticism. I have allowed for Mokyr's correction of Bourke's potato estimate, while assuming Bourke's proportion of value added.[64] This reduces the assumed consumption of potatoes on the eve of the Famine by about 10 per cent. In a private communication Peter Solar has also cast doubt on Bourke's cereal numbers: for reasons explained in the text, though not without some misgivings, I have stuck with Bourke's guesses here. In general the calculations are as explained in an earlier paper.[65] The one major change concerns hay output: there my earlier calculations were incorrect, and have been replaced for both 1840–45 and 1854.

Appendix 4 Evidence from Lewis's *Topographical Dictionary*

Antrim. A considerable portion formerly employed as grazing pastures is now under tillage . . . Great improvement has of late years been made in the agricultural implements, by introducing the best Scotch and English modes of construction . . . The breed of cattle has been very much improved within the last few years, particularly in the more fertile districts . . . The long-legged flat-sided hogs formerly reared have been superceded by the best English breeds.

Armagh. The state of agriculture in modern times has very much improved; gentlemen and large farmers have introduced all the improved agricultural implements, with the practice of drainage, irrigation, and rotation crops. Mangel-wurzel, turnips, clover, and all other green crops are now generally cultivated even on the smallest farms.

Carlow. Agriculture is in as highly improved state here as in any other part of Ireland . . . but the small farmers are generally averse to the culture of green crops. . . . The dairy farmers pay great attention to the breed of milch cows.

Cavan. Agriculture is very little improved . . . Green crops are seldom or ever grown, except by some of the nobility and gentry . . . The iron plough has been generally substituted for spade labour . . . Into the mountain districts, however, neither the plough nor wheel car has yet found its way . . . The breed of pigs has been much improved.

Clare. Great improvements have been made upon the old rude implements of agriculture . . . the Scotch plough is generally used . . . the breed of swine has been greatly improved, the small short-eared pig nowbeing universal. The breed of horses has also undergone improvement.

Cork. The tillage, except on the demesnes of resident gentlemen, presents rather unfavourable features . . . [T]he Scotch plough has been introduced by the gentry and wealthy farmers in the neighbourhood of Cork and other places . . . The cattle of the south and south-west are small, seldom weighing more than 3·5 cwts.; formerly they were all black, but at present the breed is mixed, and of various colours; they generally yield abundance of milk.

Donegal. In Boylagh and Bannagh much land is now under cultivation, though formerly scarcely sufficient was tilled to supply the inhabitants with potato and grain. [Here] turnips, vetches, mangel-wurzel and other green crops are common . . . The angular harrow is becoming very general, and all other kinds of agricultural implements are gradually improving . . . The breed of pigs has also been greatly improved.

Down. The great attention paid to tillage has brought the land to a high state of agricultural improvement.

Dublin. Considerable improvement has taken place in the system of agriculture by the more extensive introduction of green crops and improved drainage, and by the extension of tillage up the mountains.

Fermanagh. The old car with solid wood wheels has given way to the light cart with spoke wheels, and the slide car is rarely used, except in the most mountainous districts to bring turf down the precipitous roads . . . almost every sort of stock known in this kingdom is to be found here in a day's journey, but so crossed as to defy the possibility of distinguishing the original breeds . . . The horses are bad . . .

Galway. Agriculture as a system is in a backward state, except in the neighbourhood of Ballinasloe, Tuam, Hollymount, and Gort, where the rotation of green crop systems have been introduced . . . Inmost of the eastern portion of the country the iron plough and light angual harrow are generally used . . . the old wooden plough is retained in many places . . . One-horse carts with spoke wheels are so general that the old solid wooden wheeled car is now seldom seen, and the slide car never . . . In Connemara, Iar-Connaught, and Joyces Country, wheeled vehicles are almost unknown.

Kildare. In general the county is fertile and well cultivated . . . The Scotch plough is general . . . Great improvement has been made in the breed of cattle.

Kilkenny. The use of oxen in the plough seems to be rather increasing, though the proportion is very small in comparison with horses . . . The attention paid to the breeding of cattle is inferior to that of the adjoining counties of Carlow and Waterford . . . Pigs have been greatly improved . . . In all the minor departments of rural economy, except the rearing of poultry, the farmers are very deficient.

King's. The generality of the small farmers do not venture on the green crop system, except in the barony of Warrenstown where a regular rotation crop is general. Red and white clover are found on most farms; the former, with rye grass, answers bog land extremely well . . . Much has been done to improve the breed of horned cattle . . . The breed of sheep has also been much improved . . . Asses are mostly kept by the poor people, and mules are common with the small farmers . . . The Scotch plough and the angular harrow are everywhere used, except in the mountain districts and by the poorer farmers . . .

Kerry. Agriculture in a backward state . . . wheeled carriages were little known but their use is now becoming general . . . From the introduction of the improved kinds of cattle from Great Britain, the country now possesses the long-horned Leicester, the Hereford, the Holderness, and the Devon breeds: the common cattle of the country are partly of the long, partly of the short horned . . .

Leitrim. The old heavy wooden plough is generally used in the low country, while in the mountain districts the land is chiefly cultivated by the loy . . . In the southern parts of the county, and generally in the fertile districts, great improvements have been made in the breed of (horned cattle) . . . A light and useful one-horse cart has everywhere superceded the old solid wheel and slide car.

Limerick. The wheat crops are everywhere very heavy . . . The tillage, except on large farms . . . is generally conducted in a slovenly manner . . . The agricultural implements are generally of the newest and most improved construction . . . the old Irish car is quite banished, except among the very poorest people.

Londonderry. The principal artificial grass if clover, to which the annual and perennial ray are sometimes added: these seeds are generally sown as the last crop of a course, but the common farmers seldom sow anything, trusting to the prowess of the soil and the humidity of the climate to restore the herbage . . . The breeds of cattle of every kind are much improved by judicious crossing . . . All the improved agricultural implements are in general use . . .

Longford. The practice of laying down land with grass or clover seeds is gaining ground every year . . . Agricultural implements are of an inferior description, except with the gentry and wealthier farmers; one-horse carts of excellent description are universal . . .

Louth. Altogether an agricultural county . . . The agricultural implements are of the most improved kind, except in the mountain districts . . . Irrigation and draining are better understood here than in any of the adjoining counites . . .

Meath. Considerable benefit is thought to arise from a change of seed even between neighbouring baronies . . . The quantity of land applied to green crops and artificial grasses is comparatively small, in consequence of the vast tracts of natural grasses of the most productive kind . . .

Monaghan. Great improvements have been made within the last few years in almost every department of agriculture, both as to the treatment of the land and the implements . . .

Queen's. The implements and carriages employed in rural economy are generally of the most improved description . . . All the improved breeds of English cattle have been introduced into the county . . .

Mayo. The old and clumsy agricultural implements are rapidly giving way to those of a more improved description.

Roscommon. Although tillage has in later years been greatly extended, yet the general system of agriculture . . . is still in a very backward state . . . The superiority of both cattle and sheep in this county is attributable both to the excellence of the soil and attention of the breeder . . .

Sligo. Tillage has increased rapidly . . . A pair of horses abreast and driven by the ploughman is now often seen . . . The favourite breed of cattle is a cross between the Durham and the native cow . . . equal attention is paid to the breed of sheep . . .

Tipperary. Agricultural implements and carriages of improved construction are every year coming into more general use . . . in many parts, a mode of draining water off pasture lands, called pipe-draining, has been introduced from Limerick . . . In some parts of the Ormonds, and on the lands of the gentry, the most improved systems of green cropping are practiced.

Tyrone. Agriculture has made rapid advances in recent years, particularly in the eastern districts.

Waterford. Clover is becoming very general . . . The most improved implements and carriages are now in general use . . . those [pigs] in general demand are of the best description . . .

Westmeath. The most improved implements are in general use . . . Much attention is paid to the breeding of every kind of cattle.

Wexford. In the interior . . . the farmers depend in gerneral upon artificial grasses . . . Under all their various natural disadvantages, the lands of this county, by incessant industry and superior skill, are generally kept in an excellent state unknown in many other parts of Ireland . . . The farmers are by no means so attentive to the breed of cattle as in many other counties.

Wicklow. The agricultural implements are of the ordinary improved construction, and the carriages one-horse cars.

Notes

1 *Ireland and its Economy* (London, 1830), p. 7.
2 George O'Brien, 'Introduction', in E. J. Riordan (ed.), *Modern Irish Trade and Industry* (Dublin, 1921), p. xi.
3 Lance Davis *et al., An Economists' History of the United States* (New York, 1972), p. 369.
4 T. W. Freeman, *Pre-Famine Ireland: an Historical Geography* (Manchester, 1956), p. 60; Arthur Young, *Tour in Ireland*, II (Dublin, 1780), p. 75. See also George O'Brien, *The Economic History*, pp. 27–41.
5 H. S. Thompson, *Ireland in 1839 and 1868* (London, 1870), p. 29.
6 Horace Plunkett, *Ireland in the new Century* (Dublin, 1904), pp. 50-1, 131; J. Beddy, 'A comparison of the principal economic features of Eire and Denmark', *Journal of the Statistical and Social Inquiry Society of Ireland*, 17 (1943-44), 189–220; R. D. Crotty, *Irish Agricultural Production* (Cork, 1966).

7 Bourke, 'The Potato, Blight, Weather and the Irish Famine' (unpublished Ph.D. dissertation, National University of Ireland, 1965), Appendix 4; J. R. McCulloch, 'after much inquiry and consideration', gives estimates of 2·5 million, 0·45 million and 0·4 million acres for oats, wheat and barley (*id., Descriptive and Statistical Account of the British Empire*, 3rd ed. (London, 1847), p. 571).

8 I.U.P. Famine Series, vol. 2, pp. 54, 74, 139, 169; vol. 7, pp. 143-4, 392-3, 398, 480, 552; David Thomson and Moyra McGusty (eds.), *The Irish Diaries of Elizabeth Smith* (Oxford, 1980), p. 157. For more in the same vein from west Cork, Kilkenny and Mayo, John Mitchell, *The History of Ireland* (Dublin, n.d.), II, p. 419.

9 *Farmers' Gazette*, 4 September 1847.

10 John Stanley, letter to Lord Lieutenant, P.R.O. (Dublin), 1a/50/45; I.U.P. Famine Series, vol. 2, p. 240.

11 Crotty, *op. cit.*, chapter 2. Only a detailed analysis of trade data can locate the timing of any such switch; such an analysis by Peter M. Solar is nearing completion.

12 Mr and Mrs S. C. Hall, *Ireland*, p. 406; H. Townsend, 'On the improvement of Irish agriculture', *Quarterly Journal of Agriculture*, I (iii) (1829), 314; Michael McGrath (ed.), *Cinnlae*, III, p. 40.

13 E.G. Barrington farm accounts, Fassaroe, County Wicklow (held in Royal Dublin Society library, Dublin).

14 P. M. A. Bourke, 'The Potato Blight, Weather, and the Great Irish Famine' (unpublished Ph.D. dissertation, National University of Ireland, 1965), appendix 4; *id.*, 'The Irish grain trade, 1839-1848', *Irish Historical Studies*, XX (1976), 156-69.

15 The figure given for the proportion of oats marketed is based on Bourke, 'The Potato', *loc. cit.*, and Third Report of the Select Committee on Agricultural Distress', H.C. 1836 (VIII), part II, 507-45. The latter source reports the sale of oats in Irish markets at 410,000 tons. The marketed share given in the text assumes that this is something of an underestimate, and allows for some increase in the marketed production of oats between 1835 and the early 1840s.

16 The continuing importance of Irish grain was noted in Peter Solar, 'Agricultural productivity and economic development in Ireland and Scotland in the early nineteenth century', in Devine and Dickson (eds.), pp. 71-88, and Brinley Thomas, 'Food supply in the United Kingdom during the industrial revolution', in Joel Mokyr (ed.), *The Economics of the Industrial Revolution* (Totowa, N.J., 1985). While pre-Famine Ireland supplied only a small proportion of Britain's total grain requirements, it was then perhaps its biggest single supplier of grain. Hence the kernel of truth in the Halls' claim (*Ireland*, I, p. 406) that Ireland was the 'granary' of Great Britain during this period. Compare B. R. Mitchell and P. Deane, *Abstract of British Historical Statistics* (Cambridge, 1962), pp. 93-102, and Bourke, 'The Grain Trade'.

17 1841 census, p. 440. The 1·7 million assumed in Ó Gráda, 'Irish agricultural output', now seems somewhat high to me.

18 P. Deane and W. A. Cole, *British Economic Growth, 1699-1959* (Cambridge, 1967), pp. 166-7, report income from agriculture, forestry and fishing at £99·9 million in 1841 and at £106·5 million in 1851. However, as F. M. L. Thompson has pointed out to me in correspondence, Deane and Cole underestimate British agricultural income by taking Schedule B farmers' income as a guide. I have assumed instead that output was worth £120 million-130 million in the early 1840s. On the difficulties of estimating agricultural output before the 1860s, when official data become available, see Charles H. Feinstein, *National Income and Expenditure of the United Kingdom, 1855-1965* (Cambridge, 1972), pp. 41-2.

19 Patrick K. O'Brien and C. Keyder, *Economic Growth in Britain and France, 1780-1914: Two Paths to the Twentieth Century* (London, 1978), pp. 109-13.

20 Tighe, *Kilkenny*, p. 438.

21 Compare O'Brien and Keyder, *op. cit.*, pp. 109-13; An Foras Taluntais, *General*

Soil Map of Ireland (Dublin, 1969); M. J. Gardiner and P. Ryan, 'A new generalised soil map of Ireland and its land use interpretation', *Irish Journal of Agricultural Research*, VIII (1969), 95-109.

22 See J. R. McCulloch, *A Descriptive and Statistical Account of the British Empire*, pp. 549-50, whose total of £141·6 million includes £13 million for 'Meadow and Grass for Work and Pleasure Horses' and £9·1 million for clover, and fails to deduct for intermediate grain inputs. On comparing prices, Ó Gráda, 'Irish agricultural output', and A. H. John, 'British agricultural statistics, 1750-1850', in Joan Thirsk (ed.), *The Agrarian History of England and Wales, 1750-1850* (Cambridge, 1987).

23 Lord George Hill, *Facts from Gweedore* (Dublin, 1846); Liam Kennedy, 'Regional specialization, railway development and Irish agriculture in the nineteenth century', in Goldstrom and Clarkson (eds.), *Irish Population, Economy and Society*, pp. 173-93.

24 The following complaint from a County Limerick farmer (*Poor Inquiry*, Appendix E, p. 27) is an interesting case in point: 'A labourer of mine has a severe afflication of the bowels annually at the season when he begins to eat young potatoes. He suffers so much that it considerably lessens his strength, and indeed I am so well aware of it that I never give him as much hard work to do then as I do any other season of the year. None of the labourers are so strong when they first begin to eat young potatoes as at any other season, and it is commonly remarked among themselves. They also know that the white potato, commonly grown for its prolific and hardy qualities, is not such strong food, nor as supporting as the "cup" potatoes.' Such comments could be multiplied. See, e.g., 'D', 'On the agriculture of County Kerry', pp. 318-19; Kevin Danaher, *The Year in Ireland* (Dublin, 1972), pp. 163-6; W. Bence Jones, *The Life's Work of a Landlord who tried to do his Duty* (London, 1880), p. 31; R. N. Salaman, *The History and Social Influence of the Potato* (Cambridge, 1949), pp. 284-8; *Royal Commission on Labour*, H.C. (1893-4), XXXVIII, p. 340. But for a sceptical view of this hypothesis see Mokyr, *Why Ireland Starved*, pp. 223-6.

25 This is in line with the drift of recent work in development economics. See T. W. Schultz, *Transforming Traditional Agriculture* (New Haven, Conn., 1964), pp. 36-52; J. W. Mellor, *Agriculture in Economic Development* (Ithaca, N.Y., 1966), pp. 133-54. For an example nearer home see John Hunter, *The Making of the Crofter Community, 1814-1900* (Edinburgh, 1973), pp. 115-16, and A. J. Youngson, *After the Forty-five: the Economic Impact on the Scottish Highlands* (Edinburgh, 1973), pp. 191-3. See Bourke, 'The Potato', pp. 127-37, for a fine analysis along these lines. Also 'Martin Doyle', *A Cyclopedia of Husbandry* (Dublin, 1839), pp. 457-8; id., *Hints originally Intended for the Small Farmers of Wexford, but suited to the Circumstances of most Parts of Ireland* (Dublin, 1835), p. 29; C. Ó Danachair, 'The use of the spade in Ireland', in Alan Gailey and Alexander Fenton (eds.), *The Spade in Northern and Atlantic Europe* (Belfast, 1970); A. T. Lucas, 'Paring and Burning in Ireland', in Gailey and Fenton, *op. cit.*, *Report of the Committee of the Board of Agriculture appointed to Extract Information . . . concerning the Culture and Use of the Potato* (London, 1795), p. 24.

26 S. H. Cousens, 'The regional variation in population changes in Ireland, 1861-1881', *Economic History Review*, ser. 2, XVII (1969), 301-21; J. G. Williamson, 'Regional inequality and the process of national development: a description of patterns', *Economic Development and Cultural Change*, XIII (1964-65), 1-82.

27 L. M. Cullen, *Anglo-Irish Trade, 1660-1800* (Manchester, 1968), p. 70; R. D. Crotty, *Irish Agricultural Production*, pp. 266-7; Peter M. Solar, 'The agricultural trade statistics in the Irish Railway Commissioners' report', *Irish Economic and Social History*, VI (1979), 24-40.

28 Compare the estimates given by Crafts and Thomas in Joel Mokyr (ed.), *The Economics of the Industrial Revolution*, pp. 145, 159; Gregory Clark, 'Economic Growth without Accumulation or Technical Change: European Agriculture before 1850', unpublished, Stanford University, 1986; Eric L. Jones, 'Agriculture, 1700-

1780', in Roderick Floud and Donald McCloskey (eds.), *The Economic History of Britain since 1700* (Cambridge, 1981), I, pp. 67–8; E. A. Wrigley, 'Urban growth and agricultural change: England and the Continent in the early modern period', *Journal of Interdisciplinary History*, XV (1985), 683–728.

29 N. F. R. Crafts, 'Income elasticites of demand and the release of labor by agriculture during the industrial revolution: a further appraisal', in Mokyr (ed.), *The Economics of the Industrial Revolution*, pp. 159–60. Craft's numbers have, however, been cogently criticised by Joel Mokyr in 'Was the industrial revolution crowded out? Reflections on Crafts and Williamson', *Explorations in Economic History* (forthcoming).

30 *Thom's Irish Almanac 1845* (Dublin, 1845), p. 190; Donnelly, *The Land and the People*, pp. 30–3.

31 See chapter 1, and Mokyr and Ó Gráda, 'From Poor to Poorer?'. The following extract from the Grand Canal Company's report to its shareholders in April 1841 is apposite here: 'Another important fact connected with the subject arises out of the decided change which has taken place in the previous habits of a large portion of the People of this Country, which by enabling the Poor to become purchasers and consumers of Flour, Oatmeal etc to a much greater extent than formerly, has undoubtedly had the effect of decreasing the quantity of Corn bought up in distant Districts for the purpose of exportation and which was in many instances conveyed by Canal. We cannot doubt however that the general improvement of the Country consequent upon this important change, and the extension of both Trade and Agriculture growing out of it will speedily make good any deficiency arising from a cause otherwise so much to be rejoiced at.' (Quoted in Ruth Delany, *The Grand Canal of Ireland*, Newton Abbot, 1973, p. 164.)

32 Lewis, *Topographical Dictionary*, e.g. entries on Antrim and Wicklow; Mr and Mrs S. C. Hall, *Ireland*, I, p. 406; *Report of the Select Committee on Agriculture*, H.C. 1833 (V), pp. 236, 204, 494; *Third Report of the Select Committee on Agricultural Distress*, H.C. 1836 (VIII), I, p. 81, II, p. 262, 279, 324. The last reference is to the evidence of astute Armagh land agent William Blacker, who insisted that 'you cannot draw a conclusion that the farmer is getting worse from the quantity exported to this country'. See too K. H. Connell, *The Population of Ireland, 1750–1845* (Oxford, 1950), pp. 114–7, and McCulloch, *Descriptive and Statistical Account*, p. 529–30.

33 Samuel Lewis, *Topographical Dictionary of Ireland*, 2 vols. (London, 1837).

34 This and the following two paragraphs are based largely on Robert C. Allen and C. Ó Gráda, 'On the road again with Arthur Young: English, Irish and French agriculture during the industrial revolution' (Centre for Economic Research, University College, Dublin, Working Paper, October 1986).

35 B. Slicher van Bath, *European Yield Ratios* (Wageningen, 1963).

36 Arthur Young, *Tour in Ireland*, ed. Arthur W. Hutton (London, 1892), I, pp. 2, 22, 37, 86–7, II, pp. 38–9, and *passim*.

37 Compare the arbitrary dismissal of Young in M. K. Bennett, 'British wheat yield per acre for seven centuries', *Economic History* (1937), 12–29, and the more careful appraisal in Michael Turner, 'Agricultural productivity in England in the eighteenth century: evidence from crop yields', *Economic History Review*, ser. 2, XXXV (4) (1982), 489–510.

38 William N. Parker and Judith L. Klein, 'Productivity growth in grain production in the United States, 1840–60 and 1900–10', in Peter Temin (ed.), *New Economic History* (Harmondsworth, 1973), p. 83.

39 Peter M. Solar, 'Agricultural productivity and economic development in Ireland and Scotland in the early nineteenth century', in Devine and Dickson (eds.), *Ireland and Scotland*, p. 76; Patrick Chorley, 'The agricultural revolution in northern Europe, 1750–1800: nitrogen, legumes, and crop productivity', *Economic History Review*, ser. 2, XXXIV (1981), 71–93.

40 E.g. Robert A. Berry and William R. Cline, *Agriculture Structure and Productivity in Developing Countries* (Baltimore, Md., 1979), p. 225; Krishna Bharadwaj, *Production Conditions in Indian Agriculture* (Cambridge, 1974), p. 92.

41 P. M. A. Bourke, 'The average yield of food crops in Ireland on the eve of the great Famine', *Journal of the Department of Agriculture (Ireland)*, LXVI (7) (1969), 26-39.

42 Compare B. Slicher van Bath, *The Agrarian History of Western Europe* (London, 1963), pp. 330-3.

43 Wakefield, pp. 368-426, and Young, II, p. 21. J. Mokyr, 'Irish history with the potato', p. 12 n., contains a tabular analysis of Wakefield's data.

44 Quoted in McCulloch, p. 531.

45 Arthur Young, *Tour*, II, pp. 49-50.

46 Hely Dutton, *Statistical Survey of the County of Galway* (Dublin, 1824), p. 128.

47 *General View of the Agriculture and Mineralogy, Present State and Circumstances of the County Wicklow* (Dublin, 1807), p. 178.

48 Compare W. G. Burton, *The Potato: a Survey of its History and of Factors influencing its Yield, Nutritional Value, Quality and Storage* (Wageningen, 1966), chapter 3; Bourke, 'The average yields of food crops'; B. R. Mitchell, *European Historical Statistics* (London, 1975), pp. 199, 240.

49 P.R.O.N.I. D 1606, 18 January 1836.

50 *Agricultural Statistics, 1847*, p. 5.

51 C. E. B. Brett, *Court Houses and Market Houses in the Province of Ulster* (Belfast, 1973).

52 James S. Donnelly, *The Land and the People of Nineteenth-century Cork* (London, 1973), pp. 52-72; William Greig, *General Report on the Gosford Estates in County Armagh 1821*, ed. F. M. L. Thompson and David Tierney (Belfast, 1976); P.R.O. (Dublin), 978/2/4/1 (General Report of the Midleton Estate Surveyor, 1846); Trinity College, Dublin: Muniments/V/Series 78/46-61 (Descriptive Survey and Valuation of the T.C.D. Estates); N.L.I. Ms. 3829 (Lord Clement's Instructions, 1839); P.R.O.N.I., 2204/2 (Maurice Colles's Survey of the Grocers' Company Estates in Derry, 1839).

53 For an account of conacre see Michael Beames, 'Cottiers and conacre in pre-Famine Ireland', *Journal of Peasant Studies*, 2 (1974-75), 352-4.

54 R. B. McDowell, 'Ireland on the eve of the Famine', in R. D. Edwards and T. D. Williams (eds.), *The Great Famine: Studies in Irish History* (Dublin, 1957), p. 10.

55 See Tighe, *Kilkenny*, pp. 218-19.

56 On the former, P. M. A. Bourke, 'The agricultural statistics of the 1841 census of Ireland: a critical review', *Economic History Review*, ser. 2, XVIII (2) (1965), 376-91; on the latter, P. McGregor, 'The Distribution of Landholdings in pre-Famine Ireland' (unpublished, 1986).

57 See appendix 1.

58 Joel Mokyr, 'The deadly fungus: an econometric investigation into the short-term demographic impact of the Irish Famine, 1846-51', *Research in Economic History*, 2 (1980), 237-77; P. P. Boyle and C. O Gráda, 'Fertility trends'.

59 'The potato'; Mitchell and Deane, *Abstract*, pp. 80-1.

60 1851 census, p. 634, gives 383,931 farmers and 717,680 labourers and servants (male) aged over fifteen years. Other categories—ploughmen, herds, etc.—bring the total in agriculture up to 1,211,848. In 1861 the numbers were 413,309, 374,425, and about 70,000 others, but presumably a good number of those registered as general labourers in 1861—346,816 in all—were farm labourers.

61 Schultz, *Transforming Traditional Agriculture*, pp. 53-70.

62 See above, pp. 00-00.

63 E.g. Nassau William Senior, *Journals, Conversations and Essays relating to Ireland* (London, 1868); Harriet Martineau, *Letters from Ireland* (London, 1854).

64 Joel Mokyr, 'Irish history with the potato', *Irish Economic and Social History*, 7 (1981), 17-22.

65 Ó Gráda, 'Irish agricultural output'.

CHAPTER 3

The Famine:
incidence and ideology

The time will come when we shall know what the amount of mortality has been, and though you may groan, and try to keep the truth down, it shall be known, and the time will come when the public and the world will be able to estimate, at its proper value, your management of the affairs of Ireland. [Lord George Bentinck]

The most strenuous efforts which human sagacity, ingenuity and foresight could at the time devise were put into requisition . . . The various social changes forced into action at that period (were) the means most fitted ultimately to ameliorate the social condition of the inhabitants. [Sir William Wilde]

The historiography of the Great Famine is curious. For a catastrophe usually rated the key event in nineteenth-century Irish history, it has produced remarkably little serious academic research in Ireland itself. A glance through back numbers of the most likely periodical outlets for such work tells the story well. *Irish Historical Studies* is now half a century old, and on the verge of publishing its hundredth issue. So far it has carried only five contributions on famine-related topics, and two of those were written by a 'non-academic' historian. The record of *Irish Economic and Social History* is no better; it has failed to carry a single piece on the Famine since it first appeared in 1974. Equally surprising and perhaps less excusable, a recent multi-authored *Milestones in Irish History* offers essays on textbook topics such as the battle of Clontarf, the flight of the earls and the Act of Union but nothing on the Great Famine.[1]

What work there is takes some pains to debunk the accounts of 'the political commentator, the ballad singer and unknown maker of folk-tales'.[2] So too, apparently, does the orthodoxy of the third-level classroom.[3] Traditionalist appraisals that even hint at culprits and villains from across the Irish Sea tend to get short shrift. From this anti-populist perspective the current orthodoxy is doubly reassuring. On the one hand, far from being another simple case of race murder, the Famine is held to have been exaggerated in the past by 'emotive' nationalist propagandists like

John Mitchel and O'Donovan Rossa, in terms of both regional incidence and excess mortality. On the other, what deaths there were tend to be regarded as the largely inevitable or unavoidable consequence of economic backwardness.

Shattering dangerous myths about the past is the historian's social responsibility. In Ireland, where popular history is an odd brew of myth and reality, there is plenty for him to do. Perhaps a dose of cold revisionism was necessary to purge the locals of a simplistic and hysterical *Our Boys* view of the Famine as a 'British plot'? The connection between popular history and nationalist resistance is, after all, real. It was the IRA leader Ernie O'Malley who wrote of the 1916 rising: 'In the evening I was in a whirl; my economic history.'[4] Correcting nationalist misconceptions about historical grievances has been the unifying theme of revisionist Irish economic history for the last few decades. But when it comes to the Famine have Irish historians not allowed their 'generosity and restraint'[5] to run away with them? On the evidence, there is at least an argument to be put forward. Students of other famines seeking comparative insights may be impressed by the lack of Irish emotion or outrage, but they will quickly note too that themes central to mainstream famine history research have been ignored in Irish work. So, for example, the basic point of Amartya Sen's *Poverty and Famines,*[6] that starvation is not the product of food shortfall only but a function of a market solution to unjust property rights, was made (though not in so many words) by contemporaries in Ireland during the Great Famine, but finds no echo in the 'serious' Irish literature. Again, Ambirajan's classic treatments of government policy and Indian nineteenth-century famines leave little doubt but that the constraints imposed by ideology on the State bureaucracy added to mass starvation,[7] but historiography tends to be silent or apologetic on that issue too in the Irish context.

A good example of the 'generosity and restraint' view is the famous collection of essays *The Great Famine: Studies in Irish History*, edited in 1956 by the Dublin historians Dudley Edwards and Desmond Williams. Eschewing a narrative approach, the editors emphasised instead the Famine's roots deep in history, pointing to 'the scale of the actual outlay to meet the famine', and in essence making excuses for the attitudes of British bureaucrats and politicians. In tone they are much closer to William Wilde's apologetics (quoted above) than to contemporary populist rhetoric. Commenting on the human toll, Edwards and Williams are content with 'the certainty that many, many died'. Their collection is a mixed bag. The opening essays by McDowell and

Green were lazily written, using no new sources whatever. The chapters on relief policy and emigration have worn well by comparison. Yet only in those on the medical history of the Famine and on folklore sources does the reader get a true sense of what the tragedy was like for those on the receiving end. As a scholarly introduction to the Great Famine the Edwards and Williams volume lacks coherence and fairness.

What of the competition? By not attempting a general history Edwards and Williams in effect left it to the 'popular' historian Cecil Woodham-Smith to fill the void a few years later.[8] Woodham-Smith's enduring best-seller has its faults: it errs on several details, its understanding of the economic context is weak, and its interpretation of motives and events is sometimes cavalier. Still, looking back, it certainly deserved better than the chilly and delayed welcome accorded by the late F. S. L. Lyons in the trade's premier journal in 1965.[9] Lyons derided *The Great Hunger* for its naive populism and lack of humility. It was wrong of Woodham-Smith, he claimed, to criticise government outside its contemporary context; horrific descriptive accounts of the tragedy were all very well, but one must turn elsewhere for 'the reason why'. Students were asked to join in the fun of debunking Woodham-Smith; those taking an honours history degree at University College, Dublin, in 1963 were invited to write an essay on '*The Great Hunger* is a great novel'.[10] Orthodoxy has hardly changed since. The Educational Facsimiles issued for school use by the Northern Ireland Public Record Office in 1968 suffer from the same anti-populist bias. While several of the facsimile documents were well worth reproducing, the editorial introduction consists of an unenlightening or misleading collection of excerpts from three works by leading Irish historians. Some generalisations in elegant prose from J. C. Beckett are followed by an excerpt from E. R. R. Green, so effusive in its praise of government relief policy that one is left wondering now anybody could possibly have perished. Green's comments refer to the first stages of the Famine only, but the presumably unsuspecting reader is not told as much. The introduction is rounded off by a few sentences from the introduction to the Edwards and Williams volume.[11] Robert Kee's graphic and 'emotive' television history of 1980 met a worse fate than Woodham-Smith: it was heavily criticised by a leading Dublin academic for lending succour to terrorism.[12]

Sadly few of the Irish historians listed above have done what could be termed original research in this area. Among Irish historians Austin Bourke, whose pioneering research deserves far more recognition, has been the main producer. In a series of articles linked to his unpublished doctoral thesis, he has put in proportion the importance of the potato in Ireland on the eve of the crisis, chronicled the spread of the blight and its contemporary investigation by scientists, added greatly to what we know about pre-Famine weights and measures, and analysed the corn trade before and during the Famine years. Much more on the course of the crisis itself and on pre-Famine agriculture remains un-published.[13] Patrick Hickey's able account of the Famine in south-west Cork—the only comprehensive regional history of its kind available so far—also remains unpublished.[14]

Until last year no Irish historian since John O'Rourke in 1874 had attempted to write a comprehensive account of the Famine years. Meanwhile James Donnelly (an American) in his work on the rural economy of nineteenth-century County Cork and Joel Mokyr (an Israeli American) in *Why Ireland Starved* and related papers have produced a great deal of useful material, easily more than, say, the sum total of articles on the subject published by local practitioners since the great Famine itself.[15] Happily, the shortage of general accounts has been remedied to a considerable extent by the appearance of new works by James Donnelly and Mary Daly.[16] It must be said that neither embodies much fresh research, however. Daly's, an inexpensive paperback aimed at a student market, is a careful and concise review of the Famine and its economic context. Donnelly's, part of the ongoing *New History of Ireland*, provides a clear narrative guide to the complex series of policy changes enacted in the late 1840s and their impact. Since Donnelly focuses almost exclusively on the Famine years and Daly deals extensively with both the pre- and post-Famine eras, these works complement each other nicely. There is this difference, though. A cautious disciple of the 'generosity and restraint' tradition, Daly is reluctant to allocate any blame. On the pivotal issue of governmental relief, its role, she writes, should 'perhaps be seen in a more sympathetic light than it is generally regarded', since 'it does not appear appropriate to pronounce in an unduly critical fashion on the limitations of previous generations'. Donnelly has little time for apologetics. He gives the Swiftian indignation of John Mitchel—whose ghost historians still seek to exorcise—its due, and deals levelheadedly (if critically) even with British historian A. J. P. Taylor's accusa-tion of 'genocide'.[17]

Why have Irish historians shunned famine research? Why are outside historians less hidebound in their assessments? Politics is at least part of the answer; Irish historians are, by and large, a conservative bunch. There are no Irish E. P. Thompsons or Eugene

Genoveses. But the considerable rhetorical challenge posed by 'emotive' traditional accounts must also be a deterrent. Attempts at balance always risk being interpreted as making excuses. The Famine remains a sensitive subject, and perhaps that is why its economic and social history has not been written. In what follows I focus on five aspects of Famine history.[18] The outcome leaves scope, I think, for a more critical assessment of the period. First, something is added to what is already known about excess mortality. It is shown that the Famine was a graver and more protracted affair than some recent revisionist popularisation would admit. Second, an analysis of seasonal potato price movements attempts to come to grips with a theme frequently urged by those charged with relief during the crisis: the notion that unfettered competitive markets offered the best solution to the high prices induced by scarcity. For many contemporary critics of policy this faith in the market amounted to open season for hoarders and speculators of all sorts. The data used in my search for hoarding during the crisis are far from ideal, but the outcome of a simple test tentatively suggests that such hoarding was not responsible for the massive mortality of those years. If the free-market solution did not work, what, then, was the problem? An obvious third topic for consideration is the role of food availability and entitlements, recently canvassed by Sen. My analysis of food supply during the Famine finds that while Sen's approach has useful insights for the Irish case, the problem in Ireland in the late 1840s differed from that highlighted in the most striking of his twentieth-century case studies. Fourth, the part of ideology in influencing policy—an issue on which currently orthodoxy has been perhaps unduly soft—is reassessed. Finally, one remote part of Ireland, the islands of Aran, is discussed as a possible guide to the fate of nineteenth-century rural Ireland in the absence of *Phytophthora infestans*. Aran, it emerges, escaped lightly during the Famine, because it seems to have been spared the worst of the fungus. Aran's fate is interesting, since the mass mortality of these years has been invoked to paint a very fatalistic picture of the country's prospects before 1845.

1. Famine mortality

One element in the tendency to 'write down' the Famine has been either (*a*) to eschew measurement of excess mortality altogether, or (*b*) to venture cautious, conservative guesses. The traditional estimates of a million or more deaths—Woodham-Smith ventures a million and a half—give way in revisionist accounts to ones of

800,000 or even half a million.[19] What is in a number? Surely a careful guess is a useful yardstick by which to measure the effectiveness of policy. While a really accurate estimate is out of the question, two independently derived estimates by Mokyr and by Boyle and Ó Gráda suggest one million excess deaths, or over a ninth of the population.[20] Mokyr's numbers also highlight the regional contrast in fortunes. According to Mokyr's data the toll ranged from about a hundredth of the population in Carlow and Wexford to over a quarter in Mayo and Roscommon. At the provincial level Leinster seems to have lost least (forty-five per thousand), and Connacht most (254 per thousand).[21] These estimates are plausible, but they rely on rather dubious migration data, and so should be taken only as rough indicators. For instance, Mokyr's calculations produce negative excess mortality during the Famine years in Dublin. The Dublin burial statistics reported in the 1841 and 1851 censuses hardly support this. There burials are reported at 13,516 for June 1839–June 1841, and at 91,511 during the decade July 1841–June 1851. Assuming no change in the proportion of unreported burials—a generous assumption, surely—and allowing for population growth, the numbers still indicate smallish but positive excess mortality in the metropolis.[22]

Who perished from the Famine? Karl Marx's 'it killed poor devils only'[23] is a crucial, if obvious, part of the answer. Two other aspects of this massive mortality are worth examining. One broached by neither Mokyr nor Cousens is its relative impact by age and sex. Were the aged and the very young, as a west Cork rector suggested at the time, disproportionately at risk? Or did aspects of relief policy, such as task work and the infamous Gregory clause (which made small farmers and cottiers, though not their families, ineligible for relief), put males at greater risk? Or might attempts at increasing families' earnings potential through giving more of the available food to the breadwinner have affected the odds?[24] The issue is often raised in historical studies of crisis and famine mortality, with differing results. In the case of epidemics the picture is clear enough. Smallpox can be shown to have affected the young disproportionately, while cholera was more likely to attack the old. In the Irish cholera outbreak of 1849 children of six years or younger were less than 10 per cent of those hit. The Black Death is usually thought to have claimed more males and more young people.

With subsistence crises the record varies. In Pierre Goubert's Beauvaisis the elderly were apparently more starvation-prone during the subsistence crises of the seventeenth century. Turning to more recent famines, Chowdury and Chen suggest that it was the youngest and the very old who suffered most in the Bangladesh famine of 1974. In the Indian state of Maharashtra in 1970–73 it was likewise, but Sen's analysis of mortality during the great Bengali famine of 1943–44 shows that excess mortality there was a straightforward multiple of normal mortality.[25]

Our estimates of the incidence of Great Famine mortality by sex and age rely upon a range of assumptions about the structure of population and emigration between 1821 and 1841. How they were derived has been fully explained elsewhere; the results are as follows. In terms of absolute numbers there were slightly more excess deaths among males than females. However, the differential is so small and sensitive to the assumed sex composition of the emigrant outflow that not much should be made of it. As for

TABLE 24 *Excess deaths during Famine years, by age and sex*

	Males		Females	
Age groups	No. of excess deaths (total)	Average No. in population (annual)	No. of excess deaths (total)	Average No. in population (annual)
0–4	146,000 (29)	508,000 (14)	139,000 (29)	491,000 (13)
5–9	95,000 (18)	471,000 (12)	92,000 (20)	455,000 (12)
10–59	204,000 (40)	2,526,000 (68)	191,000 (40)	2,659,000 (69)
60+	66,000 (13)	211,000 (6)	52,000 (11)	234,000 (6)
Total	511,000 (100)	3,716,000 (100)	474,000 (100)	3,839,000 (100)

Source. Boyle and Ó Gráda, 'Fertility trends', 555.

incidence by age, it turns out that Famine mortality can be represented in terms of earlier, non-crisis mortality by means of a simple linear transformation of age-specific death rates. The Famine almost doubled the death rate for all ages during 1846–51.[26] In this respect the Famine toll mirrored that of the Bengali famine described by Sen.

Another aspect of Famine mortality worth more attention is its timing. Taking the period 1846–51 as a unit is a necessary step in calculating excess deaths but hardly an excuse for overlooking the intensity of the crisis as reflected in the trend of mortality during these years. That excess mortality was low in the first year after the potato failure has already been mentioned. The trend in weekly workhouse deaths charted in fig. 3 is the best guide available to crisis mortality over time. The series suffers from two opposing biases. Since workhouse capacity was presumably more of a constraint in 1846–48 than later, deaths early on are probably under-represented. The system may also have

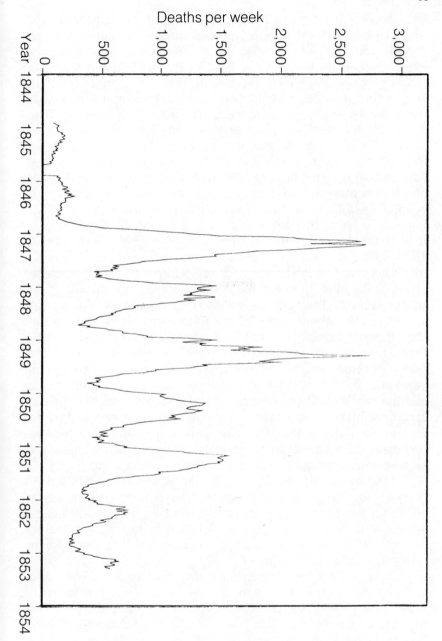

Fig. 3 Deaths in workhouses, Ireland, 1845–53

been forced to handle a rising proportion of dying people over time. However, total population was obviously falling over the period, and our series makes no attempt to account for this. Figure 3 confirms our story of light excess mortality in the wake of the 1845 potato failure. Nevertheless, by the summer of 1846, even before the failure of the new crop was known, it is clear that the previous year's poor harvest was having an effect.[27] The steep rise in late 1846 is to be expected; more striking is how slow the weekly death rate was to drop. This is interesting in view of the common tendency to discuss other aspects of the Famine as if it ended in 1848. The Irish University Press collection of parliamentary papers for all intents and purposes does not go beyond 1848,[28] while Father O'Rourke's account stops in 1847. Figure 3 suggests that the Famine was a more protracted disaster than is usually depicted. The murderous winters of 1846–47 and 1848–49 are well captured. Some of the 1849 deaths were caused by cholera, but since the starving was disproportionately cholera-prone[29] this does not greatly distort matters. Significantly the winter peaks of 1849–50 and 1850–51 equalled that of 1847–48, and were still double those of the following winters. Here again, the Bengali famine of 1943–46 mirrored the Irish version. Estimates of excess mortality in Bengal are highly sensitive to the period covered, and Sen shows that excess deaths lasted several years after an official 'end' to the crisis had been declared.[30] The continuing mortality, in turn, is an indictment of the official eagerness in both instances to announce the crisis over and try to forget about it. In the Irish case this was reflected in the unfortunate decision, taken as early as autumn 1847, to pass the entire burden of relief over to the Irish poor law system.[31]

The seasonality highlighted in fig. 3 was also a feature of 'normal' mortality in Ireland before the Famine; in Dublin in 1839–41, for example, reported burials in November–April were 40 per cent higher than in May–October.[32] But the seasonality of the 1846–51 period was clearly more marked, summer sickness giving way to winter deaths.

Broadly speaking, excess mortality was high in 1849 and 1850 where it had been high in 1846 and 1847. But in areas lightly touched by the potato failure deaths were probably close to normal by 1849.[33] The basis of these statements, William Wilde's tables of deaths, must be handled with due caution, since presumably the data for earlier years are less complete than those for 1849 or 1850. Nevertheless some regionally consistent patterns emerge (see table 25). In Leinster, Munster and Connacht the excess deaths were still very high in 1849: the pseudo-death rates in these provinces were still twice their 1846 levels. In Ulster, though, 1849 was less serious, and the rate in 1850 was nearly down to that of 1846. It is an exaggeration to claim, as Woodham-

TABLE 25 *Pseudo-death rates by province, 1845–50*

Province	1845	1846	1847	1848	1849	1850
Leinster	12·7	17·2	31·3	27·6	34·0	25·0
Munster	10·9	16·3	36·8	32·6	40·5	35·1
Ulster	9·2	13·4	28·3	20·9	21·0	15·5
Connacht	8·4	14·2	33·5	34·5	39·5	23·5

Source. Deaths as reported in British Parliamentary Papers, 1856 (XXX); population is assumed to have grown at its 1830s rate in 1841–45, and then to have declined at a constant rate between 1845 and 1851.

Smith has done,[34] that 1849 was the worst of the Famine years. Yet the bleak picture painted by Wilde's tabulations and work-house data cannot be ignored. The story of continuing crisis is lent graphic support by the pleas of some western priests to Archbishop Murray of Dublin for financial aid in the spring of 1849. This is how William Flannelly, curate in Clifden, made his case for a few pounds in April 1849:[35]

> I can assure your grace that a mile of the public road cannot be travelled without meeting a dead body, as the poor are houseless, and daily turned out of the poor house whenever they exhibit any symptom of sickness. There is not a hut without fever and dysentry, the sure precursors of cholera, which I fear is the next ordeal through which the poor Irish must pass. And how could it be otherwise, when there is no medical aid of any sort in this wild and extensive district and when the poor are obliged to live on ½ lb. of Indian meal every 24 hours. I have known men to be willing to work for a whole day for 2 pints of meal, and could not obtain work even on that low wages if wages it could be called.

By this time the public works and the soup kitchens were things of the past, and donor fatigue had set in.[36] Relief, made 'less eligible' by the Gregory clause (on which more later), was the responsibility of local Poor Law administrations. A message from the parish priest of Bangor Erris, in the Mullet peninsula, explains the result:[37]

> Our misery at the present day is not much, if any, inferior to what it had been, even at the worst time—for the outdoor relief is in great measure an empty name—to our able-bodied poor it is denied until brought to the last stages of exhaustion, and even if then admitted,

the quantity given is not more than half that allowed by law. Our distance from the workhouse is another of our grievances, the parish being in part about 26 miles from it, and yet notwithstanding the distance, some unfortunate fathers and mothers each carrying a child or two, had in the depth of winter to stand *three* reviews lest they should be too heavy in flesh for outdoor relief, and it not infrequently happened, that some after being rejected as not qualified for relief, have been found dead along the ditches in their attempt to reach their homes.

Finally a report from Ballyhaunis, again in Mayo, on how the Gregory clause went to work bears quoting:[38]

I can assure you that at no period of the distress was it required more than at the present time, when the poor landholders, who struggled this time back, are now in a most wretched state without food or seed and still they are not giving up their land lest (as they say) they would never have their own fireside again: I am certain that more in my parish will die of starvation from this time to the next harvest than died for the last three years. A poor woman was found dead the other day by the ditch at Coolnaclea in my parish, of starvation. If outdoor relief is not immediately given to the landholders and able bodied, the consequences I fear will be awful.

The great Famine had in effect been officially 'declared' over more than a year before these letters were written. It *was* over in 1849 in the sense that food prices had fallen, and that maize (Indian meal) in particular was cheap. But if data on deaths are the bottom line, the crisis did not end even then.

2. Potato prices before and after 1845

During the Famine export prohibition of grain, controls on distilling and large-scale public distribution of corn were resisted as solutions to famine. This was because government spokesmen and officials had learnt their Adam Smith well. Competition between merchants, their argument went, would quickly lead to speculators getting their fingers burnt, while to yield to popular demands would only ruin the legitimate trade in grain. Only in the remote west was there a danger of 'petty local speculators [holding] back supplies for the purpose of afterwards insisting on exhorbitant and famine prices'.[39] Was this sensible? In theory, it is true, speculation should have been self-defeating in time, for to hoard food *now* only guarantees a greater supply than otherwise *later*. Under the standard textbook conditions it can be shown that allowing buyers and sellers to determine consumption allocation over time would be the best policy in Paretian terms. The trouble is with the *now*. As Viscount Cranborne (later Lord Salisbury) stressed in a related context, anticipating a memorable quip by Keynes, 'in the long run supply and demand [might] square themselves, [but] human life was short, and men could not subsist without food beyond a few days'.[40] In practice how do speculators fare during famines? Like those at the mercy of price rises, famine researchers have a lot of trouble in sorting out purely speculative increases ('bubbles') from those reflecting supply and demand or market 'fundamentals'. Salim Rashid, for instance, has made a plausible case based on qualitative evidence for the existence of 'artificial' scarcities based on panic or ignorance during famines, citing evidence from Britain during the 1790s and the Indian subcontinent over a long time span. Convincing statistical tests for hoarding are rare, but a study of the rice market during the Bangladeshi famine of 1974 indicates that prices reflected rather poorly the perceived state of the crop. Even the possibility of such bubbles should make the steadfast application of *laissez-faire* principles to a market in food a questionable policy.[41] Was the Irish Famine exacerbated by erratic price movements, the outcome of fear and hoarding? No definitive answer can be given to this difficult question here, but there are some leads.

The following discussion is based on the analysis of Dublin weekly wholesale potato price data as reported in the *Irish Farmers' Journal and Weekly Intelligencer* (1816–25) and the *Irish Farmers Gazette* (1843–54), and monthly Dublin wheat prices over a longer period (1785–1838). Obviously price quotations from the west would have been preferable: the Dublin data have the advantages of accessability and continuous coverage. Typically data are given for three or four potato varieties in each week's issue. In the first period the varieties traded were cups, apples, whites, blacks and pink-eyes; their price histories are reproduced in fig. 4. In the second period lumpers and kemps are also included. The data for 1843–54 are the basis of fig. 5. In all cases, the solid and dotted lines represent lower and upper price quotations.

Clearly whites were a highly seasonal crop in the first period. Blacks were typically cheaper than either cups or apples, while pink-eyes were not reported before the autumn of 1819. Kemps, which came on the market in late 1819, are recorded as blacks. The data highlight bad years. The crisis of 1816–18 (already noted in chapter 1) which was particularly serious in Dublin, meant prices twice the norm. Scarcities are also indicated in the early 1810s, in 1823 and in 1825. But, above all, the graphs show how much worse the Famine years were than anything recorded earlier.

In a study of grain prices in early modern England, McCloskey and Nash have argued[42] that price seasonality can be used to infer storage costs and, in a rough-and-ready way, the rate of interest. This follows from the premise that those who store must in equilibrium cover the opportunity cost of tied-up funds and the loss from wastage during the storage period. A saw-tooth seasonality pattern is suggested, low autumn prices giving way gradually to a maximum before the new harvest comes in. McCloskey and Nash's summary results would seem to confirm such a pattern. Their calculations, based on over a thousand pairs of prices, suggest an average monthly increase in late medieval England of over 2 per cent, though with high variance. Should the increase be the same for all months and years? If the capital cost of the crop stored is what matters most, and the opportunity cost of capital remains constant, the same proportionate price increases per month would be expected in good and bad years, but if fixed costs such as buildings and security bulk large, then the increases should be less sensitive to the price of the crop. Seasonality in a well functioning market would thus mean at most proportionate increases in prices: the quality of the harvest is irrelevant. McCloskey and Nash's argument then suggests this inference: strong deviations away from the established seasonality pattern suggest speculation or 'bubbles'. Such 'bubbles' are often associated in popular reaction or memory with famine conditions, whether due to popular panic or merchant hoarding. A simple illustration may help here. In terms of fig. 6, the hypothetical price rises in years 1–4 are all 30 per cent. However, in years 5 and 6 price movements are at least consistent with hoarding and insufficient storage or panic selling early in the season. Of course, more complex seasonal movements might easily be imagined.

The popular hatred in Ireland for the 'gombeenman'—rural and small-town traders-cum-moneylenders—probably dates from Famine times.[43] That they charged high prices is obvious: that some of them extorted monopoly prices is likely, though not proven. But did they increase their monopoly exploitation in hard times? Certainly the scope for such extortion was realised by policy-makers at the time, and claims that merchants were unfairly raising prices were common.[44]

Testing for such blips in crisis times, with limited data of questionable quality, is difficult. The test outlined by Ravaillon for the Bangladeshi famine of 1974 hypothesises that forecasts of future crop loss should not affect current prices independent of realised future prices. The crop report data required for such a test

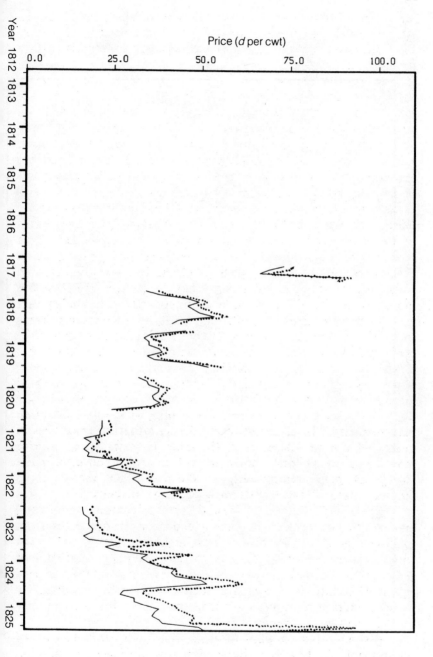

Fig. 4(a) Cups

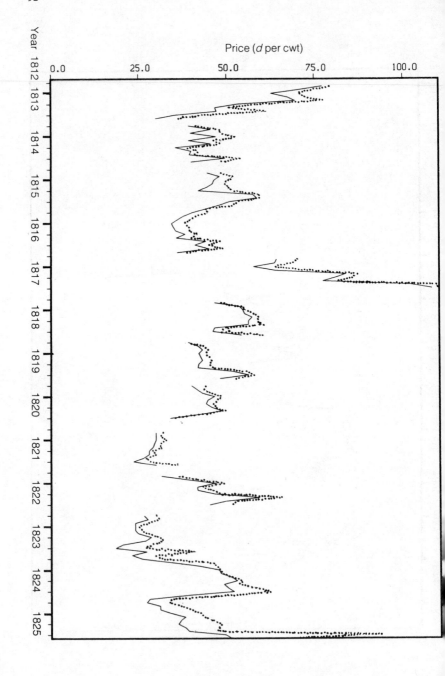

Fig. 4(b) Apples

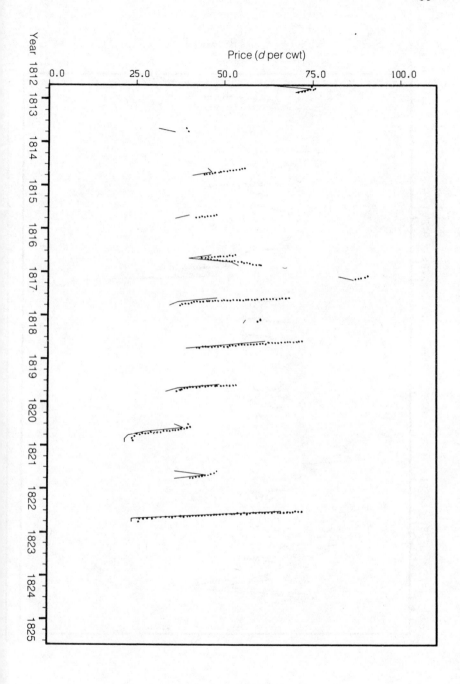

Fig. 4(c) Whites

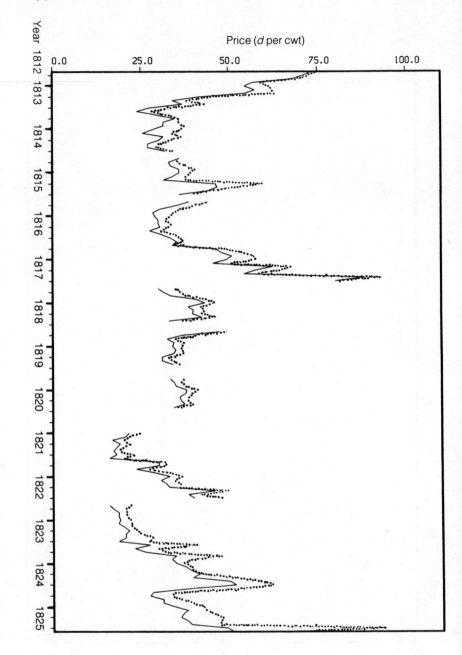

Fig. 4(d) Blacks

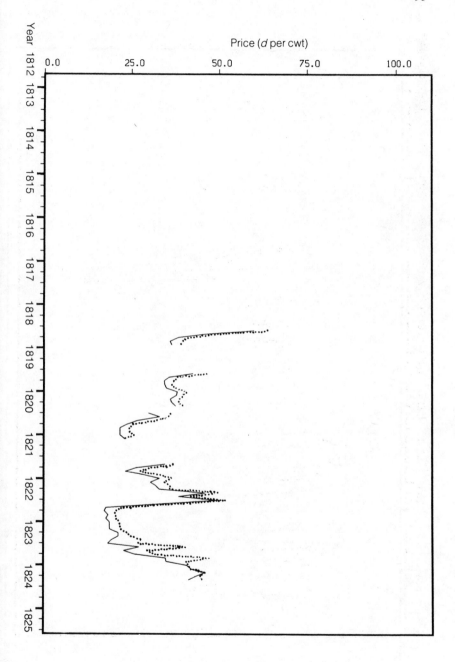

Fig. 4(e) Pink-eyes

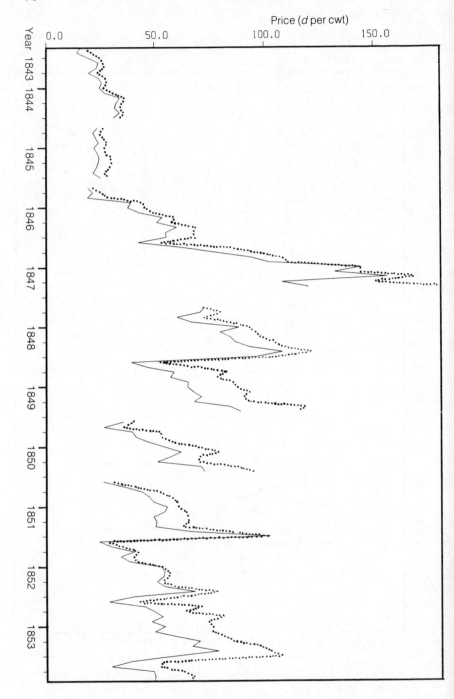

Fig. 5(a) Cups

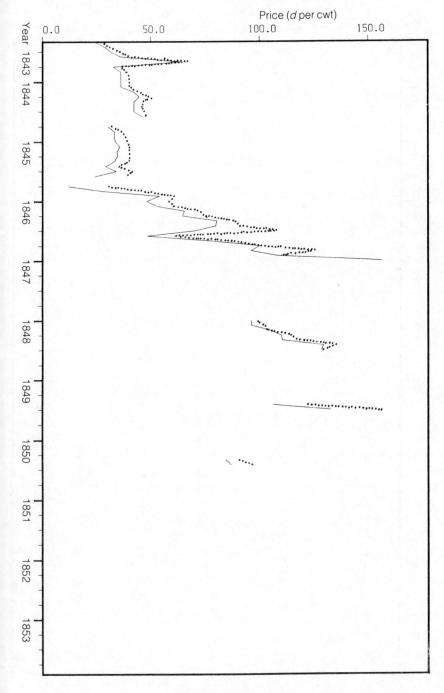

Fig. 5(b) Apples

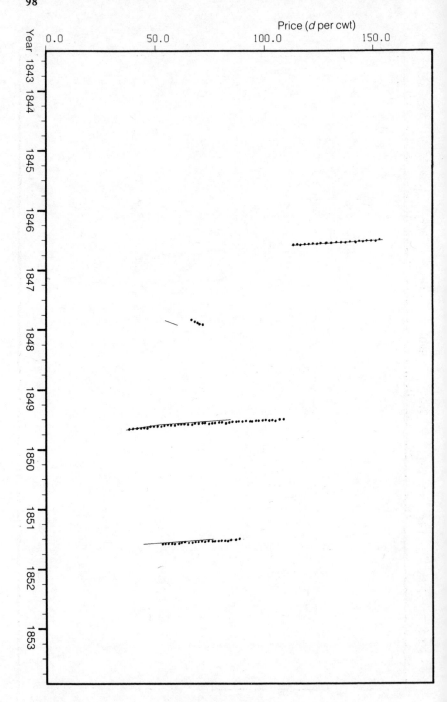

Fig. 5(c) Whites

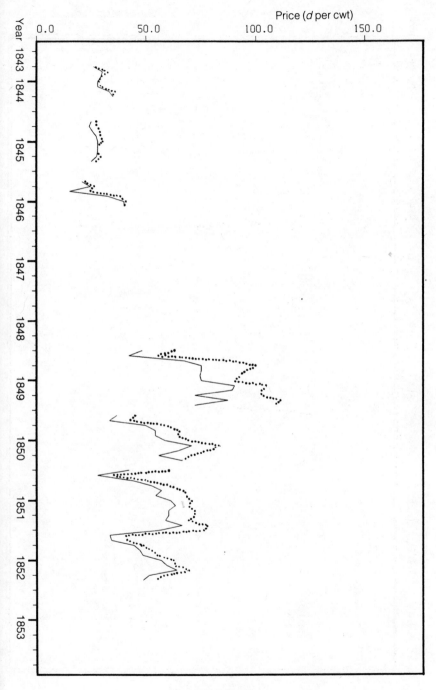

Fig. 5(d) Blacks

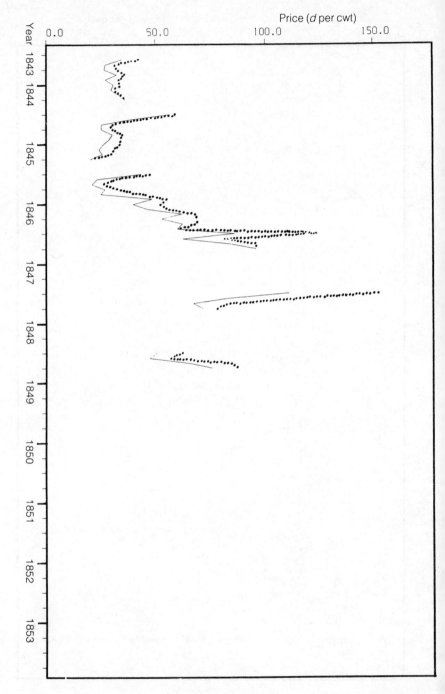

Fig. 5(e) Pinks

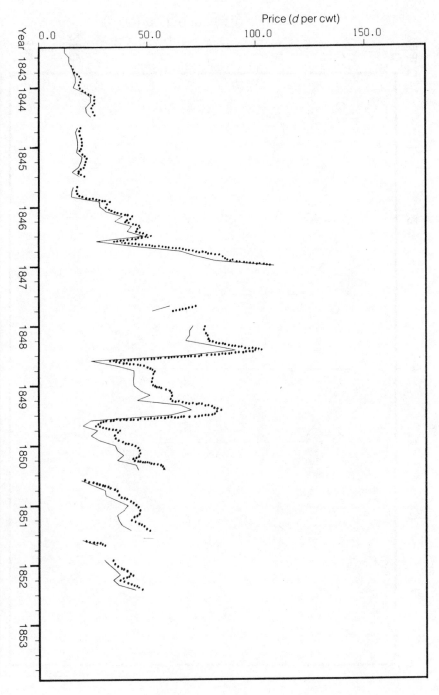

Fig. 5(f) Lumpers

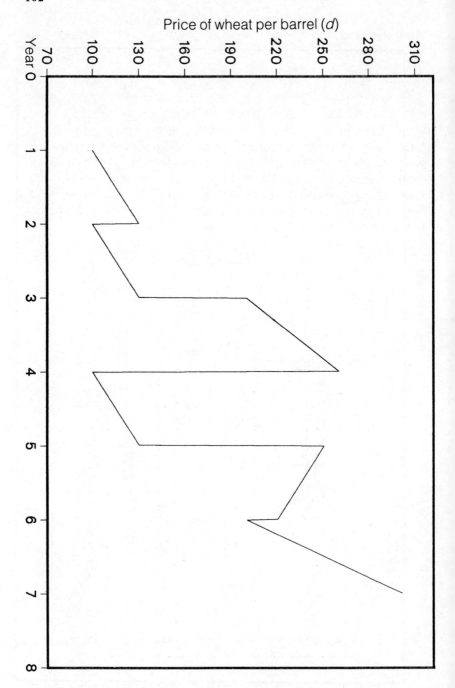

Fig. 6 Hypothetical seasonality patterns

are not available for the case at hand, but series of weekly or monthly price data would seem a rough-and-ready second-best way of seeking such blips. In particular, speculative bubbles at the onset of a poor harvest might be sought in relatively *low* trough-to-peak rises, the bubble having forced a high base price. An 'advantage' of the potato in this context is that it could not be stored from year to year, so that—if there are no bubbles—each year's data provide an independent measure of storage cost. In figs. 7 and 8 the maximum and minimum monthly prices quoted for potatoes in Dublin in 1813–25 and 1844–53 are plotted. While displaying lots of spikes, the earlier data nevertheless do reflect the kind of pattern predicted. The mean price rise between mid-September and mid-December was about 15 per cent. However, the rise was erratic, as table 26 shows.[45]

TABLE 26 *Percentage change in potato prices, (a) October to June–July and (b) mid-September to mid-December, 1812–53*

	(a)	(b)	
1812	– 55	– 9	– 13
1813	– 13	+ 18	+ 22
1814	+ 18	n.a.	n.a.
1815	– 3	– 32	– 26
1816	+ 81	+ 92	+ 92
1817	+ 18	+ 32	+ 26
1818	+ 21	– 27	– 25
1819	– 8	+ 13	+ 6
1820	– 21	– 27	– 25
1821	+ 48	– 18	– 9
1822	+ 6	+ 19	+ 20
1823	+ 95	+ 62	+ 11
1824	+ 62	+ 3	+ 11
1843	+ 67	– 4	– 4
1844	+ 8	+ 4	+ 6
1851	+ 19	+ 25	+ 17
1852	+ 36	– 6	+ 4
1853		+122	+ 29
Average	+ 22	+ 18	+ 14
1845	+158	+ 90	+105
1846	+167	+102	+ 23
1847	+ 56	+ 15	+ 7
1848	+ 52	+ 39	+ 26
1849	+ 82	+ 80	+ 68
1850	+ 70	+ 13	+ 53
Average 1845–50	+ 98	+ 57	+ 47

Typically, the rise from trough to peak was one-fifth or more, but with considerable variation from month to month and

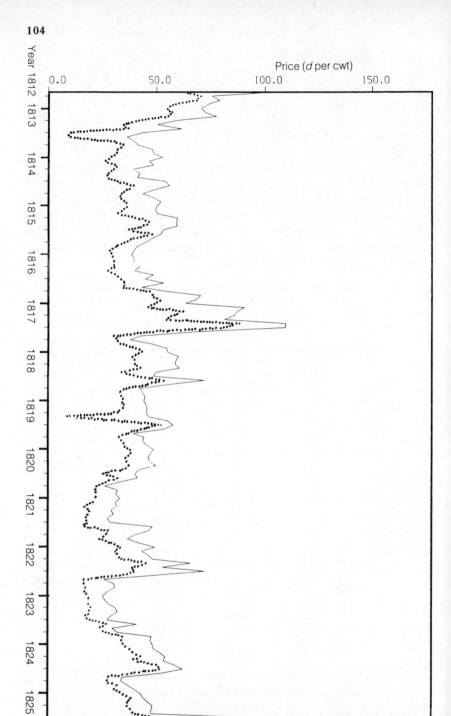

Fig. 7 Minimum and maximum potato prices, Dublin market, 1812-25

105

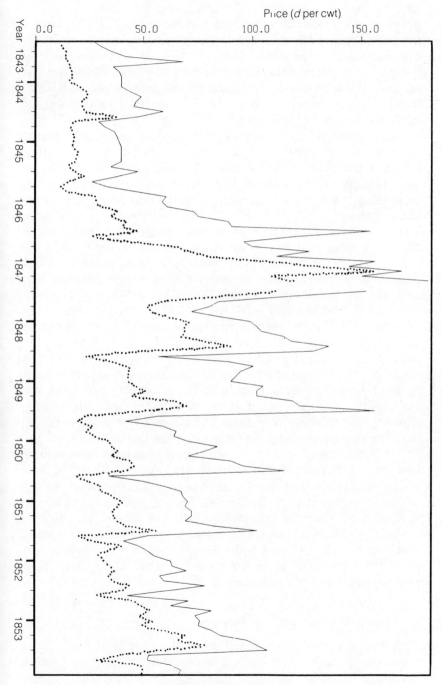

Fig. 8 Minimum and maximum potato prices, Dublin market, 1843–53

year to year. Applying the McCloskey–Nash criterion to potato prices suggests that the rate of interest facing (and paid to) potato merchants in pre-Famine Ireland was enormous. Indeed, the result is a warning that the method must be used with caution, because using a longer series of Dublin grain prices suggests quite a different picture. Between 1785 and 1810 the average annual rises from trough to peak were 13·3 per cent for oats and 13·9 per cent for wheat; between 1811 and 1838, 11·1 and 14·1 per cent.[46] Presumably grain and potato speculators faced the same risk-adjusted interest charges. The more marked rise in potato prices thus reflects higher storage charges and risk premia, pure and simple.

Turning to the Famine proper, let us concentrate on the seasonality displayed by the series with the best coverage, that for cups. Strikingly, the seasonality is more regular but hardly more marked during the Famine years than earlier. Seasonality varies too much from year to year for strong inferences, but focusing on the movement from October to June–July seems to tell us someting. Thus between 1814–15 and 1824–25 the average rise was 28·8 per cent, while in 1843–44, 1844–45, 1851–52 and 1852–53 it averaged 32·4 per cent (see table 26). However, between 1845–46 and 1850–51 the average rose to almost 100 per cent. This hardly supports the notion of hoarding: on the contrary, if anything it suggests that potatoes were being brought to market 'too quickly'. Now these data refer to Dublin only: whether their message holds in areas more directly affected must await the availability of data from farther south and west. Meanwhile, allowing the market for potatoes to operate freely seems not to have the consequences feared by some in the late 1840s.

Finally, the numbers are a reminder of the permanent resurce cost of the Famine. Prices did not drop back to their previous levels, partly a reflection of higher production costs, but mainly of lower average yields. Before the Famine oatmeal cost five to six times as much as potatoes, weight for weight. In 1849–50 oatmeal, containing twice the food value, was not much more than double the price of potatoes. Farmers who had plenty of potatoes apparently preferred to sell them, 'living, with their servants, on oaten and Indian meal'.[47]

3. Food shortage and entitlements

That famines stem from shortfalls in the supply of food might seem tautological. However, a generalised food shortage is not a necessary condition of mass starvation. In a work that focuses primarily on famine in the modern Third World Amartya Sen has

argued that typically the fundamental reason for mass starvation
is not an aggregate shortage of food. The paradox arises from poor
people's inability to *buy* the food available. Those without land
lack the funds, and the authorities lack the will to transfer the
food to them through political means, relying instead on market
forces. In such circumstances some groups—traders, farmers
whose output remains intact, employers of labour—may stand to
gain from famine conditions. Thus:[48]

> market forces can be seen as operating *through* a system of legal rela-
> tions (ownership rights, contractual obligations, legal exchanges, etc.).
> The law stands between food availability and food entitlement. Starva-
> tion deaths can reflect legality with a vengeance.

Sen's framework was originally inspired by a context far
removed from the Ireland of the 1840s. The victims of the great
Bengali famine of 1943–46 were more likely to have been urban
artisans and labourers, who paid for their food in money. Moreover that famine was *not* caused by a natural disaster like the
potato blight. The Bengali case prompted Sen to examine other
modern famines in Ethiopia, the Sahel and Bangladesh. These
were indeed prompted by harvest failures, but the striking conclusion that starvation was due not to inadequate food but to the
poor's inability to command enough food to live, held firm.[49]
What is the relevance of Sen's model to Ireland in the 1840s and
earlier? Certainly there are loose anticipations of his argument in
contemporary Irish sources. During the famine of 1816–18 high
food prices pointed to scarcity as the problem, but the *Irish
Farmers Journal*, admittedly an interested party, focused on 'the
want of employment as the chief cause' of the distress. In 1812,
it pointed out, similarly high prices had caused no problems,
while in the summer of 1817 a substantial drop in prices would
do no good as long as unemployment persisted. Thus 'the
difficulties . . . evidently proceed not from absolute want of food
but from the want of means to purchase it'.[50] Again, the Irish
famine of 1822 fits Sen's pattern; a parliamentary committee
reported at the time than it was due less to the shortage of food
'than from the want of adequate means of purchasing it'.[51] But
the potato's failure in 1846–48 meant the destruction of about
30 million tons, or 5 million acres, enough to feed almost 5
million daily for three years. There is thus no question but that
food supply was drastically cut. But was there still enough,
suitably divided out, to feed everybody? How much grain or other
food would it have taken to feed those without potatoes in 1847
or 1848?

In Arthur Young's day feeding eight people on potatoes would have taken eight quarters or two Irish acres, but 'to feed on wheat those eight persons would require eight quarters, or two Irish acres, which at present imply two more for fallow, or four in all'.[52] Young's assumption that the fallow yielded no calories is questionable, but less than two decades later a committee of the Board of Agriculture also proposed a food production ratio of about two to one.[53] Such rather crude assessments are consistent with modern calculations based on dietary requirements. According to Burton, the potato today no longer outstrips grain in food production efficiency, but that finding is based on assumed yields of twenty-five and four metric tonnes per hectare respectively.[54] On the basis of pre-Famine yields, and assuming no change in relative calorific quality in the interim, the potato's advantage would thus have been of the order of two to one. About 3 million acres of grain would therefore have been needed annually to make up the shortfall in potatoes after 1845. It was not grown; indeed, the destruction of the potato crop probably induced (for reasons explained in chapter 2) a decline in grain production. Comparing Bourke's acreage estimates with those in the agricultural statistics of 1847–49 implies little change in barley or wheat production but a fall in the acreage under oats from 2·5 to 2·1 million.[55]

Yet the notion that the famine was not due to an aggregate shortage of food was common in Ireland. When the first agricultural census of 1847 showed the value of gross tillage produce at £45 million, the *Evening Mail* (no radical journal) was quick to point out that:

> enough (wheat, oats, barley, bere, rye, and beans) has been gathered in the past harvest to feed double the number of people actually existing in Ireland for a period of twelve months. But this is only a small fragment of the marvel; there were . . . green crops enough to feed 4,000,000 of human beings; and all this is exclusive of the stock of cattle, sheep, pigs and poultry . . .

This is true in the following sense: if a quarter of grain *per capita* was enough to hold body and soul together, then the 3 million acres under grain provided potentially enough food for everyone. Whence the populist inference that most of the food which 'would have saved every human being in the country from famine was shipped to England to pay rents and the salaries of bailiffs, police, and an army of officials', leading to the verdict that 'the word "famine" is a mere euphemism for what happened'.[56] Another reading of the figures, still in the spirit of Sen, is less nationalist in its implications: by showing more generosity to their labourers Irish landlords and Irish farmers could have alleviated the misery.

Yet these interpretations are too simple in two respects. First, trade data show (see table 27) that Ireland switched from substantial exporter to net importer of grain during the Famine years. In 1846–48 *net* grain exports were about 700,000 tons below the level of the early 1840s. Ireland, for decades a large-scale exporter of grain, imported massively during the Famine.[57] But the populist story is not all wrong here. Donnelly makes a cogent case for the view that a *temporary* embargo on exports in late 1846 or early 1847, while foreign supplies were being obtained, would have saved lives. However, the notion that an export prohibition would have solved the problem of food shortfall over the longer haul is an exaggeration.

TABLE 27 *The grain trade during the Famine ('000 tons*

Year	UK imports	Irish imports
1840	700	−294
1841	646	−377
1842	694	−313
1843	271	−465
1844	502	−394
1845	392	−485
1846	766	− .87
1847	1,869	+743
1848	1,308	+123
Average 1840–45	534	−388
Average 1846–48	1,314	+290

Second, the calculations above assume away the likely effects of redistribution on production, and make no allowance for seed and animal input requirements. It is too much to hope that a reallocation or requisitioning of available domestically grown food in 1846–47 would have produced no cutbacks in grain output in 1847–48 and later. Simple political arithmetic thus suggests that famine could probably not have been avoided on Ireland's own resources. In this sense, the Malthusian emphasis on food supply is not misplaced. Nevertheless, the lack of generosity from the rest of the United Kingdom guaranteed the outcome. So, ultimately, the starvation was in part at least due to how politics limited entitlements.

The Gregory clause, which removed relief entitlements from those holding more than a quarter of an acre of land, also lends itself to interpretation along Sen's lines. Tellingly, only two Irish members voted against the clause in the House of Commons.[58] By depriving those on relief of the prospect of supplementary income from the land this measure, and the clearances inspired by it, were probably directly responsible for thousands of deaths. While some landlords and farmers connived with their tenants at obtaining relief without surrendering possession, more had no compunction about using the Gregory clause to clear estates, and many areas showed 'strong marks of the march of the enemy [from] the multitudes of ruined cottages or cabins'. In Carrick-on-Shannon a local official who would 'give no opinion on the propriety or expediency of this step' admitted that it gave rise to a situation that could not be coped with locally.[59]

Finally, it is unlikely that any significant group in Ireland *gained* during the Famine. In this sense too the Famine differed from the typical scenario described by Sen. In a world where starvation is the outcome purely (or even mainly) of an entitlement shift, gains are necessarily part of something close to a zero-sum setting. In Ireland landlords (a large minority of whom were bankrupted) and the landless (of whom a majority starved or emigrated) and near landless were the obvious losers. But who gained? Commercial grain producers can hardly have gained, either. For them grain prices were largely exogenously determined by world markets rather than by local famine conditions. More important, the destruction of the potato undermined their chosen rotation, and forced on them the need to pay those workers they retained a higher efficiency wage.[60] During the Famine a bare subsistence on oatmeal cost much more than a bellyful of potatoes had cost a few years earlier. For such farmers the Famine, far from being a boon, spurred the shift from a grain-based to a live-stock agriculture. The acreage under grain dropped from 3·3 million acres in 1847 to 2·7 million in 1854.[61] Only to those specialising in cattle—and employing little labour—can the crisis have been a boon, since the price of their main input (land) fell. But such farmers were few in Ireland in the 1840s.

4. Policy and ideology

In *Economic Thought and the Irish Question* Professor R. D. C. Black has shown that the analysis of those classical economists who wrote most about Ireland before the Famine amounted to more than 'merely a policy of *laissez-faire*'. His survey reveals instances of support for some far-reaching remedies, including public investment in a railway network, State-supported emigration schemes, and more funding for education. In this sense

Black's findings could be interpreted as evidence against those who 'regard the Classical conception of the functions of the State as sufficiently characterized by Carlyle's phrase, "Anarchy plus the constable", or by Lasalle's simile of the night watchman'.[62]

Yet as Black also admits—and this is surely much more to the point—the impact of economists on public opinion and on economic policy, through their parliamentary spokesmen and the media, was certainly against government intervention in Ireland. The message to be distilled from the work of luminaries such as Nassau Senior, Harriet Martineau or John Ramsay McCulloch was that public help for Ireland would prove counter-productive. It would stifle private enterprise and private charity, produce corruption rather than 'real jobs', and increase idleness. And so the notion grew that *laissez-faire* was the best cure for poverty:[63]

> unshackled industry left to seek its own reward is the best relief for distress . . . to give one man a right without exertion, one the labour and capital of another, is to subvert the fundamental law of property on which all property depends . . .

This was the fashionable brand of economics learned by those responsible for famine relief, including the energetic but dogmatic Charles Trevelyan, permanent under-secretary at the Treasury. In the British context it had much going for it. It put an end to many monopolistic privileges, and promoted economic growth. In Ireland in the 1840s 'sound political economy' was dangerous stuff, though. By captivating leading members of the Whig government that came to power in July 1846 it influenced and constrained policy during the height of the Famine. Lord John Russell at its head and his Chancellor of the Exchequer, Charles Wood, were certainly not immune.[64] A nice example of Russell's style is his riposte to Daniel O'Connell's warning of impending disaster in the summer of 1846:[65]

> We have been informed from various parts of England and Scotland that there is the greatest difficulty in getting in the harvest from the absence of Irish labourers who, when they come over to those districts, usually earn good and even high wages at this season. The inference has been that they found employment in their own country.

During the Famine the belief that free markets would cure the shortages caused by the blight, and that public relief risked perpetuating the problem, were constantly aired. *Private* charity and *local* responsibility for funding famine relief were also stressed and insisted on, a reflection of an attitude to property rights rooted in political economy.

According to this view, government had no obligations towards those in need, though some local responsibility on the part of the rich was admitted. And so in late 1846 and early 1847, when deputations from Ireland began to make representations in Whitehall, they were presented 'not with relief . . . but with extracts from the fifth chapter of the fourth book of Adam Smith's *Wealth of Nations*'.[66] Smith's belief in the virtues of the market during famines underlay the government's refusal to intervene in the grain trade. The rest of political economy's message was broadcast incessantly by the infant *Economist* ('it is no man's business to provide for another') and by able controversialists such as Henry Brougham and Nassau Senior. In the House of Lords Brougham warned early on that the Irish 'were too sanguine in their hopes when encouraged, and too confident in their own delusions once deluded', adding pre-emptively that 'nothing could be worse for Ireland herself than that . . . the whole empire should contribute to the removal of a temporary misfortune which no human agency had brought upon Ireland'. The ever abrasive Brougham was soon reminding Ministers of cases 'when it was more difficult to do nothing than to do something, although the trying to do something were almost certain mischief'.[67]

Nassau Senior was a distinguished economist, and in the 1830s and 1840s one of the most influential intellectuals in the United Kingdom. He had written previously on Ireland; indeed, his 1843 article on the Irish question was all but a Whig manifesto, cleared by most of the Cabinet. Senior's public pronouncements during the Famine amounted to little more than a catalogue of the abuses of relief administrators and recipients. In a masterpiece of distortion published in the *Edinburgh Review* in 1849 he presented relief as the *problem*, and bluntly refused to suggest any other cure: 'we are not sure that this is a question which an objector to outdoor relief for such a population is bound to answer'. In private Senior went further. Apparently an erstwhile believer in government investment in railways as a weapon in the 'war against poverty', it was he who confided to Jowett (later the celebrated master of Balliol College) that a million deaths 'would scarcely be enough to do much good'. That aside to Jowett has become deservedly famous, but less known is the comment to his friend Alexis de Tocqueville:[68]

> We are to have committees in each House on the Irish poor laws. They will contain illustrations valuable to a political economist. Experiments are made in that country on so large a scale, and pushed to

their extreme consequences with such a disregard to the sufferings which they inflict, that they give us results as precious as those of Majendie.

No hint here of Senior's own back-room role in designing and defending these 'experiments'! Both Senior and Brougham belonged to the 'hard left' of radical Whigdom, but more decent men than they let the dismal science get the better of their humanity. This was hardly the ideal time for John Stuart Mill to announce that 'no one has a right to bring creatures into life, to be supported by other people', or for the Limerick Whig landlord Lord Monteagle to fret about the 'idleness of the Irish people, of their reliance on others, their mendicant propensities'.[69] The belief that things should be 'let . . . take their natural course' soon gained 'a philosophical colour, and many individuals, even of superior minds, seem to have steeled their hearts to the sufferings of the people of Ireland, justifying it to themselves by thinking it would be going contrary to the provisions of nature'.[70] The novelist Maria Edgeworth, a long-time fan of political economy, caught the mentality of Nassau Senior and the others well, though her comments to Richard Jones (successor to Malthus at the East India College in Haileybury) were probably closer to the bone than she knew:

> To leave all the misery consequent upon improvidence and ignorance, to say nothing of imprudence and vice, to their own *reward* (anglice *punishment*) and to refuse any relief by charity to those who are perishing and perhaps before the very eyes of the anti-charitable . . . in their death-struggle, would require a heart of iron—a nature from which the natural instinct of sympathy or pity have been expelled or destroyed.[71]

The final irony is that when these ideologues played fast and loose with people's lives they did so not out of genocidal intent—far from it—but from a commitment to their vision of a better world. Even the unlovely Senior's eagerness to sacrifice hundreds of thousands of Irishmen and Irishwomen was for the greater good of both survivors and 'all that makes England worth living in'.[72]

While economists tended to rationalise economy, government nevertheless felt politically bound to do something. The political conjuncture was hardly auspicious for those in want, however. During the worst of the crisis a divided Irish representation, weakened by O'Connell's failing health, faced a minority Whig administration bent on making Irish landlords (mainly Tories, of course) pay for the damage, and headed by people who had little faith in intervention as a solution. It was also a period of financial and economic trouble on world markets.[73] What of the policies actually pursued? Donnelly gives a clear account of the succession of attempts to cope with the crisis in his forthcoming *New History of Ireland* contribution.[74] The less ideologically constrained policies of the Peel administration (autumn 1845 to summer 1846) were popular in Ireland and are widely rated a success by historians, but the challenge faced in that first famine year was less serious too. The new Whig Ministry first expanded the public works (October 1846 to spring 1847) started by Peel, then tried the famous soup kitchens (spring 1847 to September 1847), and finally reliance on the amended Irish Poor Law. At all stages policy was guided by the principles of local financing and 'less eligibility'. Local financing entailed eliciting local contributions by both carrot (matching funds from London) and stick (legal remedies), 'less eligibility', erring on the side of caution (i.e. death) in doling out relief. While calculating the minimum cost of reducing famine deaths by any given amount is hardly possible, it is clear that the policies actually pursued failed, even subject to the chosen budgetary constraint. Not only was aid ungenerous, the criteria used in doling it out were hardly geared to need. In terms of the notation of our earlier discussion of vulnerability, ideological constraints undoubtedly increased what we called in chapter 1 the conditional probability of disaster, $P(D/H)$, during the Great Famine.

Whitehall insisted from the outset that the costs of dealing with the crisis be met mainly by local taxpayers. In the west of Ireland this determination to offer aid 'in exact proportion to local contributions' had disastrous results. Land-holders refused to pay rates, and while the Poor Law commissioners and local Guardians played cat-and mouse the poor died. In Castlebar in January 1847 workhouse paupers were going without breakfast for 'the want of funds', patients were kept in bed for the lack of turf for fires, and the coffin contractor was refusing to supply coffins. Guardians at the Ballina workhouse soon began to refuse applicants from Erris, Cahirciveen was rejecting applicants owing to 'a sacrcity of provisions', and the difficulties of the Clifden workhouse were a boon to local creditors who were 'charging an exhorbitant rate for the goods they supply'. One macabre incident from south-west Cork, recounted by Hickey, highlights the uselessness of relying on local funding. When a rate-collector found no answer at the home of one Patrick Regan of Rosbinn he pushed the door open, to find the 'ratepayer' and his wife on the point of death. Their son had been dead for five days.[75] The principle of local funding, despite its obvious and oft repeated implications for mass mortality, was never fully abandoned during the Famine.

Local responsibility also explains the massive clearances by Irish landlords, who between 1849 and 1854 alone put over a quarter of a million people on the roadside. The poor rate fell largely on landowners, directly or indirectly. Those who, like the ruthless Lord Sligo, felt 'under the necessity of ejecting or being ejected', evicted *one-tenth* of the entire population of County Clare and only slightly lower proportions in Counties Galway and Kerry during the same period.[76]

Many cases where a less doctrinaire line might have saved lives might be cited from the parliamentary record and newspapers. The official response in 1847–48 to Patrick Dawson, Catholic priest in Carrick on Shannon, County Leitrim, is one telling example. Again and again, since local funds had dried up, Father Dawson pleaded 'most respectfully, but most earnestly' to the Poor Law commissioners and the Lord Lieutenant in Dublin for a 'trifling' loan for his area; each time he was curtly reminded of local obligations. Not even a last-ditch claim that the annual valuation of the Union would be insufficient to feed the poor made an impression. There can be no question here of officials 'not knowing' what was happening in Leitrim. The local Poor Law inspector, caught in the crossfire between Dawson and Dublin, apologised for the turbulent priest's 'unreasonableness and importunity'. The inspector had reason to eat his words two months later when he and a colleague were forced to pay out of their own pockets for a coffin. It was for a Kilmore woman they had found dead by the roadside 'with five children around her'.[77]

The rate-in-aid imposed in 1849 on the more prosperous parts of Ireland was another application of the principle of 'local responsibility'. The controversy provoked by this tax was out of all proportion to what the sums raised—about half a million—could have done to stop the continuing mortality. Yet while the landlords of Ulster deserved little sympathy for not wanting to help the poor of Connacht or Munster, their claim that 'Ireland [was] an integral part of the United Kingdom, and that Ulster has no relations with Connaught which are not equally shared by any other division of the British Empire' had a broader validity. In Westminster Russell's rationale for passing the back to Ireland was that it had been under-taxed since the Union, but—even if true—1849 was hardly the time to force it to make amends. Even George Nicholls, inspirer and historian of the Irish Poor Law, later admitted as much.[78]

Nor was the money spent during the Famine sensibly

distributed. The policy of limiting outdoor relief in 1846–47 to those on public works and paying them by task not only bred corruption and waste: it was less likely to help those who needed help most. In famine conditions the effect of food intake on productivity is paramount. Piece rates discriminated against the hungry, and healthy workers equipped with wheelbarrows and crowbars might earn two to three times as much as the weaker. An unrealistically low 'ordinary' wage, delays in payment and the policy of setting a low standard wet-time rate combined to progressively debilitate the poor. Soon the Chancellor of the Exchequer was being forced to concede in the Commons that 'crowds flock to the works who are unable from weakness to perform their task, who faint and die upon the works . . . who a few months ago, could earn enough to procure themselves subsistence'. By January–February 1847, with 500,000 on the books, relief officials were already impressing on London the wisdom of providing food instead of work, and Trevelyan was being reassured that 'it is now beyond a spirit of idleness and unwillingness to work; there is a *physical* incapability'. Many, it seems, chose the public works because they were unable for the work which would have gained them much higher wages from farmers. By showing up on the public works instead and shivering through the day they won their 8*d* or 10*d*.[79] The soup kitchens which replaced the public works were a great deal more economical and, however demeaningly, at least tackled the problem of starvation head-on. At its peak in early July 1847 the new system was providing food to over 3 million people; through it, ventured Trevelyan, 'the famine was stayed'.[80] The truth of the matter is that the soup was passed out in September 1847, before its effectiveness could be properly assessed. Whether continuing it for the following winter would have prevented the massive mortality that ensued (see fig. 3) is impossible to determine.

The net public outlay? Between 1846 and 1853 Whitehall spent £7 million on famine relief, while Ireland through poor rates and landlord borrowings spent over £8 million.[81] The comparison rather flatters Whitehall, since much of what ended up being given was originally granted as a loan only, thereby hindering its effectiveness as famine relief. Thus the Board of Works, in their assessment of proposals of their 'reproductiveness', routinely turned down applications for help from the neediest areas.[82] Still, Professors Edwards and Williams seemed awestruck in 1956 by 'the scale of the actual outlay to meet the famine', while Mary Daly pleads that 'it remains difficult to conclusively argue that greater sympathy with the Irish case would have automatically guaranteed a dramatically reduced mortality'. By what yardstick, though? Spread out over a five-year period, the sums sanctioned by Westminster amounted to only about 0·3 per cent of United Kingdom GNP annually. Both Mokyr and Donnelly have contrasted what they consider government's lack of generosity during the Famine with its readiness to spend nearly £70 million a few years later on 'an utterly futile adventure in the Crimea'. This guns *v.* butter comparison is neither fanciful nor anachronistic, because critics of government policy at the time argued likewise. In late 1846 the leader of the opposition, Lord George Bentinck, was reminding Parliament (with some exaggeration, it is true) that a country which had spent £100 million annually for three years fighting Napoleon should not be 'downhearted' about providing properly for Ireland. For Edward Twistleton, the increasingly disillusioned dispenser of Irish Poor Law relief, 'the comparatively trifling sum with which it is necessary for this country to spare itself the deep disgrace of permitting any of our miserable fellow subjects to die of starvation' was nothing compared to 'the expenses of the Coffre War'. Twistleton knew his facts, if anybody did; surely his protest is answer enough to Daly's doubts. Again, when Daniel O'Connell in late 1846 wanted the government to give Ireland £30 million to £40 million to 'ransack the world for food and buy it at any price' he pointed to the £20 million that had been given to West Indian slave owners a few years earlier to compensate them for emancipation.[83] The O'Connell–Mokyr–Donnelly analogies are a reminder that if poverty was the death warrant of many after mid-1846, a more generous government might have prevented the deaths of hundreds of thousands more.[84]

It is instructive to compare the public parsimony of the 1840s with the sums lavished on Ireland only a few decades later for the relief of what were minor crises by comparison. Harvest failures and bad weather continued to cause 'exceptional and acute distress' in parts of the remote west in 1880–83, 1890–91, 1894–95 and even as recently as 1904–05. Between 1880 and 1905 over £4 million was provided in grants and loans out of the public purse, and £2·6 million was concentrated on just ten Poor Law Unions along the western seaboard. This takes no account of the moneys spent on light railways and other 'reproductive' schemes, investments which were geared towards eliminating the root cause of the distress. Such outlays exceeded £3 million in the same period. Government support for far more viable main-line routes had been proposed by Bentinck and others in 1846–47, but their plans had been laughed out of Parliament by the Whigs. Nor should government help for development schemes fostered by the Irish Agricultural Organisation Society and the creation of the Congested Districts Board in the 1890s and after be forgotten, for they are also part of the story. While some of the extra generosity in this later period was due to economic growth, attitudes, individuals and ideology surely played their part. The legacy of the Famine years through its impact on public opinion must count for something. So must the democratisation of politics. Politicians both in Ireland and in Britain were forced to focus more on the plight of the Irish poor in the 1880s than in the 1840s. If only *Phythophthora infestans* had waited on Gladstone, Balfour and William O'Brien![85]

5.   The Aran Islands

It has become fashionable to argue that the Famine did not cause but merely acclerated, many of the post-1850 changes highlighted by Irish social and economic historians. Thus (as noted in chapter 2) the shift towards pasture has been pushed back to 1815 or so by Crotty, and hallmarks of demographic adjustment such as lower fertility and emigration have also been traced to the pre-Famine decades. The pre-Famine commercialisation of economic life and the reform of estate management have also been stressed. Other changes attributed to the Famine are seen as due, in part at least, to separate tough contemporary developments, notably the building of a railway network and cheaper ocean transport.[86] Nevertheless, the impact of the Famine should not be underestimated.

It would be nice to have a control, somewhere in Ireland that the potato blight did not reach, or let off lightly, in the late 1840s. Let us end this chapter with a district that, curiously enough, goes some way towards fitting the bill, the three islands of Aran off the coast of County Galway. On the eve of the Famine Aran was one of the poorest and most isolated places in Ireland. Its people, mostly (85 per cent) illiterate, lived in one- and two-bedroomed cabins on a diet consisting almost exclusively of potatoes and fish. The islands' population had risen from 3,079 in 1821 to 3,521 in 1841. Surely Aran was as likely a candidate for positive Malthusian checks as anywhere else in the country?[87] Yet on the islands themselves the tradition remains that they came off lightly in 1845–48,[88] and the poet-antiquarian Samuel Ferguson drew attention to the fact as long ago as 1853: 'the islanders have had the singular good fortune never to have been visited by the potato blight; never to have had a death from destitution, and never to have sent a pauper to the poor house'.[89] Other evidence is consistent with this. Famine graves, very numerous on the mainland, seem to be absent on Aran.[90] Moreover—turning to contemporary bureaucratic evidence—the total advance under the soup kitchen legislation for relief purposes per head was less than in any other electoral district o Galway Poor Law Union, and the maximum number of public food rations at any stage during the Famine was less than in all but one (Ballinacourty).[91]

TABLE 28 *Famine relief in Galway*

	Population in 1841	Maximum No. given food in any one day
Galway	32,511	22,009
Annaghdown	4,941	3,765
Aran	3,521	1,538
Athenry	1,770	1,629
Ballinacourty	3,407	1,136
Claregalway	3,873	2,966
Killanin	11,501	8,952
Lackagh	3,753	3,361
Moycullen	7,343	6,610
Oranmore	4,486	2,792
Oughterard	10,601	10,921
Stradbally	1,264	757

Source. IUP Famine Series, vol. 8, p. 322.

Still, there is an implausible ring to Ferguson's claim that Aran escaped completely from the blight that had crossed Europe like a brush fire in the summer of 1845. Indeed, evidence in the Relief Commission papers contradict it. Several reports in late 1845 refer to damage from potato blight on Aran, and one dated 2 December estimates overall losses to be one-third on the 'large island', about a quarter on the 'middle island', with only the 'south island' escaping blight-free. Now the country-wide loss was put at 40 per cent in 1845, so Aran escaped relatively lightly. But it is hard to believe that the blight passed it by completely in the destruction of 1846–48. Perhaps, however, freak weather conditions again spared the worst of *Phythophthora infestans*.

Not that this was an idyllic period for the islanders: life on Aran even in normal years was bleak, and after 1846 immigration from the mainland seems to have put further pressure on meagre resources. That hardship is reflected in the pleas of the parish priest, who was forced to act as a one-man relief committee. He wrote to the Relief commissioners:[92]

I have now to state to you, that in order to rescue the wretched inhabitants of Aran from starvation, there is no alternative left me, in regard to their salvation, but to desire them to leave this desperate and forlorn place ...

I have the honour to state in compliance with your desires that the Islands of Arran County of Galway contain a population of four thousand souls, who are at present in extreme distress, without food or employment by public works up to this period and situated thirty miles from Galway. There is no gentleman save myself and one lay person, who generously subscribed fifty pounds towards the relief of the destitute. And for my part, I have left myself penniless in the vain endeavour to relieve the most destitute of this vast population, the people themselves are too poor to entitle themselves to the donations of government, so that the unfortunate Islanders, packed I may say on a barren rock, must inevitably perish, unless promptly relieved from this melancholy doom by the timely interposition of government or some other charitable source.

Yet Father Harley may have been driven here less by literal famine than by a desire to obtain something for Aran from the big city. During the Famine years potatoes, blight or no blight, continued to be the mainstay of the islanders. The picture given by the *Agricultural Statistics* is summarised in tables 29 and 30.

TABLE 29 *Acreage under potatoes and turnips in some Galway electoral districts, 1847–48*

| | Potatoes | | Turnips | |
	1847	1848	1847	1847
Annaghdown	116	754	78	368
Aran	457	723	1	1
Athenry	84	143	95	75
Ballymacourty	146	516	174	206
Claney	161	324	147	114
Galway (part of)	408	1413	232	222
Killanin	472	706	165	135

TABLE 30 *Agriculture in Aran, 1847–51*

	1847	1848	1851
Potatoes (acres)	457	723	564
Grain (acres)	173	138	128
Turnips (acres)	1	1	-
Cattle	725	664	816
Pigs	373	437	447
Goats	116	132	347
Poultry	1,487	1,008	1,004
Horses	185	185	139
Donkeys	88	34	88
Sheep	2,785	2,040	1,494
Stockholders	449	432	391

In Aran the potato acreage rose less in 1848 than elsewhere, and surely this was because the 1847 shortfall was less serious there. The 'refusal' of the islanders to bother with turnip-growing in the late 1840s may be explained in the same way. Like other coastal populations they presumably had recourse to fish, seaweed and the eggs of seabirds. Tradition has it that fish were plentiful during the Famine years, and one piece of boastful but telling apocrypha speaks of shoals of fish coming into Loch an Charra, like manna from heaven, to be caught by hand. There were rabbits too: a few years later William Wilde (wearing his antiquarian hat) pleaded with the people not to ruin the prehistoric fort of Dun Aengus 'for the paltry advantage of catching a few rabbits'.[93]

An important point: the islands' population dropped only marginally in the 1840s, less than that of any other Galway barony (see table 31). A quick comparison with the other Irish

TABLE 31 The population of Galway baronies, 1841 and 1851

	1841	1851	Change (%)
Aran	3,521	3,333	- 5·4
Athenry	8,179	5,859	-28·4
Ballymoe	28,666	21,388	-25·4
Ballinahinch	33,465	24,349	-27·2
Clare	45,412	32,371	-28·7
Clonmacowen*	14,715	14,045	- 4·6
Dunkellin	28,207	17,474	-38·1
Dunmore	28,092	20,342	-27·6
Galway	15,236	10,362	-32·0
Kilconnell	17,162	11,582	-32·5
Killian	17,122	11,695	-31·7
Kiltartan	27,565	19,695	-28·6
Leitrim	32,590	19,664	-39·7
Longford	33,069	21,500	-35·0
Loughrea	18,797	13,862	-26·3
Moycullen	29,445	21,990	-25·3
Ross	9,758	7,692	-21·2
Tyaquin	31,522	21,361	-32·2

*This barony contained a large workhouse in 1851.

islands may be of interest. While Aran's population dropped from 3,521 to 3,333 (or by 9·5 per cent) between 1841 and 1851, that of other islands off the Galway coast fell by almost 25 per cent. Numbers on Achill (in Mayo) fell by over 22 per cent, on Cape Clear (in Cork) by 22 per cent, and on Valentia and the Blaskets (in Kerry) by 15 and 29 per cent. Only islands off the coast of Donegal, always less dependent on the potato and linked to the world outside through seasonal migration, fared better.[94] Numbers on Aran continued to drop, though slowly. In 1881 the population was 3,163, in 1926 it was down to 2,157. Here, as in most of Ireland, the numbers reached in the 1840s could not be maintained in comfort in the long run. But Aran's was by no means demographic adjustment through 'inevitable' deaths. The history of traditional, poverty-stricken Aran provides a clue to that counterfactual will-o'-the-wisp, an Ireland spared the potato blight in the 1840s.

6. Conclusion

The current orthodoxy described at the start of this chapter tends to view the great Famine as both unavoidable and inevitable. I see it instead as the tragic outcome of three factors: an ecological accident that could not have been predicted, an ideology ill geared to saving lives and, of course, mass poverty. The role of sheer bad luck is important: Ireland's ability to cope with a potato failure would have been far greater a few decades later, and the political will—and the political pressure—to spend more money to save lives greater too. If this post-revisionist interpretation of events of the 1840s comes closer to the traditional story, it also keeps its distance from the wilder populist interpretations mentioned earlier. Food availability *was* a problem; *nobody* wanted the extirpation of the Irish as a race.

Notes

1 Liam de Paor (ed.), *Milestones in Irish History* (Middleton, Mass., 1986).
2 R. Dudley Edwards and T. Desmond Williams (eds.), *The Great Famine: Studies in Irish History* (Dublin, 1956), p. viii.
3 As lampooned in *In Dublin*, 13 December 1984.
4 *Our Boys* was a 'patriotic' monthly for schoolboys, produced by the Irish Christian Brothers. Ernie O'Malley is quoted in Peter Gibbon, 'Colonialism and the great starvation in Ireland 1845–49', *Race and Class*, XVII (1975), 138.
5 The phrase is Cecil Woodham-Smith's. See her *The Great Hunger: Ireland, 1845–1849* (London, 1962), pp. 75–6.
6 A. Sen, *Poverty and Famines: an Essay on Entitlement and Deprivation* (Oxford, 1981).
7 Srinivasa Ambirajan, 'Political economy and Indian famines', *Journal of South Asian Studies*, 1 (1971), 20–8; *id.*, 'Malthusian population theory and Indian famine policy in the nineteenth century', *Population Studies*, 30 (1976), 5–14; *id.*, *Classical Political Economy and British Policy in India* (Cambridge, 1978).
8 Woodham-Smith, *The Great Hunger*.
9 *Irish Historical Studies*, 14 (1964–65), 76–9. Fairer and less condescending is the review by Kevin B. Nowlan in *Studia Hibernica*, 3 (1963), 210–11.
10 I am grateful to Ronan Fanning for telling me about this and to Kyra Donnelly for directing me to the old exam papers. Several other questions set in 1963 reflected a horror of Woodham-Smith's account.
11 P.R.O.N.I., *The Great Famine* (Belfast, 1968). Professor Green's survey in T. W. Moody and F. X. Martin (eds.), *The Course of Irish History* (Cork, 1984), pp. 263–74, is more balanced. There those ultimately responsible for relief are termed

'callous, parsimonious, and self-righteous' (p. 273).

12 Robert Kee, *Ireland: a History* (London, 1980), pp. 77–101. The attack on Kee occurred on a television discussion of the series on which his book was based ('Today Tonight Special', 24 February 1981).

13 P. M. A. Bourke, 'The Potato, Blight, Weather and the Irish Famine' (unpublished Ph.D. dissertation, National University of Ireland, 1965); 'The Irish grain trade, 1839-48', *Irish Historical Studies*, XX (1976), 156–69; 'The average yields of food crops on the eve of the Famine', *Journal of the Department of Agriculture (Ireland)*, LXVI, No. 7 (1969), 26–39; 'The agricultural statistics of the 1841 census of Ireland: a critical review', *Economic History Review*, ser. 2, XVIII (1965); 'The use of the potato crop in pre-Famine Ireland', *Journal of the Statistical and Social Inquiry Society of Ireland*, 21, Part 6 (1967-68), 72–96; 'Notes on some agricultural units of management in use in pre-Famine Ireland', *Irish Historical Studies*, 14 (1965), 236–45; 'The scientific investigation of the potato blight in Ireland in 1845-6', *Irish Historical Studies*, 3 (1962), 26–32. Most of Bourke's work appeared while he was in charge of a greatly expanding Irish meteorological service. In 'Half a lifetime with potato blight', forthcoming in a volume to mark the fiftieth anniversary of the service, Bourke amusingly reminisces about his long preoccupation with the potato in Irish history.

14 Patrick Hickey, 'A Study of Four Peninsular Parishes in Cork, 1796-1855' (M.A. thesis, National University of Ireland, 1980).

15 O'Rourke, *op. cit.*,; Donnelly, *Land and People*; Mokyr, *Why Ireland Starved; id.*, 'Industrialization and poverty in Ireland and the Netherlands: some notes towards a comparative case study', *Journal of Interdisciplinary History*, X (3) (1980), 429–59.

16 Mary E. Daly, *The Famine in Ireland* (Dublin, 1986); James Donnelly, 'The great Famine, 1845-50', forthcoming in T. W. Moody *et al.* (eds.), *A New History of Ireland*, vol. 5 (Oxford, 1876/8).

17 Donnelly, 'The great Famine'; Daly, *The Famine*, p. 113.

18 I attempt a more rounded survey of the Famine in a pamphlet in preparation for the Economic History Association.

19 E. R. R. Green, 'Agriculture', in Edwards and Williams (eds.), p. 126; W. A. McArthur, 'Medical history of the Famine', in Edwards and Williams, p. 312; M. Daly, *The Economic History of Ireland since 1800* (Dublin, 1980), pp. 20–1; Garvin, *Evolution*, p. 54.

20 Joel Mokyr, 'The deadly fungus: an econometric investigation into the short-term demographic impact of the Irish Famine, 1846-1851', *Research in Population Economics*, II (1980), 237–77; Boyle and Ó Gráda, 'Fertility trends'. Both studies invoke emigration data that leave something to be desired. To the extent that migrants escaped enumeration the estimates exaggerate mortality. Against this, the migration data are mostly gross, while in Boyle and Ó Gráda no allowance has been made for the mortality *en route* of famine emigrants. The pioneering work in this area is by S. H. Cousens; see his 'The regional variation in mortality during the great Irish Famine', *Proceedings of the Royal Irish Academy*, 63, Section C (1963), 127–49, and 'Regional death rates in Ireland during the great Famine', *Population Studies*, 14 (1960), 55–74.

21 Mokyr, *Why*, pp. 266–7.

22 1841 census, 'Tables of Death', p. lxxii; 1851 census, 'Tables of Death', B.P.P. 1856 (XXIX), c. 770–80.

23 *Capital*, I (Moscow, 1954), p. 704.

24 This and the following two paragraphs draw on results reported in Boyle and Ó Gráda, 'Fertility trends'. The Cork rector is quoted in W. McArthur, 'The medical history of the Famine', in Edwards and Williams (eds.), p. 289.

25 L. Dechene and J. C. Robert, 'Le choléra de 1832 dans le bas-Canada: mesure des inégalités devant la mort', in Henri Charbonneau and Andre Larose (eds.), *The Great Mortalities: Methodological Studies in Demographic Crises in the Past* (Liège, 1981), pp. 229–56; Report of the Commissioners of Health, Ireland, on the Epidemics of 1846 to 1850, H.C. 1852-3 (1562), XLI, p. 29; M. F. and

T. H. Hollingsworth, 'Plague mortality rates by age and sex in the parish of St. Botolph with Bishopsgate, London, 1603', *Population Studies*, 25 (1971); A. K. M. Choudhury and L. C. Chen, *The Dynamics of Contemporary Famine* (Dacca, 1977); Pierre Goubert, *Cent Milles Provinciaux au XVIIe Siècle: Beauvais et le Beauvaisis de 1600 à 1730* (Paris, 1968); Elizabeth Oughton, 'The Maharashtra droughts of 1970-3: an analysis of scarcity', *Oxford Bulletin of Economics and Statistics*, 44 (1982), 169; Sen, *Poverty and Famines*, pp. 210-14; S. C. Watkins and J. Menken, 'Famines in historical perspective', *Population and Development Review*, 11 (1985), 647-76.

26 Boyle and Ó Gráda, 'Fertility trends'.

27 This did not prevent Lord John Russell from claiming in Westminster that 'there has not been a single case of starvation throughout [Clare]' (Hansard, 17 August 1846, p. 770).

28 Irish University Press (I.U.P.) Famine Series, 8 vols. (Shannon, 1968).

29 Mokyr, 'Industrialization and poverty'.

30 Sen, *Poverty and Famines*, pp. 195-202.

31 Woodham-Smith, pp. 296-8; 302-3.

32 1851 census, 'Tables of Death', p. lxxiv.

33 Compare Deborah Guz, 'Famine in the Punjab: a Case Study of the Famines of 1896-7 and 1899-1900' (M.Sc. dissertation, London School of Economics, 1982).

34 Woodham-Smith, p. 377.

35 Dublin Diocesan Archives, Archbishop Murray Papers, Flannelly to Murray, 6 April 1849. The persistence of the Famine is also stressed in S. H. Cousens, 'Regional death rates during the great Famine from 1846 to 1851', *Population Studies*, 14 (1960), 55-74, and in Daly, *The Famine*, p. 114. See too William Steuart Trench, *Realities of Irish Life* (London, (1868) 1966), pp. 58-9.

36 Thus the generosity of even the decent Quakers had waned by late 1847. See *Transactions of the Central Relief Committee of the Society of Friends during the Famines in Ireland in 1846 and 1847* (Dublin, 1852), pp. 68, 468-71.

37 Woodham-Smith, p. 377; Archbishop Murray Papers, 32/5a/Reily to Murray, 15 March 1849.

38 Murray Papers, Eugene Coyne to Murray, 9 March 1849.

39 Hansard, vol. 89, pp. 28-9.

40 Hansard, 3rd ser., vol. CLXXXIX, pp. 809-10, 2 August 1867, quoted in S. Ambirajan, *Classical Political Economy*, p. 273.

41 S. Rashid, 'The policy of *laissez-faire* during scarcities', *Economic Journal*, 90 (1980), 493-503; Martin Ravaillon, 'The performance of rice markets in Bangladesh during the 1974 famine', *Economic Journal*, 95 (1985), pp. 21-2.

42 Donald N. McCloskey and John Nash, 'Corn at interest: the extent and cost of grain storage in medieval England', *American Economic Review*, 74 (1) (1984), 174-87. For an earlier articulation of the idea see Holbrook Working, 'The theory of the price of storage', *American Economic Review*, 39 (1949), 1254-62.

43 See C. Ó Gráda, 'Solathar creidmheasa don isealaicme in Eirinn san 19u Aois', *Central Bank of Ireland Quarterly Bulletin*, (1974), 120-35. These traders figure prominently in two Famine novels, William Carleton's *Black Prophet* (Dublin, 1847) and Liam O'Flaherty's *House of Gold* (London, 1933).

44 E.g. R. D. C. Black, *Economic Thought and the Irish Question, 1817-1870* (Cambridge, 1960), p. 119 n; Public Record Office (Dublin), 1A-50-69, Captain Hutcheson on 'huxters' in Lettermore, County Galway.

45 The data refer to the wholesale price of 'cups'. The final two columns refer to 'low' and 'high' prices.

46 Based on data in National Library of Ireland Ms. 4168, 'Register showing Prices and Quantities of Corn, Meal, and Flour Sold at Dublin Markets', 1785-1839.

47 I.U.P. Famine Series, vol. 8, pp. 427-8.

48 Sen, p. 160.

49 For further analysis along these lines see John Seaman and Julius Holt, 'Markets and famines in the Third World', *Disasters*, 4 (3) (1980), 283-97; Louise A.

Tilly, 'Food entitlement, famine and conflict', *Journal of Interdisciplinary History*, XIV (2) (1983), 333-49; Mohiuddin Alamgir, *Famine in South Asia: the Political Economy of Mass Starvation* (Cambridge, Mass., 1980); Ajit Kumar Ghose, 'Food Supply and Starvation: a Study of Famines with Reference to the Indian Subcontinent', *Oxford Economic Papers*, xx (1986), 368-88. In a review of Joel Mokyr's *Why Ireland Starved* (*Journal of Economic History*, XLIV, 1984, 839-40) Barbara L. Solow points to the challenge that Sen's work poses for analysis of the Irish Famine.

50 *I.F.J.*, 9 August 1817.

51 O'Rourke, p. 32. As Sen notes, David Ricardo made the same point about Ireland in 1822. See A. Sen, 'Food, Economics and Entitlements', Wider Working Paper No. 1, Helsinki, February 1986, pp. 14-15.

52 Young, II, p. 46.

53 *Report of the Committee of the Board of Agriculture appointed to Extract Information from the County Reports . . . Concerning the Use and Culture of Potatoes* (London, 1795), pp. 73-4.

54 Burton, *The Potato*, p. 181.

55 Bourke, 'The Potato', appendix 4.

56 T. Shea, 'The Minute Book of the Ballineen Agricultural Society, 1845-47', *Journal of the Cork Historical and Archaeological Society*, ser. 2, LI (No. 173) (1946), 58; John Mitchel, *The History of Ireland from the Treaty of Limerick to the Present Time*, 3rd ed. (Dublin, n.d.), II, chapter 26.

57 Bourke, 'The Irish grain trade'.

58 Hansard, ser. 3, vol. 91, 29 March 1847, pp. 585-94.

59 I.U.P., vol. 3, 12 February 1848, p. 726; Hickey, 'Four peninsular parishes', pp. 491-2.

60 The higher wage entailed a 'deadweight loss' for the whole economy. The point may have a bearing on the issue of Famine entitlements in other contexts too.

61 These farmers' difficulties are well captured in the comments of pamphleteer John Stanley referred to in chapter 2.

62 R. D. C. Black, *Economic Thought and the Irish Question, 1817-1870* (Cambridge, 1960); Lionel C. Robbins, *The Theory of Economic Policy in English Classical Economics* (London, 1952), p. 34.

63 Monteagle Papers, National Library of Ireland, Spring Rice to George Ensor, 15 January 1837 (quoted in T. P. O'Neill, 'The State, Poverty, and Distress in Ireland, 1815-45', unpublished Ph.D. thesis, National University of Ireland, 1971, p. 209).

64 Trevelyan is the main villain of the piece in Woodham-Smith's *Great Hunger* but this is somewhat unfair. His dogmatism, his ignorance of Irish affairs and his weaknesses as an administrator are well known (see Jennifer Hart, 'Sir Charles Trevelyan at the Treasury', *English Historical Review*, LXXV, 1960, 92-110), but in the final analysis Trevelyan was merely a public servant carrying out the policies of Russell and the Whigs. Without them his enthusiasm for harsh policies would have been wasted. The point about responsibility is strongly put in Austin Bourke, 'Apologia for a dead civil servant', *Irish Times*, 5-6 May 1977.

65 Woodham-Smith, p. 87; Maurice O'Connell (ed.), *The Correspondence of Daniel O'Connell*, VIII (Dublin, 1980), p. 84.

66 Hansard, 3rd ser., vol. 77, p. 83. See also Christine Kinealy, 'The Irish Poor Law, 1838-1862' (Ph.D. thesis, Trinity College, Dublin, 1984), p. 131. Edmund Burke's *Thoughts and Details on Scarcity* (London, 1800) enjoyed a similar vogue.

67 Hansard, 3rd ser., vol. 89, January-February 1847, pp. 54, 1329-30; see also *The Economist*, 23 September 1848, p. 1075, for more in the same vein.

68 S. Leon Levi, *Nassau W. Senior, 1794-1864* (New York, 1970), pp. 132-43; British Library, Add. Mss. 34623, f. 622 (Senior's correspondence in the early 1840s with Macvey Napier, editor of the *Edinburgh Review*; Nassau W. Senior, 'Relief of Irish distress in 1847 and 1848', in *Essays, Journals and Conversations relating to Ireland*, vol. 1 (London, 1868), pp. 195-264; Senior to Monteagle, quoted in Black, *Economic Thought*, p. 113; Woodham-Smith, pp. 373-6; M. C. Simpson (ed.), *Correspondence and Conversations of Alexis de Tocqueville with*

Nassau William Senior from 1834 to 1859, vol. 1 (London, 1872), p. 52; *The Economist, 1843-1943: a Centenary Volume* (Oxford, 1943), p. 39.

69 *The Times*, 25 March 1847; Mill, *Principles of Political Economy*, II, chapter XII (2) (London, 1871, originally published in 1848), p. 445.

70 Twistleton, quoted in Hansard, ser. 3, vol. 105, p. 300.

71 N.L.I. Ms. 22822. In the same vein, G. Poulett Scrope, *Reply to the Speech of the Archbishop of Dublin, delivered in the House of Lords, Friday March 26 1847* (London, 1847), especially pp. 8, 18, 40.

72 Senior, *Journals*, I, p. 264.

73 A. Gayer, W. Rostow and A. Schwartz, *The Growth and Fluctuations of the British Economy, 1790-1850* (Oxford, 1953), vol. 2, pp. 611-16; R. Dornbusch and J. A. Frenkel, 'The gold standard crisis of 1847', *Journal of International Economics*, 16 (1984), 1-27.

74 Donnelly, 'The great Famine'. Also Thomas P. O'Neill, 'The organisation and administration of relief', in Edwards and Williams, pp. 209-59.

75 I.U.P. Famine Series, I, 'Copies of Extracts of Correspondence relating to the State of Union Workhouses in Ireland', pp. 1-62; Hickey, 'Four peninsular parishes', p. 374.

76 Donnelly, 'The great Famine'; also N.L.I. Ms. 8717, correspondence of Robert French of Monivea, 1847. There are some well known cases of landlords going bankrupt in their struggle to help their stricken tenants, but Donnelly's numbers surely suggest that tough, no-nonsense landlords were the norm.

77 I.U.P. Famine Series, II, pp. 461-2 III, 12 February 1848.

78 George Nicholls, *History of the Irish Poor Law* (London, 1856), p. 356; Newry Board of Guardians resolution, 24 February 1849, facsimile No. 16 in P.R.O.N.I., *The Great Famine* (Belfast, 1968); Woodham-Smith, pp. 379-80. For a thorough account see Kinealy, 'The Irish Poor Law', pp. 235-43.

79 Donnelly, 'The great Famine'; Hansard, ser. 3, vol. 89, January–February 1847; I.U.P. Famine Series, vol. 7, p. 537 (Captain Burgoyne to Trevelyan, 23 February 1847); Patrick McGregor, 'The impact of the blight upon the pre-Famine rural economy of Ireland', *Economic and Social Review*, 15 (4) (1984), 289-303.

80 Woodham-Smith, p. 296.

81 Donnelly, 'The great Famine'.

82 An exasperated Kilrush Relief Committee questioned the Board's right to quibble with 'very urgent applications [from] the cess payers and the rate payers who hereinafter will be called to reimburse the government in a portion of the outlay'. The Board suspected the viability of the schemes proposed, probably correctly, but its caution was hardly geared to aiding the starving. Cf. Public Record Office (Dublin), 1A-50-45, 23 March 1846. On the operation of the Board of Works see A. R. G. Griffiths, 'The Irish Board of Works in the Famine years', *Historical Journal*, XIII (4) (1970), 634-52; on the issue of Poor Law Guardians being pressed to repaya dvances, Kinealy, 'The Irish Poor Law', pp. 135-140.

83 Hickey, 'Four peninsular parishes', p. 378. On the generous terms granted the slaveowners, R. W. Fogel and S. L. Engerman, 'Philanthropy at bargain prices: notes on the economics of gradual emancipation', *Journal of Legal Studies*, 3 (1974), 377-401.

84 Edwards and Williams, p. xi; Daly, *The Famine*, p. 114; Mokyr, *Why*, p. 292; Donnelly, 'The great Famine'; O'Rourke, p. 339; *Select Committee on the Irish Poor Law*, H. of L., 1849 (182), XVI, p. 947. A character in Thomas Murphy's *Famine* (Dublin, 1984), p. 58, makes the same point: 'If it was needed for a war against the Afghans . . . Maybe economics can only survive to cater for the catastrophe of war.' The relevant GNP figures are given in R. Floud and D. McCloskey (eds.), *The Economic History of Britain since 1700*, I (1981), p. 136.

85 Royal Commission on Congestion in Ireland, 'Memorandum on the Financial Aspect of the Relief of Distress in Ireland', 1907. My thanks to Tim O'Neill for showing me this document and for impressing on me this comparison between government ideology in the 1840s and later.

86 Crotty, *Irish Agricultural Production*, chapter 2; J. M. Goldstrom, 'Irish agri-

culture and the great Famine' in Goldstrom and Clarkson (eds.), pp. 155-71; Donnelly, *The Land and the People*, pp. 52-72.

87 1821 census, p. 322; 1841 census, pp. 374-5; Stephen Royle, 'The economy and society of the Aran Islands, County Galway, in the early nineteenth century', *Irish Geography*, 16 (1983), 36-52.

88 Antoine Powell, *Stair Oileán Árann* (Dublin, 1984), pp. 59-60; personal communications from Antoine Powell and Tim Robinson. Robinson's *Stones of Aran: Pilgrimage* (Dublin, 1986) touches on many aspects of the natural history and topography of Aran. According to Seán Ó Giolláin, a fine *seanchaí* from Fearann a' Choirce, 'things were not so bad in Aran. To be sure, news came in of the plight of people outside. A few arrived full of tales of woe. But nobody died here, as far as I know, from hunger. Many other things killed them.' [From a recording made by Tim Robinson c. 1976, my translation.]

89 Samuel Ferguson, as quoted by Stephen A. Royle, 'Irish famine relief in the early nineteenth century: the 1822 famine on the Aran Islands', *Irish Economic and Social History*, XI (1984), 56.

90 Tim Robinson, personal communication.

91 I.U.P. Famine Series, vol. 8, p. 322.

92 P.R.O. (Dublin), 1A-50-69, Harley to Routh, February 1847.

93 Robinson, personal communication, and *Stones of Aran*, p. 74.

94 Hickey, 'Four peninsular parishes', p. 603, suggests that islanders in his region were less affected than mainlanders partly because of the fishing but partly too because crop loss from blight was less serious.

CHAPTER 4

Of bullocks and men: agricultural change after the Famine

You and Robert both know what my opinions are, the estate is not fitted for agriculture but stock, and never lose sight of that. [Galway landlord, 1847[1]]

Although Ireland, almost in every part where the industry of husbandry applieth itself thereto, bringeth good corn plentifully, nevertheless hath it a more natural aptness for grass. [Boate, *Natural History of Ireland*, 1652[2]]

Between the 1850s and the 1920s Irish agriculture underwent a transformation which can have had few parallels at the time. One curious indication of the change is that the farmyard hen and duck were contributing more to agricultural value added in 1908 than wheat, oats and potatoes combined, crops which in the early 1840s had accounted for almost half total output. The change was accompanied by a dramatic fall in the numbers working on the land, and by marked shifts in regional specialisation in both livestock and crop production. But, most historians argue, it brought little sustained increase in the aggregate value of farm output. This failure of output to grow despite auspicious demand conditions across the Irish Sea has often been bemoaned.[3]

However, analysed int erms of productivity growth, the performance of Irish agriculture between the Famine and the 1920s was quite impressive. Though output per worker remained low throughout by the standard of neighbouring Britain, the gap narrowed in time, and total factor productivity growth was higher than Britain's and on a par with Japan's and the United States'.[4]

This is shown in the following pages. Table 32 presents a new output estimate for 1876, along with the official one for 1908. By combining the official figure of £57 million for the value of the Irish Free State's output in 1926/7 with that of Northern Ireland's output in 1925, valued at Free State prices, an estimate of £72·6 million is obtained for the island as a whole in the mid-1920s. The result is also given in Table 32.[5] We thus have data for three arguably distinct sub-periods in the history of post-Famine agriculture. The period 1854–76 might be considered one of 'post-

TABLE 32 Irish agricultural output at current prices in 1876, 1908 and 1926 (£ million)

Item	1876	1908	1926
Crops			
Wheat	0·9	0·3	0·2
Oats	2·6	1·4	1·3
Barley	1·2	0·8	0·9
Flax	1·7	0·4	0·1
Potatoes	3·2	1·9	6·2
Hay	0·8	0·8	0·3
Other	0·6	0·9	2·9
Subtotal	11·0	6·5	11·7
Livestock			
Cattle	11·3	11·0	17·8
Milk, etc.	10·6	10·7	15·7
Pigs	5·5	5·9	10·1
Sheep	3·6	2·2	3·4
Wool	0·9	0·4	0·8
Eggs	2·1	4·1	8·9
Other	1·9	1·8	4·3
Subtotal	35·7	39·1	60·8
Total	46·7	45·6	72·6

Famine adjustment'. The traditional view that agricultural progress in this period was smothered by tenurial restrictions is no longer popular. Nowadays these years are seen as ones of prosperity and innovation: approaching it from three quite different perspectives, Vaughan, Solow and Crotty have depicted it as the Indian summer of landlordism in Ireland.[6] The period 1876–1908 roughly encompasses the Land War and the so-called 'agricultural depression', while 1908–26 marked the almost universal transition to peasant proprietorship. Despite the shakiness of some of the assumptions underlying them, the data invite calculations for each sub-period, and comparisons between the results. When these are combined with estimates of the labour force on the land, landlord income, the capital stock in agriculture, and changes in agricultural prices and the cost of living, some idea is obtained of the trends in labour and total factor productivity, and in living standards during the post-Famine decades.

The main results are given in table 33. They do not support the claim that output, after allowing for price change, failed to increase over the period as a whole, though they do indicate that it continued to fall till the 1870s at least, and that it took eighty years to reach its pre-Famine level once more. The results confirm accounts of a continuous rise in non-landlord incomes after the

TABLE 33 Changes in agricultural income and productivity, 1854-1926

	1854	1876	1908	1926
Output (£ million)	46·7	47·5	45·6	72·6
Labour force (million)	1·15	0·9	0·81	0·684
Rent (£ million)	10	12	(8)	(8)
Non-landlord incomes per head (£)	31·7	39·4	46·4	96·2
Labour productivity	100	121	151	199
Total factor productivity	100	113	134	177
Output (adjusted for price change)	100	95	107	119
Share of capital in agricultural income	0·06	0·07	0·08	0·10

Famine. Curiously, though, the rise in real terms in 1876–1908 seems to have been greater than in 1854–76. It thus seems that the lion's share of the pre-Land War gains was reaped in the immediate post-Famine decade. This becomes plausible when it is remembered that the post-Famine decades were years when livestock prices rose faster than tillage prices, benefiting landlord more than farmer or labourer. It also emerges that for the Irish farmer of the late Victorian era there was no real sustained 'Great Depression'. Almost three decades ago Fletcher laid the ghost of the same 'Great Depression' so far as the majority of British farmers were concerned.[7] With no problem of turning cold, heavy land over to grass to contend with, and having won substantial reductions in his rent in the wake of the Land War, it would have been surprising indeed to have found the Irish farmer *not* prospering. This does not exclude the presence of some trying years—after all, the particularly bad patch in the late 1870s and early 1880s sparked off and fuelled the Land War—but the data suggest worthwhile improvement over the period taken as a whole.[8]

Labour productivity seems to have risen by just short of 1 per cent annually between the 1850s and 1920s, while total factor productivity grew at a rate of 0·7 per cent. How do these numbers emerge in perspective? Total factor productivity growth turns out to have been a good deal higher than that recently calculated for Britain over a similar period, and also higher than that calculated for the United States for 1840–1900. Kelley and Williamson have proposed similar rates for Japanese agriculture at the time. Overall the Irish results are reassuring enough—indeed, striking in the light of historiographical tradition. Moreover the differences between the 1854–76 and 1876–1908 subperiods raise doubts about the strong emphasis in the work of Crotty and Solow on a turning point (for the worse) in the fortunes of Irish agriculture around the 1870s. My calculations suggest an annual total factor productivity growth of about 0·5 per cent in both periods.

The results bear out neither the more optimistic assessments of pre-1876 development, nor the doleful depiction of agricultural conditions before and after the Land War. Almost certainly the sharp rise in estimated total factor productivity after 1908 owes something to the conservatism of the official estimate of output in that year—in which case the Land War period emerges more impressively—but they may also be due in part to the impressive gains noted elsewhere, which are associated with the diffusion of twentieth-century farm technology and the external economies which that brought in train. These numbers, though rough and tentative, prompt a reassessment of some of the reasons offered in the literature for what has passed for a 'poor performance' in the post-Famine period.

1. The land question

This used to be by far the most popular and resilient explanation of agricultural backwardness. Its largely apologetic character is now recognised, but there is no harm in reviewing the argument from an economic perspective. Much of the controversy revolves around the issue of rent determination. In popular accounts before William Vaughan and Barbara Solow, landlords typically 'rack-rented', that is, squeezed the full Ricardian rent out of the hapless tenant on threat of eviction, and sometimes all or the lion's share of the return on tenant investment outlays in addition.[9] The pursuit of this policy, it is argued, explains the large number of recorded evictions.

From an economic historian's perspective it is worth noting that the optimal eviction rate for efficiency was not necessarily zero. To have kept incompetent tenants who paid little or no rent, while others who could pay remained landless, could only have reduced rent and output. In this revisionist view, associated especially with Raymond Crotty and Barbara Solow, the 'bad' landlord was the indulgent proprietor who chose not to exercise his property rights fully. Both Crotty and Solow imply that rents not squeezed out of the tenantry are most likely to have been dissipated in bad management and idleness, and the former's sombre view of Irish agricultural trends since the Land War is entirely predicated on the absence of some mechanism, be it landlord or land tax, that would prevent dissipation.[10] In the case of a troublesome tenant who encumbered a property the revisionist case surely makes sense. But in general the main conse-

quence of lower rents may merely have been redistribution—
poorer landlords, richer tenants—since there is no theoretical
presumption that lower output would automatically have followed
the demise of landlordism. Lazy tenants could have let some or all
of their holdings to the more industrious. Or they *could* have used
up their increased welfare on a hefty rise in leisure, leaving their
money income net of rent much the same as before. The post-
Land War record belies this, however.

Rent levels are closely linked to the next issue, insecurity of
tenure. The notion that 'a good landlord is as good as a good lease'
pervades the traditional literature. In general, leasehold problems
have been exaggerated, for several reasons. First, tenancy-at-will
was never as prevalent in the Irish case as the criticism implies.
Even as late as 1870 two-fifths of all holdings over £15 valuation
(or over twenty-five to thirty acres) and almost two-thirds of all
holdings over £50 valuation were held on lease or freehold. The
problem was potentially greatest, then, on smallholdings, where
by 1870 five-sixths of holdings were tenancies at will.[11] Yet even
there institutional arrangements, formal and informal, sometimes
mitigated the dangers of under-investment in cases where fixed
investment on the part of farmers stood to benefit agriculture. For
instance, an eighteenth-century law protected those who sought
to plant trees on their holdings as an investment, while more
generally tenant-right arrangements provided some guarantee
against insecurity.[12] Finally, an insolvent or greedy landlord might
occasionally succeed in creaming off his tenants' returns and deter
them from further ventures. But to assume that landlords as a
group could continually do so is quite a different matter: only
gross irrationality could have enabled them to get away with that.
The notion that the absence, or presence only in attenuated form,
of tenant right outside Ulster before 1870 could have made a
difference rests on a confusion as to what 'Ulster custom' really
was.

Unlike English tenant right, the Ulster version was mainly—
some would say exclusively—about the right of outgoing tenants
to charge for occupancy. In England tenant right was rarely
worth more than two or three years' rent, but in Ulster it was
often sold for fifteen or twenty times the rent. Still, though, the
right to dispose of landed property was the key, a by-product of
the system was a mechanism for realising the value of unexhausted
improvements, an aspect stressed by the economist John Stuart
Mill. Surely, the argument went, if tenants could not recover the
full value of unexhausted improvements on relinquishing a holding,
and landlords under-invested for fear of tenants' 'overusing' the

investment and then leaving, agriculture suffered as a result? Under tenant right, by contrast, the incentive to run a property down would disappear, since the tenant would bear the cost of any abuse himself. The Land Act of 1870 may be viewed, then, as motivated in part at least by efficiency considerations. The testable implications of the 'efficiency' view are clear enough. If optimal investments required such a change, then relatively more landlord and tenant investment might be expected in the rest of Ireland than in Ulster, where the benefits of tenant right had long been available.[13]

Unfortunately direct evidence on the most straightforward test, the trend in tenant investment, is lacking. The annual agricultural statistics provide the material for an indirect test, though, for although yield and stock levels in different areas may have differed for climatic and other reasons at any point in time, rises in stocks and yields should follow tenant investment. The efficiency hypothesis is thus consistent with a disproportionate jump in yields and stock numbers outside the north in the wake of the Land Act.

No marked variation that could be attributed to tenurial change can be detected in the agriculture statistics. Ulster, the 'control' province, seems to have responded to the legislation much like the country as a whole. Another way of showing this is to regress the Connacht–Ulster and Munster–Ulster grain yield ratios on time over the period 1870–1917. The results are:

	Constant	Time coefficient	R^2
Connacht–Ulster			
Oats	1·140	–0·001	0·09
	(0·047)	(0·001)	
Barley	0·958	–0·000	0·00
	(0·093)	(0·001)	
Wheat	0·763	0·002	0·07
	(0·084)	(0·001)	
Munster–Ulster			
Oats	0·921	0·002	0·12
	(0·087)	(0·001)	
Barley	1·101	–0·001	0·02
	(0·089)	(0·001)	
Wheat	0·773	0·002	0·15
	(0·074)	(0·001)	

Note. Standard errors in parentheses.

Table 34 tells a similar story over a shorter time period. Qualitative evidence on greater tenant investment in the southern provinces after 1870 is lacking. The earliest firm quantitative evidence to hand appears in the census reports of 1901 and 1911: it concerns farm outhouses (table 35).

TABLE 34 *Percentage change in yield and stock data, 1861/70 to 1872/81*

	Ulster	Connacht	Ireland
Wheat	6·0	23·0	18·7
Oats	11·5	11·4	10·7
Barley	8·4	9·5	6·7
Potatoes	–0·6	0·7	–1·9
Horses over two years	–6·7	–12·9	–9·4
Cattle	10·8	18·6	14·8
Sheep	5·0	1·6	0·0
Pigs	6·0	8·6	1·1

TABLE 35 *Number of outhouses and farmsteadings, per holding, adjusted for value of holding, 1901 and 1911*

Province	£4–£10	£10–£15	£15–£20	£20–£30
	(a) 1901			
Leinster	3·33	4·45	5·26	6·03
Munster	3·22	4·09	4·68	5·31
Ulster	3·40	4·56	5·42	6·47
Connacht	2·76	3·54	4·06	4·33
	(b) 1911			
Leinster	3·23	4·29	4·95	5·83
Munster	3·47	4·44	4·96	5·53
Ulster	3·49	4·68	5·55	6·55
Connacht	2·99	3·73	4·13	4·41

Since these data (tables 34–5) indicate no worthwhile difference between Ulster and the other provinces either, the revisionist hypothesis that under-investment—if such there was—was equally serious in all parts of Ireland, cannot be rejected.

Comprehensive data on landlord investment before and after the Act are not available, either. However, official returns of the sums loaned to proprietors under the various Land Improvement Acts may be taken as a fair proxy, since such loans probably accounted for a substantial share of all worthwhile landlord investment at the time.[14] Data on landlord borrowing from govenment for investment purposes lend little support to the efficiency hypothesis, either. The investment share of the northern counties rose from 15·6 per cent inthe 1850s to 18 per cent in the 1860s, and then fell to 16 per cent in the 1870s; their share in the number of projects supported fell from 14 per cent in the 1860s to 13 per cent in the 1870s. Such trivial changes prove nothing (see table 36).

TABLE 36 *Loans issued under the various land improvement Acts, 1852-81 (£)*

	1852-60	1860-70	1870-81
North	40,162	107,457	199,870
Midlands and East	93,672	220,215	487,502
West	50,666	124,559	258,310
South	72,455	146,288	302,175
Total	256,955	598,519	1,247,857

Source. Calculated from reports of the Commissioners of Public Works for 1852, 1870, 1881. In these reports 'North' includes Ulster minus Cavan and Monaghan.

Why is the outcome so disappointing for the efficiency hypothesis? In part because the Ulster *v.* 'the rest' dichotomy has been exaggerated both by contemporaries and by historians. Tenant right was recognised by many landlords outside Ulster, if in a less thoroughgoing form, while others 'winked at' or fought in vain against deals between outgoing and incoming tenants.[15] A second reason is that such a mechanism was not so urgently required. Even with the massive emigration of the post-Famine period, farms rarely changed hands outside the family, being passed on instead from father to son or son-in-law. The hypothesis that would so closely link the increase in emigration with an increasing need for 'free sale' fails to take account of the family character of the emigration.[16] In sum the supply of tenant right was greater, and the necessity (i.e. demand) for it less outside Ulster before the Gladstonian reforms than these arguments suggest.

Those traditional historians who took an anti-landlord stance sought to indict landlordism on both political and economic grounds. Like the neo-abolitionist historians of US slavery, they let their indignation sometimes get the better of them. Hardly surprising, then, that early revisionist work in this area went 'soft' on landlords. Two decades on, the neo-revisionist message seems to be that Irish democracy achieved its victory over landlordism at a very low cost indeed.

2. 'Indolence'

Between the early seventeenth century, when they were deemed 'the sluggishest, nastiest, rudest, least painful and industrious of all civil countries', and the great Famine the rural Irish were the butt of ever louder criticism from outside observers of their work habits. To fill a whole paper with colourful contemporary quotations would be an easy task.[17] After the Famine the stereotype hardly changed, and many later accounts imply a labour supply schedule that was backward-bending above some undefined, but low, level of income.

Horace Plunkett, high priest of the rural co-operative movement, wrote in exasperation of farmers confining their energies to 'opening and closing gates', while his friend Robert Gibson pleaded with others to trade their winter mornings in bed for an alleged 50 per cent return on their capital. But probably the high point in neurosis about the problem was reached in the 1870s when A. H. Herbert, proprietor of a large estate near Killarney, was:

> wont to visit his tenants . . . beg a brush, and with his own hand proceed to sweep down offensive cobwebs. On the top of a hill with an opera-glass, at four or five in the morning, he would turn out to see which of his tenants made the earliest start, while to the laggards he would forward a bundle of nightcaps.

Less dramatically, the Scottish 'agricultural commission' which surveyed Irish agriculture fleetingly, though at first hand, in 1906 reported seeing 'good land going to waste for want of energy on the part of farmers'. Particularly in the south, they noted, 'waste and neglect [were] much in evidence'.[18]

Certainly those, like Gookin in the seventeenth century and McLysaght and Bulfin in the early twentieth,[19] who questioned the charge of 'indolence' were a small minority. The temptation to go along with the (irrefutable) hypothesis that the lazy Irish were simply maximising their utility is considerable. Yet it must be noted that the traffic was not *all* one way. The evidence from those directly involved in farming, particularly farm labourers, tells a different tale. Throughout the post-Famine period analysed here labourers—admittedly, like their bosses, inveterate complainers—seemed to protest more, in verse and in prose, against the physical demands of their daily work than their pay or food. Personal reminiscences tell the same story. A small sampling of such (usually neglected) evidence may not come amiss:[20]

> The cows and all the animals would be stalled in then about the 15th of November, and I should be threshing oats from the time I'd ate my breakfast until I'd ate my dinner, and then I'd clean out the houses with a pike and shovel and spread sand under 'em, I'd draw up the oaten straw in *bearts* with a rope, four *bearts* to the cows and two to the calves, one to eat and one for a bed. I'd get the supper then and

carry a lantern and a candle and hang it up in the barn and start threshing then until ten o'clock with a flail, and come in then and go to bed,
and be up again then at five in the morning.

About six in the morning, from then until seven in the evening, these
were our hours. In some houses it might be till eight or nine. When you
got back to the house, then, you might be put doing something else.
That's how it was. There was no work harder than spring harrowing,
because the ground was very wet and the weather cold and hard. You
were exhausted in the evening after a day's harrowing, and after a week
of it you could scarcely walk because, you see, you'd feel yourself
always sinking in the clay.

Paddy, get up. The clock is alright if yer goin' for a train, it wouldn't
pay us to go be the clock . . . The worst feature was the constant nag
of jobs waiting to be done, for ever and ever, it was a circle, and a
vicious one at that, a wheel without a spoke of time missing.

> Do bhí allas im' léine, is is tréan mar
> do shilfeadh mo ghrua
> Is mo dhá ghéigín chaola ag pléascadh le
> hiomarca dua
> Deargadh mo phíopa ní bhfaighinn i mbun
> ná i mbarr
> Is nárbh é an tinpinní tuillte, céad díth air.
> ba dheacair é dh'fháilt.

    The issue cannot be decided by another battle of quotations,
however.[21] Other considerations suggest that the nineteenth-
century Irish agriculturalist was not quite as bad as he was painted.
The first is an increasing reluctance by economic historians and
anthropologists to explain observed differences in behaviour
simply in terms of 'taste'. This should prompt us not to ignore
other possibilities such as limited markets, poor endowments or
institutional constraints. In the light of such currents perhaps the
onus is on those who would argue that the Irish were exceptionally
lazy to prove their point. 'Idleness', after all, cannot be taken
simply as revealed preference for 'laziness'. Perhaps contemporary
observers of Irish farming sometimes mistook seasonal lulls in
agricultural activity or even a lack of strength or stamina for
laziness, and switches to more profitable, if less arduous, forms of
production (e.g. from dairying to grazing, or from tillage to
pasture) as part of the unending quest for leisure.[22]
    Second, high agricultural yields suggest that when hard work
really counted for something it was forthcoming. 'The crops are
large: the utmost pains are taken to cultivate them; and the
industry and care the people display in the business, contradicts
entirely the charge of inherent and inconquerable idleness,' claim-

ed the economist John Bicheno in 1830.[23] Yields dropped after the Famine but, given the low capital inputs and, for grain crops, land of different quality and an unfavourable climate, remained impressive by the standards of the day. Claims such as Nassau Senior's that 'the land of Ireland does not return a fourth, perhaps not an eighth, of what might be obtained from it by fair industry and competent skill'[24] quickly lose their plausibility. Farmers' reluctance to remove offending manure heaps, cobwebs and even weeds, if bad for tourism and the gentry's sensibilities, probably only marginally affected output. Theproverbial pig in the parlour or the dungheap half obscuring the doorway were no harm if the diary was kept clean—as indeed it must have been while Irish butter continued to command a price on home and foreign markets.

Take the case of common weeds, a perennial cause of criticism and target of extermination campaigns from the Registrar General's office in the post-Famine decades and from the Department of Agriculture and Technical Instruction (DATI) after the turn of the century. It was claimed, rather dramatically, in 1872 that weeds were costing Irish farmers as much as £1·5 million to £3 million annually—or 3–6 per cent of total output. Naturally enough, proper data on the problem are hard to come by. Official weed statistics were collected, however, between 1853 and 1856: they imply that over 5 million acres in Ireland were then 'generally free from weeds' and another 5 million 'partially attended to'. Since the total acreage under crops, including meadow and clover, was then less than 6 million, it is difficult to see from the aggregate data—even if the statistics exaggerate somewhat—how further weed control would have much improved the quality of farm produce or crop yields. Throughout most of Leinster and east Munster, and in Galway and Roscommon, there was more land reportedly weed-free in 1854 than under all crops, and everywhere weed-free and 'partially attended to' land exceeded the cropped acreage.[25] Generally the ratio of weed-free to cropped acreage was lowest in the north and west, where yields were also lowest. This should not be taken to mean that farmers in those areas were

TABLE 37 *Weeds and cropped acreage, 1854 ('000 acres)*

	Weed-free	Partly weeded	Extent under crops
Leinster	1,948·6	1,309·5	1,665·6
Munster	1,336·0	1,305·5	1,379·0
Ulster	1,226·3	1,289·9	1,811·5
Connacht	605·2	864·4	714·5

Source. Agricultural Statistics, 1854.

greater idlers than the rest, however, since soil and climatic disadvantages almost certainly reduced their marginal return from weed control. Ireland may still have been under-weeded, if only for the following reason: in the absence of control, graziers and others relatively unconcerned with weeds could frustrate the efforts of tillage farmers to keep their crops clean. But even that much is far from obvious, since the cost of greater weed control to the grazier may well have exceeded the gain to the arable farmer from such activity. In sum, given the paucity of data, suffice it to note that, first, the problem seems not to have been too serious in the 1850s at least, and, second, that anything like the complete removal of weeds in a damp climate such as Ireland's is unlikely to have been an optimal strategy.

3. Diffusion of innovation

That the Irish farmer was unresponsive to relative price changes during the nineteenth century is readily refuted by the evidence. Estimated supply elasticities of some of the main items marketed by farmers in the post-Famine period suggest 'rational' behaviour, roughly on a par with that of farmers elsewhere at the time.[26] The characterisation of the Irish farmer as 'an innocent, simple being, unable to take care of his own interests or make a bargain for himself' may be discounted at this level at least. But could technological conservatism, the result of excessive risk aversion or ignorance, have inordinately delayed the diffusion of new machines and process innovations, and thus have hampered productivity growth? Research in the area has hardly proceeded beyond the anecdotal remark.

One recent study of the diffusion of process innovations, that of the milk separator, suggests a creditable performance. After a hesitant start the number of creameries rose rapidly during the 1890s, and on the whole it is likely that the innovation had spread as far as was viable in the Irish context by 1910. By then somewhat less than half the total milk supply was being processed in creameries. In lush dairying areas such as the Golden Vale the switch to the new technique was almost complete, but in poorer places such as Clare and west Connacht, where land quality dictated a lower cattle density, traditional methods persisted. In such areas 'a community of those small holders of only two or three cows each would be slow to launch into an enterprise meaning an expenditure of two or three thousand pounds': indeed it was sometimes stated that over-eagerness to set up creameries was more of a problem than a reluctance to do so. In the wake of some failures a writer in the *Farmers' Gazette* mused that 'it would have been better to have had too few of them than too many'. In sum, the creamery caught on where the commercial opportunities were present. Perhaps special factors had some influence here, for other process innovations lacked their coterie of country gentlemen and priests, enthusiasts for rural co-operation, to help them along. Arguably, however, amateurs influenced the organisational form more than the extent of the diffusion. Barbara Solow's claim that 'the introduction of modern techniques, especially in dairying, never occurred at all' is absurd.[27]

The speed with which a humbler innovation, the Champion variety of potato, spread throughout the island is well known.[28] Introduced from Scotland in the late 1870s, prolific and rich in flavour, the Champion was given a great boost by the near total failure of older varieties such as the Rock in 1879. Already the single most important variety in 1880, it had swept the board a few years later, and retained its dominance till the 1910s. Indeed, as late as 1917 it was still the most common variety, and accounted for 45 per cent of the acreage under potatoes. Regional variations in the rise and fall of the Champion can be documented from the agricultural statistics. The new variety caught on first in the market gardens around Dublin and Cork, where it had won three-quarters of the acreage in 1880. In that year the remoter parts of the west had hardly been touched—4 per cent of the acreage in Erris, 6 per cent around Dungloe, 7 per cent around Clifden—but by 1883 the Champion was being more widely sown along the western seaboard than it was nationally. Its rapid diffusion is proof, if proof be needed, that the farmer was eager to change when he had little or nothing to lose.

The later record of the Champion is less clear. Several accounts suggest that its fertility and reliability began to wane around the turn of the century. Yet, despite persistent coaxing from the DATI and others, most of the country's farmers continued to place their trust in Champion seeds. Only in the north and east did a dramatic switch to the new varieties such as the Up-to-date occur. An instance of entrepreneurial incompetence in the poorer parts? Qualitative accounts suggest as much. However, yield data do not support the view that those countries which stuck by the Champion suffered through relatively lower yields. After 1890 the province of Connacht remained loyal while Ulster switched to new varieties. Yet the Connacht–Ulster yield ratio regressed on time (1890–1914) gives:

$$Y_{c/Y_u} = 0.926 - 0.00027T$$
$$(2.29) \quad (0.00)$$

$RSQ = 0.00$, t statistics in parentheses.

An important reason for the 'failure' to switch in the west and south seems to have been that the main new varieties were less appetising than the Champion. As James Robinson put it in 1890, 'there appears to be something in the Champion that, potato for potato, makes it more satisfying as a staple article of food than any other variety . . . it is essentially a variety thoroughly suited for conditions under which the potato is a large constituent of the people's food'.[29] The east and north forsook it because the opportunity cost of not doing so—losing the British and urban markets where round potatoes with deep eyes such as the Champion commanded a lower price than varieties more suited to the frying pan or the chip pan—was greater. Thus while farmers in the exporting areas opted for the Champion like the rest in the early 1880s for its blight-resistant qualities, they switched almost as soon as alternatives became available.

Resistance to change was thus far from universal. On the other hand, the flail, the spade and the reaping hook, all archaic survivals suggesting farmer inertia, have been used within living memory.[30] How widespread was their persistence? Were they used by the typical farmer in some specially circumstanced areas or merely by the old and particularly backward? Can their survival be rationalised in terms of relative factor costs, as with the sickle in much of nineteenth-century England, and the caschrom in highland Scotland? The historians of material folk culture have so far not addressed these problems, and the lack of hard data is too serious for the economic historian to make any definitive pronouncements. What is quite clear is that the early decades of this century saw an unprecedented degree of mechanisation in Irish agriculture. Oral reminiscences usefully capture the initial scepticism towards, and then the great popular interest in, the new technologies:[31]

> Steam threshers did not come to this locality until about thirty years ago, and the first one that came . . . had to be removed from haggard to haggard with horses. It was a steam engine but did not haul, it only worked the mill. Small farmers were usually afraid to put their horses to haul it from place to place. It was only big haggards that employed it, so me and my equals had to thresh our own little handfuls with our capaleens.
>   Our day came too when Hurley bought a set that could haul itself . . . The old men used to say when they used to see it travelling the

road, 'That'll never come in this boreen anyway.' But it wasn't long until it was going in every boreen where there was corn to be threshed.

You'd hear an old fellow saying, 'What's the world coming to at all, what will they invent next?' And some other fellow would start about the old prophecies about yokes going the road without a horse pulling them . . . People would come to the haggard to see the thresher working, and the children coming home from school would come in and stay looking at it for hours. You'd hear some of them imitating it afterwards—they'd be puffing with their mouths like the engine, and they'd make a humming sound like the drum.

The agricultural statistics give a firmer impression of the transformation on the farm (table 38). The number of tractors on Irish farms jumped from seventy in 1917 to almost 800 in 1929. In general, though, such data do not prove that Irish farmers were

TABLE 38 *Farm machinery stock, 1908-28*

	1908	*1912*	*1929*
Potato sprayers (hand)	29,698	59,783	86,122
Do. (machine)	688	2,773	2,593
Harrows	185,342	204,270	252,951
Gas, oil and steam engines	402	1,542	3,010
Reapers and mowers	61,056	96,766	106,472
Self-binders	6,210	9,394	17,558

good entrepreneurs. Studies of diffusions such as that of the reaper and binder, the potato sprayer, the threshing machine and the tractor are both feasible and overdue. The early history of the adoption of the mechanical mower and reaper, for instance, has yet to be researched, but considering that a machine could cut several acres in a day, and about fifty to a hundred acres in a season, official 1917 data seem to suggest that, given a reasonable distribution across farms, diffusion had gone quite far enough in this case at least (table 39).

TABLE 39 *Reaper and mower diffusion* c. *1917*

Farm size (acres)	Acres of corn/hay per mower/reaper
Less than 30	25·4
30–50	12·6
50–100	15·0
Over 1,000	27·1

Sources. *The Output of Agriculture in Saorstat Eireann, 1925-26* (Dublin, 1929).

Finally, the earliest Irish experiments with the new Bordeaux mixture against potato blight were carried out at the Albert College in 1890. Forty years later it was proudly claimed that potato-spraying was practised more widely and successfully in Ireland than anywhere else.[32] There is some circumstantial evidence for rapid diffusion here: sales of bluestones and prepared anti-blight mixes rocketed in the late 1890s, and bluestone was being applied on the Great Blasket by 1900 at the latest.[33] Diffusion soon made for bigger yields: output per acre in the 1900s was almost 20 per cent more than in the 1880s and 1890s. Why, then, the repeated complaints from the Congested Districts Board in the interim that their offer of hand sprayers at bargain prices were being sniffed at by a recalcitrant peasantry?[34] Part of the answer must be that at the outset the machines easily broke down and were difficult and expensive to service, so that in the remote west at least caution may have been the best policy. But the Board was also disregarding the rather strange 'intermediate technology' developed by west-of-Ireland smallholders during the 1890s and 1900s, and apparently in wide use then. The playwright John Synge came across the new method in the wilds of Erris, and describes with glee an elderly woman spraying her potato patch with an old broom dipped in bluestone solution as evidence of how quick people were to try out promising new methods.[35] The initially slow diffusion of hand sprayers—their number grew from seven per hundred acres of potatoes in 1908 to nine in 1917, and then jumped to twenty-three in 1926—should thus not be equated automatically with farmer pig-headedness.

4. Ageing and the brain drain

Crotty and Lee have suggested that a steep rise in the proportion of elderly farmers in the labour force impeded modernisation after the Famine.[36] The hypothesis that a preponderance of older men (and women) should have led to misallocation is plausible, and censal data (see tables 40–1) seem to support it. The proportion of farmers aged sixty-five years and up increased steeply between 1861 and 1926. In neighbouring countries at the time the trend seems to have been far less marked or, as in England and Wales absent.[37] Increasing life expectancy and emigration cannot account for the discrepancy, especially after 1900. Thankfully, the true explanation for most of this 'ageing' is quite straightforward. It is that both in 1911 and in 1926 a great number of farmers exaggerated their age on the census form in the

TABLE 40 Age of Irish farmers, 1861-1926 (%)

Year	Men and women			Women only		
	45+	55+	65+	45+	55+	65+
1861	54·8	33·1	13·2	4·2	2·7	1·0
1871	59·2	38·6	16·1	5·5	3·8	2·0
1881	65·3	–	21·8	10·1	–	3·6
1891	68·4	–	21·7	13·0	–	4·6
1901	68·4	–	22·8	14·5	–	5·2
1911	71·4	–	32·7	12·6	–	7·3
1926	80·0	53·0	30·2	16·0	12·7	8·3

hope of—or because they were—benefiting from the provisions of
the Old Age Pensions Act, introduced in 1908. This is confirmed
by some cross-section data in the 1926 census (see table 41). Since
the pension involved a means test, the poorer farmers had a greater
incentive to lie, and hence the greater 'ageing' on smaller holdings!

TABLE 41 Irish farmers' ages by farm size, 1926

Farm size (acres)	Farmers 65+	Farmers 55+	Women 65+	Women 55+
1–4	42·6	63·1	16·2	22·4
5–9	37·7	59·2	11·9	16·6
10–14	33·3	55·4	9·6	13·9
15–29	30·3	53·6	8·0	11·9
30–49	27·6	50·8	6·8	11·0
50–99	19·9	49·8	6·5	11·0
100–99	18·6	48·7	6·1	10·9
200+	18·1	49·1	6·0	10·9

Another explanation of the supposedly low productivity
growth in Irish agriculture is the post-Famine exodus to Britain,
America and farther afield. It was repeatedly claimed that emigration took away 'the fairest and the bravest', 'the bone and sinew'
of the country, leaving behind the over-cautious, the elderly and
the incompetent. The agrarian activist Lawrence Ginnell put the
argument forcefully in 1907:[38]

> Alarming as is the decline in numbers, the decline in efficiency is
> greater still . . . While the physically and mentally healthy and energetic
> emigrate, the physically and mentally inefficient and dependent stay at
> home—some for want of courage, and some because they would not be
> admitted into a new country . . . Hospitals and lunatic asylums [in
> Ireland] are constantly being enlarged . . .

It is at best an unproved hypothesis. It seems to rest in part at least on a confusion between rates and levels, for though Irish farming in the wake of the great Famine and after may have been hurt by heavy emigration, the *rate* of emigration fell slowly, but more or less steadily, thereafter. Of itself this should have reduced any resultant constraint on productivity over time. This does not dispose of the issue, since in theory at least the exodus could have reduced living standards and labour productivity throughout the period: there may have been a 'brain drain' effect. *A priori* what is the more likely outcome? Theory provides no clear-cut answer. In so far as people who were relatively productive in agriculture earned incomes related to their specific complementarities with respect to other inputs, there is *some* presumption that they would stay. Professional sport provides an analogy: 'super-stars' are on average less mobile than mere journeymen. But if these same people had a comparative advantage in whatever they turned their hand to abroad, the presumption against them leaving no longer holds. However, since the majority of first-generation Irish emigrants took ordinary labouring jobs in urban centres, the point is worth making.

Perhaps empirical work will resolve the issue one day. Meanwhile one admittedly crude test for the presence of a 'brain drain', the analysis by age cohort of literacy patterns from decade to decade, lends it little support. Emigrants who could read and write had probably received some formal schooling and so had at least a rudimentary command of productivity-increasing skills. Therefore if the 'best' of each generation left a reduction in the literacy level of what remained of a particular age cohort might be expected. Table 42 provides the results of a simple exercise for a spread of counties. The results, as far as they go, are negative: what is surprising is how closely the later data match the earlier.

5. Conclusion

The historiography of post-Famine agriculture has dwelt over-long on factors which 'make and keep Irish farming backward'.[39] I have argued that some of those factors were of secondary importance, and hardly put Irish farmers at a disadvantage. This does not exclude the possibility that in some other respects the same farmers faced special problems. Special positive influences should not be forgotten, either, however. An increasingly literate and healthier labour force must have counted for something, as must the improvement in communications. Certainly the post-Famine decades saw marked changes in regional specialisation.

TABLE 42 The 'brain drain': age-cohort analysis of selected counties, 1851-71

(a) Percentage of the population aged 15-29 in 1851 and 25-39 in 1861 who could neither read nor write

	1851				1861			
	15-19		20-29		25-29		30-39	
	M	F	M	F	M	F	M	F
Leitrim	35·8	42·5	30·4	44·5	25·9	34·1	28·6	41·7
Mayo	61·1	72·3	57·2	75·4	49·9	68·1	54·0	75·4
Donegal	44·2	49·5	42·3	52·7	38·9	47·4	40·9	53·4
Longford	34·6	37·6	27·1	35·4	25·6	29·9	25·3	34·2
Tyrone	27·4	27·5	22·1	27·3	22·1	25·7	23·7	28·6
Kerry	51·0	63·5	46·5	67·9	41·9	58·0	42·7	64·6

(b) Proportion illiterate in selected age-cohorts, 1861 and 1871

	Men		Women	
Year	1861	1871	1861	1871
	(10-29)	(20-39)	(10-29)	(20-39)
County:				
Kerry	39·2	35·7	47·8	47·4
Longford	24·9	21·8	26·5	23·7
Tyrone	22·1	19·1	25·0	23·0
Donegal	39·7	36·6	46·2	45·1

Source. Calculated from the censuses of population, 1851-71.

Pig farming concentrated more on the west and south-west, and sheep numbers grew in Connacht, Ulster, Kerry and south Leinster while they declined elsewhere. Most impressive, and far more far-reaching than anything occurring in Britain at the time, were the shifts in cattle herds, which are captured in table 43. The impressive jump in the coefficient of variation provides a good short-hand summary of the trend. While the share of cows in the total declined, the midlands concentrated more and more on fattening and the west on supplying stores.[40] Average farm size grew, increasing the scope for economies of scale from the innovations of the 'second agricultural revolution'.

Finally the increasing role of governmental and government-supported agencies was probably a benign influence. Though I have not attempted to carry out cost-benefit analyses, I suspect that support for bodies such as the Department of Agriculture and Technical Instruction, the Congested Districts Board and the Irish Agricultural Organisation Society was not money wasted in the pre-1925 period. Such bodies mobilised volunteer support, collect-

TABLE 43 Regional specialisation in livestock farming (cows and heifers)

	Cattle two years plus per 100			Cattle under two years per 100		
	1854	1874	1904	1854	1874	1904
Carlow	53·97	80·49	117·74	110·25	171·19	195·93
Dublin	76·93	162·25	181·24	87·13	110·55	117·50
Kildare	207·88	315·92	414·48	177·63	215·45	270·46
Kilkenny	29·30	52·04	70·80	84·97	147·11	179·83
Laois	68·04	115·21	124·64	97·05	151·58	195·82
Longford	42·51	69·73	94·54	93·80	139·11	183·12
Louth	81·72	143·76	164·24	140·23	177·94	198·47
Meath	352·00	635·39	810·80	225·71	274·96	308·22
Offaly	107·32	172·50	188·26	119·76	176·43	213·76
Westme	126·83	266·20	330·35	166·80	243·61	310·17
Wexford	35·69	50·71	92·71	103·90	144·30	187·22
Wicklow	52·25	71·42	95·63	100·15	131·99	164·06
Clare	46·95	69·54	55·60	88·24	140·60	163·22
Cork	22·01	21·96	28·17	63·80	88·71	110·04
Kerry	29·12	26·32	25·68	60·94	70·92	101·97
Limerick	21·97	22·83	31·61	57·97	87·13	97·21
Tipperary	42·35	59·39	71·37	78·28	130·39	160·28
Waterford	23·42	27·16	53·24	68·50	99·38	135·27
Antrim	33·55	38·81	26·58	80·88	111·55	114·19
Armagh	20·36	37·74	34·48	74·76	121·76	157·17
Cavan	24·56	34·77	34·27	79·89	111·53	130·45
Derry	34·57	36·20	37·24	86·06	112·87	141·34
Donegal	40·20	51·70	37·54	86·89	102·71	136·30
Down	24·13	32·93	39·44	90·38	128·33	158·72
Fermanagh	26·96	36·31	33·20	70·41	93·05	111·09
Monaghan	16·93	33·37	34·93	83·14	124·59	142·87
Tyrone	23·11	28·18	25·62	76·29	104·28	134·28
Galway	140·75	157·52	131·08	119·54	135·55	182·69
Leitrim	27·78	39·63	34·87	72·53	97·27	119·77
Mayo	88·08	93·50	89·42	90·71	99·64	152·55
Roscommon	96·16	93·27	91·55	101·99	138·73	181·37
Sligo	49·46	58·04	55·73	84·11	113·29	159·48
Mean	64·59	94·83	114·17	97·58	134·27	167·03
S.D.	66·27	117·7	150	20·23	44·33	51·93
C.V.	1·03	1·24	1·31	0·21	0·33	0·31

ed and produced statistical data of high quality, standardised and improved the quality of output, accelerated the diffusion of information about techniques, protected farmers from unscrupulous traders, and improved educational skills throughout the countryside.[41]

Appendix 5 On the 'cost' of negotiating rent cuts after 1881

Irish farmers took up with alacrity the opportunities offered to them by the land legislation of 1881 and after. The 1881 Land Act created special courts to decide between landlord and tenant claims as to what constituted a 'fair' rent. What the courts sought to impose was not an 'economic' rent but something less, in recognition of the tenants' shared ownership of the land. However, the courts' judgements were not based on any clear formula, and inevitably many landlords were left unhappy with what was deemed 'fair'.

All tenants had the right to apply to have their rents settled for a fifteen-year term—hence the saying that Ireland lived 'under a regime of lawsuits lasting fifteen years, and renewable for ever'. Alternatively landlord and tenant might register out-of-court settlements with the Land Commission with the same effect. The average reduction in percentage terms obtained from the courts exceeded that granted by landlords out of court. This is true at both aggregate and individual estate level, yet a sizable minority of tenants accepted out-of-court settlements. There are several possible reasons. One obvious consideration is the cost associated with the court procedure, making litigation not worth while for the smallest tenants. Second, information from some estates suggests that tenants sometimes preferred the security of a deal with the landlord to risking the judgement of the court. One might expect a risk-averse tenantry to trade off a larger expected decline in rent against a smaller variance in the decline. On the Mercers' estate, for instance, the average out-of-court settlement was a reduction of 18·9 per cent with a standard deviation of 5·8 per cent, while for court settlements the figures were 21·6 and 8·7 per cent. Other examples might be given, though the picture is by no means uniform. Third, landlords were in a strong position with tenants in arrears, and so could force them to settle out of court. Finally, it is likely that some tenants who settled out of court did so because they were paying low rents to begin with, and preferred a more personal and informal relationship with their landlord than that implied by third-party decisions.

Tenants and landlords unsatisfied with court decisions had a remedy: they could appeal to the Land Commission for a review. They frequently did so, to the great annoyance of those who saw the procedure as a waste of time and money to all concerned. 'The changes made in the fair rents fixed are on the whole small; and the expenses incurred are greatly in excess of the pecuniary advantages resulting from them': so judged the Morley committee in 1898. According to the Fry Commission of 1894:

> [T]he rents fixed by the Subcommissioners in the 19655 cases subject to rehearing amounted to £431,398; the net result of the rehearings was to increase this amount by £1,282, or only 0·2 per cent . . . The . . . rehearings must have cost the parties at least £250,000 and this vast expenditure was incurred, in the case of nine-tenths of the cases . . . in order to subject the decision of the Court, two of the three members of which are agricultural experts, who themselves inspect the holding, to be reviewed by another court, no member of which inspects the holding,

and no member of which need be an agricultural expert . . .

The thrust of the argument is rather misleading. The evidence against it is to be found in the appendix to the Fry Commission's report. This contains data on 31,013 cases, of which the bulk—24,867—were withdrawn, struck out or rejected. However, in the 3,136 cases in which landlord appeals resulted in a changed rent the net rent increase was £8,008·62, while in the 1,982 cases in which tenant appeals resulted in a change the net *reduction* was £7,997·18. These sums, taken together, must be regarded as the annual return to plaintiffs on outlays spent in litigation. If one assumes that court costs were £5 on average, then we have an annaul return of £(8,008·82 + 7,997·18) on an outlay of £(31,013)(5). That comes to 10·3 per cent.

Litigation, the data suggest, was not such a risky business. Only in 117 cases did a landlord's appeal result in a reduced rent: only in thirty-six did a tenant's result in an increased rent. Thus the worst that could happen to a plaintiff in 99·5 per cent of the cases was that the original judgement would be upheld. The private return to litigation was thus respectable. In the wider sense one must bear in mind the running costs of the appeal procedure and the cost to the losers, and remember that the judgements of the appeal tribunal probably had an impact too on out-of-court settlements. The costs were the *faux frais* of recognition of 'dual ownership' in law.

Appendix 6 A note on the output estimates

Barbara Solow's earlier calculations[42] have been used for many items, and her estimate of value added and mine differ little. However, our estimates for several individual items differ considerably, for reasons explained below.

Potatoes. An output ratio of 1 : 3 was used for 1876, and the 1908 price was used rather than the market price quoted in the parliamentary papers.

Butter and milk. A milk yield of 385 gallons is assumed, and the deductions made for mortality, dry cows and calf and pig feed are as in *Agricultural Output, 1908.* Butter output has been estimated on the assumption that three gallons of milk produced a pound of butter. Milk consumption at the rate of fifteen gallons per person is assumed.

Pigs. An average pork output of 1·5 cwt per pig was allowed. This agrees well with Professor Thomas Baldwin's guess that in 1874 'about as many pigs are annually sold in Ireland as the country contains at the time of taking the government returns'.[43]

Cattle. My calculations follow the method used elsewhere for 1854.[44]

Michael Turner has provided an output series covering the period from 1850/5 to 1906/13[45] He estimates output valued at current prices to have risen from £41·6 million in 1850/5 to £47·0 million in 1866/75, and then to have fallen to £44·6 million in 1876-85, while agricultural prices moved from 67 to 94 and 97 (base 1900 = 100) over the same period. Thus his results also rule out the possibility of any sustained rise in real agricultural value added in the interim. Between 1876-85 and 1906/13, however, Turner has the value of output rising from £44·6 million to £51·5 million, while his index of agricultural prices rises from 97 to 113·7.

Notes

1 National Library of Ireland, Ms. 5717, letter from Robert French, Monivea, to his son (and estate agent).

2 Gerard Boate, *Ireland's Naturall History* (London, 1652).

3 Most notably, perhaps, by Barbara L. Solow. See her *Land Question and the Irish Economy, 1870-1903* (Cambridge, Mass., 1971), pp. 170-2, 200-10; also *id.*, review of Devine and Dickson (eds.), *Journal of Economic History*, XLIV (3)) (1984), 852, where it is argued, 'There has been extraordinarily little change in the volume and structure of Irish agriculture since the early nineteenth century. Hardly a brilliant success story.' Raymond D. Crotty's classic *Irish Agricultural Production* (Cork, 1966) also highlights agriculture's failure to expand.

4 Compare A. C. Kelley and J. G. Williamson, *Lessons from Japanese Economic Development* (Chicago, 1974), p. 181; R. Gallman, 'Changes in total United States factor productivity in the nineteenth century', *Agricultural History*, 46 (1972), 191-210; C. Ó Gráda, 'Agricultural decline, 1860-1914', in R. Floud and D. N. McCloskey (eds.), *An Economic History of Britain since 1700: 1860 to the 1970s* (Cambridge, 1981), pp. 176-9.

5 Department of Agriculture and Technical Instruction, *The Agricultural Output of Ireland, 1908* (Dublin, 1912); *Agricualtural Output of Northern Ireland, 1924-5* (Belfast, 1928); *The Output of Agriculture in Saorstat Eireann 1925/6* (Dublin, 1929). Details in appendix.

6 Solow, *The Land Question*, chapter 3; Crotty, *Irish Agricultural Production*, chapter 2; W. E. Vaughan, 'Landlord and tenant relations in Ireland between the Famine and the Land War', in L. M. Cullen and T. C. Smouth (eds.), *Comparative Aspects of Scottish and Irish Economic and Social History* (Edinburgh, 1977), pp. 216-26.

7 T. W. Fletcher, 'The Great Depression in English agriculture, 1873-96', *Economic History Review*, XIII (2) (1960-1); see also P. J. Perry, 'Where was the "Great Agricultural Depression"?: a geography of bankruptcy in late Victorian England and Wales', *Agricultural History Review*, XX (1972).

8 This suggests an analogy with the post-Napoleonic period, where a few bad years make people forget the broader trend.

9 Traditional and modern views are well explained in W. E. Vaughan, *Landlords and Tenants in Ireland, 1848-1904* (Dublin, 1984).

10 Solow, *Land Question*, pp. 50-88; Crotty, pp. 84-107.

11 *Returns showing the Number of Agricultural Holdings in Ireland, and the tenure under which they are held by the Occupier* [c. 32], H.C. 1870, lvi.

12 E. McCracken, *Irish Woods since Tudor Times* (Newton Abbot, 1971), pp. 31-2; E. D. Steele, *Irish Land and British Politics* (Cambridge, 1974), pp. 8-10, 20-2.

13 J. M. Guttman, 'The economics of tenant rights in nineteenth-century Ireland', *Economic Inquiry*, 18 (1980), 408-24.

14 C. Ó Gráda, 'The investment behaviour of Irish landlords, 1850-1880: some preliminary estimates', *Agricultural History Review*, 23 (1975), 139-55.

15 *Report of the Commissioners of Inquiry into the Working of the Landlord and Tenant (Ireland) Act, 1870 and the Acts amending the same (c. 2779)*, H.C. 1881, XVIII, pp. 7-9; E. D. Steele, *Irish Land and British Politics: Tenant Right and Nationality, 1865-1870* (Cambridge, 1974), pp. 19-22.

16 E.G. *Commission on Emigration and other Population Problems* (Dublin, 1956), pp. 122-3.

17 G. O'Brien (ed.), *Advertisements for Ireland* (Dublin, 1925), pp. 43, 58; C. H. Hull (ed.), *The Economic Writings of Sir William Petty* (London, 1899), pp. 201-2; H. L. Lindsay, 'On the agriculture of the County of Armagh', *Quarterly Journal of Agriculture*, 7 (1836), 62-3; N. W. Senior, *Journals, Essays, and Conversations relating to Ireland* (London, 1868), I, pp. 22-31; Thackeray, *Sketchbook*, pp. 43,

75, 123.
18 Horace Plunkett, *Ireland in the New Century* (Dublin, 1904), p. 43; *Irish Farmers' Gazette*, 6 October 1906; Finlay Dun, *Landlords and Tenants in Ireland* (London, 1881), pp. 80-1; *Report of the Scottish on Agriculture in Ireland* (Edinburgh, 1906), p. 34.
19 V. Gookin, as quoted in E. McLysaght, *Irish Life in the Seventeenth Century* (Dublin, 1950), p. 39; Liam Bulfin, *Rambles in Eirinn* (Dublin, 1906), p. 182; E. McLysaght, *Changing Times* (Dublin, 1978), p. 26.
20 The first and fourth are taken from the archives of CBE; the third from P. Kavanagh, *The Green Fool* (1971 edition, Harmondsworth), pp. 125-6; the second from a Radio na Gaeltachta programme on migrant workers, 1976 (my translation). The fourth is another tirade against the demands of fieldwork for farmers.
21 Compare S. de Canio, *Agriculture in the Post-bellum South: the Economics of Production and Supply* (Cambridge, Mass., 1974), pp. 16-121.
22 J. Meenan, Minority Report, *Commission on Emigration*, p. 376; R. Kane, *Industrial Resources*, pp. 301-2.
23 Bicheno, *Ireland and its Economy*, pp. 20-1.
24 Senior, *Journals*, I, p. 32.
25 *Returns of Agricultural Produce in Ireland in the Year 1853*, H.C. (1854-5), XLVII, vii, 223; *Returns . . . Year 1854*, H.C. (1856), LIII, xxi-iii, 225.
26 T. Barrington, 'A review of Irish agricultural prices', *Journal of the Statistical and Social Inquiry Society of Ireland*, 15 (1927), 269-80; H. Staehle, 'Statistical Notes . . .'. C. Ó Gráda, 'Supply responsiveness in nineteenth-century Irish agriculture', *Economic History Review*, ser. 2, 28 (1975), 312-7. See also Lee, *The Modernization*, pp. 10-11.
27 C. Ó Gráda, 'The beginnings of the Irish Creamery system, 1880-1914', *Economic History Review*, ser. 2, 30 (1977), 284-305; Solow, *Land Question*, p. 198.
28 The following three paragraphs are based on data culled from *Agricultural Statistics*, 1880 to 1917; *Department of Agriculture and Technical Instruction Journal*, 1889-1913, especially 11 (1910-11), 311-12; 8 (1907-08), 256; 13 (1912-13), 766; *Extracts from Reports on the Potato Crop, 1890, made for the Irish Land Commission*, H.C. (1890-1) LXIII; *Report from the Select Committee on the Potato Crop*, H.C. (1880) XII; R. N. Salaman, *Potato Varieties* (Cambridge. 1928).
29 *Extracts from Reports*, p. 52.
30 E. E. Evans, *Irish Folk Ways* (London, 1939); T. P. O'Neill, *Life and Tradition in Rural Ireland* (London, 1977).
31 C.B.E., Mss. 462, pp. 282-6; 38, pp. 179-80; 1174, pp. 371-3; 1158, pp. 480-2.
32 Department of Agriculture, *Potato Blight and its Prevention* (Dublin, 1934), p. 4.
33 Evidence from the account books of a Dingle merchant.
34 E.g. *DATIJ*, 11 (1910-11), 311.
35 John Millington Synge, *In Wicklow, West Kerry and Connemara* (Dublin, 1919), p. 214; Congested Districts Board, *Tenth Annual Report*, pp. 14-15; J. Maguire, *Come Day, go Day, God send Sunday* (London, 1971), p. 29; *Reports on recent Experiments in checking Potato Disease*, H.C. (1892) LXIV, pp. 51-73.
36 Crotty, *Irish Agricultural Production*, pp. 106-7; Lee, *Modernization*, pp. 10-1.
37 Comparison of data on individuals from the 1901 and 1911 manuscript returns yields some hilarious results. See also T. de Bhaldraithe (ed.), *Seanchas Thomáis Laighléis* (Dublin, 1978), p. 61; Henry Robinson, *Further Memories of Irish Life* (London, 1924), frontispiece; A. Birrell, *Beyond Recall* (London, 1939), p. 210-11. Genuine ageing was a more serious problem in the post-1926 period. See R. C. Geary, 'Variability in Irish agricultural statistics on smalland medium sized farms in an Irish county', *Journal of the Statistical and Social Inquiry Society of Ireland*, 20 (1956-57), 2-32; J. Scully, *Agriculture in the West of Ireland* (Dublin, 1971).
38 Lawrence Ginnell, *Land and Liberty* (Dublin, 1907), p. 30.
39 Quoted in Moritz Bonn, *Modern Irish Farming* (Dublin, 1906), p. 58.

40 Department of Agriculture, *Agricultural Statistics, 1847-1926* (Dublin, 1930), p. xviii; J. O'Donovan, *The Economic History of Livestock in Ireland* (Cork, 1939), chapter II; Edith H. Whetham, 'The changing cattle enterprise of England and Wales, 1870-1910', *Geographical Journal*, 129 (3) (1963), 378-400.

41 On these activities see W. L. Micks, *History of the Congested Districts Board* (Dublin, 1925); annual reports of the Congested Districts Board, the Irish Agricultural Organization Society and D.A.T.I.

42 Solow, *Land Question*, pp. 171, 213-17.

43 Thomas Baldwin, *Introduction to Irish Farming* (Dublin, 1874), p. 87.

44 Ó Gráda, 'Agricultural Output'.

45 Michael Turner, 'Towards an agricultural price index for Ireland, 1850-1914', *Economic and Social Review*, 18 (1987).

CHAPTER 5
Inheritance, emigration and fertility

Son. When we were small boys an' we sitting there at that table, who always used to be given the white loaf, an' who used to get the strong cake?
Mother. Sure, ye were only the same to me as two lambs that would be on the same hill, only one o' ye being a bit stronger like than the other. [T. C. Murray, *Birthright*]

Subdivision of farms in Ireland is not so much the consequence of laws of equal inheritance—it sprang rather from the fact that but for the soil the father had nothing which he could leave his children. [Moritz Bonn, 1907]

Much of the recent spate of historical writing on rural inheritance customs and their consequences focuses on spatial contrasts. Le Roy Ladurie's introduction to the work of Jean Yver is a famous example: it highlights the difference between a *preciput* or patrilineal impartible inheritance zone in the south of France and one of automatic impartible inheritance in the west.[1] Spatial variations in succession regimes have also been examined at a more micro level for parts of Italy, Germany, and France and their implications for social and demographic change convassed. Further afield, Alston and Schapiro have tried to explain the coexistence of primogeniture in the colonial American south and multigeniture in the north.[2]

In Ireland it seems more natural to focus on the shift from partible to impartible as a temporal phenomenon. The former, popularly associated with the pre-Famine era, is seen variously as a cause and effect of 'backwardness' and poverty, and ultimately of mass starvation. Malthusian pressures before the Famine, and possibly also a reduction in optimal holding size, dictated subdivision. The partitioning effect on the landscape is captured by the first Ordnance Survey maps and contemporary estate surveys.[3] In his *Descriptive and Statistical Account* McCulloch describes the process thus:

The practice of subdividing small farms was still on the increase . . .

'One great obstacle to improvement,' says Mr. Ross, 'and which is too general in Ireland, is their notion of the equal and unalienable right of all their children to the inheritance of their father's property, whether land or goods. This opinion, so just and reasonable in theory but so ruinous and absurd in practice, is interwoven in such a manner in the constitution of their minds, that it is next to impossible to eradicate it. In spite of every argument, the smaller Irish occupiers continue to divide their farms among their children, and these divide on, till division is no longer practicable; and in the course of two or three generations, the most thriving family must necessarily go to ruin.' . . . The extent to which this ruinous practice has been carried is such as sometimes almost to exceed belief. Dr. Kelly, late Catholic Archbishop of Tuam, stated, in his evidence before the Committee of 1830 on the 'State of Ireland', that he knew a farm in his neighbourhood which was originally leased, on the partnership system, to about twenty families, and he afterwards recollected to have seen sixty families living on the same farm, an augmentation that grew naturally out of the increase of population . . . This splitting of the land into minute portions, and the direct dependence of so large a portion of the people on it for subsistence, form the principle obstacles to the improvement of agriculture, and make the condition and prospects of the population exceedingly unfavourable.

Such a process could not have persisted for ever. The crisis of 1846–50, it is argued, merely occasioned or accelerated the switch to impartible inheritance. This model is clearly over-simplified. On the one hand, subdivision long outlasted the Famine in parts of the west; on the other, impartible inheritance was encouraged by relative price movements which dictated a shift from tillage to pasture. But it is still a useful model. By implication the pre-Famine rural family was poor and rudely egalitarian: the change created a more patriarchal regime, often beset by squabbles about the succession. Predictably the new system was sometimes seen as inequitable; it was only because 'family loyalty was stronger than brotherly jealousy' that it could last.[4]

Some alleged features of the post-Famine system are dear to writers of the Irish literary renaissance. Loveless marriages, class conflicts, sibling rivalry, mother *v.* daughter-in-law—what author could fail to be inspired? The literature highlights the bitter division occasioned by patriarchal decision-making and unfair inheritance patterns. In *Birthright*, by T. C. Murray, for example, a powerful play set in rural mid-Cork just after the turn of the century, it is the younger of farmer Bat Morrissey's two sons who feels slighted: dedicated to the land but selected by his parents for emigration, the 'hundred or more distinctions' made between him and his brother ultimately prove too much, and the action ends in fratricide.[5]

Conflict about succession is also a central theme in Sean O'Faoláin's first novel, *A Nest of Simple Folk*.[6] When Judith O'Donnell in the end prevails on her dying farmer husband to leave the best land to their youngest son there are anguished protests from others. 'Was that free farm,' urges the family lawyer on their behalf, 'to go over the heads of six sisters and six brothers to their last child, who has never done a stroke of work on the land?' The will breeds resentments that sustain the plot.

In Patrick Kavanagh's *Great Hunger*, by way of contrast, it is the lotof the sons who must stay at home that is lamented:[7]

> Maguire was faithful to death
> He stayed with his mother till she died
> At the age of ninety-one.
> She stayed too long
> Wife and mother in one
> When she died
> The knuckle bones were cutting
> The skin of her son's backside
> And he was sixty-five.

The same theme is taken up by the anthropologist Hugh Brody's *Inishkillane*.[8]

When the dramatic element is discounted, that parental choice regarding property should arouse some rivalry seems natural. Even an absolutely equal sharing of the estate—or parental efforts towards that end—might not be seen as such by some interested party. But literary sources reinforce the suspicion that the succession stakes were inherently unfair, a price to pay for the continuation of a way of life. In this view of post-Famine peasant society inequality begins within the family.

Such a view is also supported by much research on impartible inheritance elsewhere in Europe. What the practice involved, according to the economic demographer Ronald Lee, was the property passing to 'one favoured child, who can marry', the others being forced to move on or find menial employment locally, 'in which case they would marry late or not at all'.[9] Bourdieu and Goy's detailed investigations into custom in the Béarnais of south-west France describe an extremely inegalitarian regime 'which resolutely puts the integrity of the family holding above all else'.[10] Berkner's analysis of eighteenth-century practice around Hanover in lower Saxony has equally gloomy implications for the lot of all siblings but the heir.[11]

Of the two Irish writers to pay most attention to the issue in practice, Kenneth Connell and Conrad Arensberg, Connell comes closest to the position just described. In a series of classic papers he claimed that the practice of impartible inheritance (and its associated trappings, such as the 'match') made sacrificial victims of all siblings but one. These were 'the men (and the women too, unless they prefered spinsterhood) [who] should be ready to slip down the social scale, beneath their brother to whom the family's land was committed'. So, according to Connell, 'family loyalty, even at a personal loss' was a fundamental feature. Arensberg's discussion—based on field work in west Clare in the 1930s—is more equivocal. In tune with his more harmonious view of rural life, the portioning off of siblings is emphasised, yet the disadvantaged lot of those who 'must travel' is also hinted at: 'It is the very fortunate farmer indeed who can provide for all his sons and daughters so. Usually only the heir and one daughter are married and dowered, the one with the farm, the other with the fortune. All the rest, in the words of Luogh residents, must travel.'[12]

1. Some probate evidence

Before the Succession Act of 1965 Irish law supported the right of the testator to do exactly what he liked with his property. There was plenty of scope therefore for the kind of outcome predicated above. Only when the farmer died intestate could his issue in law lay claim to a share of the property.[13]

In my own view, giving pride of place to this temporal dichotomy between partible-equitable on the one hand and impartible-inequitable on the other is not helpful in the Irish case. The historical record sits more comfortably with the hypothesis that parents by and large tried at all times to be fair to all their children. Sometimes it might mean 'share and share alike'; sometimes, that apparently deprived siblings be granted special treatment. Parents, in other words, would try consciously to reduce inequality between their offspring. Practical difficulties of interpretation or execution could complicate the outcome, and exceptions blur the picture. But I find it instructive to regard both succession systems as the product, in different circumstances, of a common desire for intrafamilian equity or 'fairness'. The transition from partible to impartible—eased or accelerated by the Famine—may then be interpreted as a reflection of increased opportunities off the land for other siblings, and the differences between the two systems due more to socio-economic circumstance than to culture.

A corollary of this way of looking at things, that the infighting usually associated with the post-Famine regime was not new, finds some support in recent work on rural crime.[14] Another clear corollary, that even before the Famine impartible inheritance was common among the better-off, will not be tested here. Before leaving that period, however, a nice example of such coexistence is worth mentioning. It comes from Elizabeth Smith, busybody wife of a small west Wicklow landlord and useful chronicler of estate and farm life. On the eve of the Famine, after one of her frequent rounds of the property, she described one home that she entered as that of a 'thriving man with a wife well deserved of him . . . the daughters of this house are well married, the sons in trades, and the youngest Philip will worthily succeed his father . . .' Not far away, however, she found the Widow Quin's daughter, who had made a wretched marriage; 'she yook a sickly labouring lad who is often laid up, but to whom she has brought seven children. They live in the mother's cowhouse where she had no right to put them and thus settle a whole family of beggars on us, but we did not look after things as we have learned to do now.'[15]

For some insight into the workings of impartible inheritance in Ireland after the Famine I have used the evidence of late nineteenth and early twentieth-century wills and probate records.[16] By the century's end will-making had become quite common, even for small farmers. The selection of that period for analysis therefore guarantees a fair spread across the socio-economic spectrum. For reasons of availability and convenience the analysis concentrates on wills from Cork and south Ulster. All usable wills for the late 1890s and 1900s were used.

The strategy followed (see table 45) was to compare the value of estates with the terms laid down in the will. Some of the wills, it is true, were grist to the mill of the 'inequity' view, but the check satisfied me that impartible inheritance *usually* worked in the manner posited at that time. This is a subjective judgement, for who can tell for sure that what is interpreted as 'fair' on the basis of cold documentary evidence, may not have been intended by parents or regarded by resentful siblings as rank favouritism? Matching wills and probate valuations seems a promising way, nevertheless, of checking the relative good fortune of the successor on the land against other members of the family.

The wills confirm the view that physical subdivision of estates was rare at this juncture. Curiously enough, it was far more likely to occur on the lands of the very rich than of the poor.[17] If the poor had the will to subdivide they had not the means. Wills also suggest that sibling ranking alone is no great predictor in the succession stakes.[18] When the father died young the eldest son almost invariably took over as surrogate father, immediately or on reaching his majority. Examples of the youngest son being left the property by default also occur. I quote a case in point, partly in order to illustrate a common will format:[19]

> In the name of God Amen. I Patrick McDonagh of Abbey Loughrea and the parish of Ballinakill being now in full possession of my senses but not knowing how soon God may call me am going to settle my affairs with God and man. I have eight children all of whom are married except the youngest namely John McDonagh and Kate McDonagh. It is my full intention and wish to leave will and bequeath my house furniture land and farm implements and stock horses cows cattle and sheep to my youngest son John McDonagh he to pay my daughter Kate McDonagh the sum of £80 0s 0d sterling within a reasonable time after my death. Should any of the rest of my children who are married make any claim to my property or stock after my death I hereby will and bequeath them one shilling each . . .

The elder McDonagh had not long to live, and his last-minute preoccupation with the welfare of those not adequately 'provided for' is quite typical. Here is another example:[20]

> My daughter Mary got her fortune at her marriage. I now bequeath her seventy pounds. I have arranged for the advancement in life of my son Luke Lee. I confirm same and bequeath him seventy-five pounds. I bequeath to my son Thomas one hundred pounds. It is my intention during my life to provide for my said daughter and two sons by securing to them benefits equal to the money above bequeathed to them and the said legacy shall abate by the value of such benefits as shall be given in satisfaction of such legacies. And to my son James I advise and bequeath all the property which I may [be] possessed or entitled to not otherwise disposed of in this will or any codicil thereto. In witness whereof I hence hereunto put my hand.

In both these cases the wife had predeceased the man who made the will. Had she not, doubtless her comforts would also have been catered for. The 'one shilling clause' is a common feature, most usually invoked against previously married or emigrant siblings, though occasionally in bitter, despotic or sectarian fashion against a 'black sheep'. Power of exclusion to executors of minors who later married somebody not deemed suitable is also characteristic. The 'fairness' analysed here is always constrained by such patriarchy.

Probate valuations undoubtedly sometimes underestimated the true worth of an estate. Since valuations were the benchmark for charging estate duty, farmers and their representatives were eager for this to happen. Assessment thus might include references to 'weakly' cattle, remote location, and the like, or imply implausibly spartan housing and furniture. Take for instance Martin Downes, a west Clare smallholder, who left his farm at Congriff, 'together with five in calf cows, five yearlings, horse and car, farming implements, household furniture, dairy utensils, together with hay and all farm produce on the land' to his son John in 1899. The probate put the value of house and humble farm, forty acres at a rent of £4, at £100. However, household goods were valued at £2, and the stock and farm implements at only £30. Compare this with a case such as that of Simon Hickey, a very prosperous (by Irish standards) Cork farmer: his animals were assessed at £1,027, close to their market value, though his household effects were put at only £40. In general livestock and land were less loosely assessed than household goods. On balance the wills are nevertheless a useful proxy for bequeathed wealth.

The wills which formed the basis of tables 44–5 are neither numerous enough not sufficiently representative regionally for definitive inferences, but they illustrate an approach and a new interpretation. Table 44 summarises two aspects of wills of interest here: the role of subdivision and the share of other siblings. Table 45 shows the average number of sons and daughters provided for, at least to some extent, in the wills examined.

TABLE 44 Probate values and inheritance terms

Probate range (£)	Mean	n	Total No. subdivided	Average to sons (£)	Average to others (£)
(a) Cavan district					
1–199	101	49	5	10	36
200–1,600	429	30	9	110	124
(b) Cork district					
1–199	105	24	4	21	78
200–499	332	65	17	97	156
500–1,500	818	23	7	332	236

Note. Financial provision for wives, daughters and others is included under 'Others'. Annuities are capitalised at ten times their annual value; no account is taken of stock or bed and board. When a property is to be subdivided, or sold and the proceeds split, this is reflected in the totals.

Three obvious preliminary points need to be remembered. First, some compensation for the financial and psychic costs of caring for elderly relatives and, in many cases, for the funeral and testamentary expenses of the deceased is to be expected. Second, the son who inherited the farm usually had to wait his turn,

TABLE 45 Average number of sons and daughters provided for

Probate range (£)	n	Sons	Daughters
(a) Cavan			
0–199	48	1·38	1·08
200+	32	2·12	1·47
(b) Cork			
0–199	25	1·36	1·40
200–499	62	1·87	1·50
500+	22	2·32	1·32

postponing marriage and receiving a low income in the meantime; sometimes the wait would spoil his marriage prospects entirely.[21] The post-1881 Irish censuses make a mockery of the model whereby in the words of Ronald Lee 'the property passes to one favoured child, who can marry', forcing the other children to marry late or not at all.[22] By 1926 one-third of thirty-five to forty-four-year-old farmers remained unmarried, and one-sixth of fifty-five to fifty-nine-year olds.[23] Hardly surprisingly, those holding least land were most likely to remain single. Third, transfers *inter vivos*, which are likely to have benefited those who left, are for the most part not captured by the wills. On all three counts a 'fair' division of the estate would indicate a larger share to the remaining son. Some of the wills in table 44 may still seem to favour the successor to the farm. Quinlivan, for instance, left the farm to his eldest son, and that was that. The overall impression, however, is surely closer to a balanced division of the estate than the lopsided distribution sometimes envisaged. Two or more sons are often bequeathed something. Note, moreover, that in some of the cases listed in appendix 7, and in many more inspected, the 'encumbrances' on the legacy were greater than the probate value! In these and other cases we suspect that the wills must have reflected the testator's aspirations rather than the eventual outcome—though that does not exclude a 'fair' outcome, either. Even that Quinlivan farm may have been no great boon, since the father clearly had serious doubts about any of his sons wanting to remain on.[24]

So far we have been arguing for a greater measure of fairness among siblings than is indicated in the literature. Perhaps, though, a little *caveat* should be entered in so far as the eldest son is concerned. Neither the wills nor other evidence support the claim that primogeniture was dominant or even widespread. But that need not necessarily indicate random choice of successor on the farm: the eldest may simply have chosen not to exercise a customary right when the inheritance was not worth much. I have presented some tentative evidence in favour of that notion elsewhere.[25] here, however, it is the stronger assertion that all sons except one came very badly out of the inheritance regime that is being discussed.

There remain one group rarely mentioned in wills, and thus possibly hard done by the succession system. These are the siblings who emigrated, and it is to them that we now turn.

2. Disinherited emigrants?

Between the great Famine and the great Depression emigration accounted for more than half of each rising generation, including millions 'set free' by impartible inheritance. As has been suggested, emigrants were usually either not mentioned in bequests or specifically excluded. This seems to support the view that those who 'must travel' were badly treated by the system. Others have argued, however, that it was those who remained who suffered: Robert Kennedy explains large families in the post-Famine era as a form of insurance, increasing the prospect of an heir remaining on.[26] What may be usefully added here about the relative fortunes of those who stayed and those who left?

Let us suppose that the alternative for the 'disinherited' son who was not helped to emigrate was to become a labourer in Ireland. The portion of sons who emigrated may then be regarded as their excess lifetime earnings, appropriately discounted, over the Irish standard. The mid-1870s provide a good starting point, since quite comprehensive wage and price data survive from that period.[27] However, the crude calculations underlying what follows should be taken as no more than suggestive. In the United States, where most Irish were destined, money wages were two to three times their Irish level in the mid-1870s. American prices were generally higher too, though some staples (notably meats, flannel, coffee) were cheaper there. A near doubling of the real wage for the typical emigrant, of £200 to £400 added to the present value of lifetime earnings, is indicated.

Looking forward, between the 1870s and 1920s Irish agricultural output rose by about a third, while the labour force dropped by another third. Let us assume for the sake of argument that the implied rise of two-thirds in agricultural income per head was equally spread between the labourers and small and strong farmers alike. Now to turn to the US side, the David–Solar United States real wages index[28] doubled over the same half-century, implying some improvement in the lot of the emigrant relative to the stay-at-home. Between the 1850s and 1870s, however, it would seem to have been a different story. Non-landlord income per head in Ireland grew by at least one-fifth, while in America real wages rose by less than a tenth. Our conclusion, then, from such rough-and-ready numbers: the relative lot of the emigrant worsened in the pre-1875 period, and steadily improved thereafter. Irish demographic behaviour in the latter period—the dramatic rise in the proportion of never-marrieds and in mean marriage age—is consistent with this, and we suggest that the 'unfair' treatment of emigrants in wills is a reflection of it also. If these guesses at their expected extra earnings are in the ball park, tables 44–5 and the appendix indicate that, the case of very large estates apart, 'disinherited' sons fared just as well as, if not better than, the inheritors who remained around the turn of the century.

The County Roscommon smallholder who in 1911 ordered that 'my son James Padian shall pay to my eldest son John Padian who lives in the United States the sum of one pound at the same time regretting that [he, the father] cannot conscientiously do more for him or take from James Padian what he actually earned himself' is a good case in point. In the rare instance when an entire farm was bequeathed to an emigrant, his return was never taken for granted. Overall the wills indicate that parents who had children abroad sensed that they owed them nothing. Indeed, the sizable and rising flow of emigrant remittances, in cash and in kind, during these years may bespeak a compensatory intra-familial transfer, an implicit admission by those who emigrated that they had fared relatively well. In the late 1860s it is estimated that 2 million Irish-born in north America were remitting home about £1 million annually; four decades later a considerably smaller stock of emigrants was sending back over $10 million, or between double and treble the earlier sum in real terms.[29]

One suspects that changes in remittance flows and bequests reflected the altering fortunes of those who left and those who remained, all the time attempting to support 'equitable' outcomes among siblings, though establishing this would require a detailed time series study and more. Meanwhile it is worth mentioning that several aspects of socio-economic stratification in Ireland between Famine and Treaty—the high proportion of farmers' sons among traders and publicans in the villages and towns, the almost complete absence of farmers' sons among the ranks of labourers in Dublin city, the comfortable socio-economic background of most of the clergy and rural professional classes—argue in the same direction.[30]

While by no means wishing to deny the tensions occasioned by the intergenerational transmission of wealth, I would maintain that the evidence belies Connell's argument about a firm link between the shift to impartible inheritance and greater inequity. Perhaps those accounts in Lee, Berkner, Goy *et al.* are also somewhat overdrawn? But, finally, why does Connell seem to have got it wrong? Over-reliance on folk lore and anecdotal evidence may be that answer. Such sources are prone to highlight the dramatic and the unusual. Relying on direct, preferably quantitative, evidence seems a better way out. The point arises in other contexts too: for instance, Connell's use of impressionistic evidence prompted him to underestimate mean age at marriage on the eve of the Famine.[31]

3. Migration and fertility

It is over two decades since Kingsley Davis[32] warned social historians against seeing inheritance customs as exogenous determinants of population change in the long run. The relative autonomy of the superstructure in this sphere has its supporters still, however, and customs such as primogeniture and impartible inheritance generally are identified with the Malthusian preventive check and a low rate of natural increase. In France the rule 'one farm, one household; one household, one family' is held by Jacques Dupaquier to have played a crucial role in stemming population growth; in Germany Berkner has allowed custom considerable autonomy in the long run.[33]

In Ireland's case it is tempting (and probably simplistic) to link the great reduction in nuptiality between the 1850s and the 1930s to a switch to impartible succession. More interesting, though, is the coexistence for decades of apparently high fertility levels and what other studies would envisage as a restrictive succession regime. That Irish fertility remained high after the Famine is universally agreed, though convincing evidence on trend is elusive.

The fruits of one effort at monitoring the trend is spelt out in appendix 7. The apparent rise after 1841 (see appendix 7) may turn out to be a statistical mirage. The subsequent slow but steady fertility decline—confirmed in independent calculations by David Fitzpatrick[34]—suggests that Ireland was a participant, but only a half-hearted one, in the demographic transition mapped out by the Princeton research unit for a growing number of European countries. The implication that after 1881 at least the Irish were not following a 'natural fertility' regime to the letter is interesting, though the concurrent increases in marriage age and celibacy rates were much more significant demographically. Yet fertility levels after the turn of the century remained very high by contemporary European standards. The implied drop in *Ig* between the late 1870s and 1900s was only 5–10 per cent.[35]

Emigration helps explain the sustained coexistence of high fertility and impartible inheritance. The regression analysis in table 46 suggests that the considerable variation in fertility across counties around the turn of the century is associated with their emigration experience. Regressions 1 and 2 are in terms of fertility levels, while in 3 the dependent variable is the proportionate change in fertility. LOWVAL is the proportion of farms valued at under £7. Inferences about causality from

TABLE 46 Fertility and emigration regressions

	Dependent variable		
Variables	(1) FERT 81	(2) FERT11	(3) DFERT
EMIGR	286·69 (43·02)	463·99 (65·81)	84·48 (57·22)
PRCATH	0·631 (0·236	1·006 (0·362)	–0·249 (–0·32)
LOVAL			2·781 (0·622)
Constant	460·69	320·40	–160·36
RSQ	0·691	0·732	0·572
F	35·67	39·68	12·49

Note. FERT81 and FERT 11 are the marital fertility estimates for adjusted *Ig*, as explained in appendix 7. DFERT is simply FERT11–FERT81. EMIGR is calculated as the cohort depletion of those up to fifteen years of age between 1881 and 1911. This crude measure is probably more reliable than the official emigration statistics. Standard errors are given in parentheses.

emigration to fertility are perhaps not warranted: the argument may equally run the other way. And yet it is the failure of Irish fertility to follow a common European pattern that is to be explained.

As cross-section estimates go, the regression results are not bad. The implied fertility elasticity, calculated at the mean values of the variables, is statistically significant but low; of those who emigrated, less than half were 'replaced' through higher fertility.

Nineteenth-century American demographic history provides

an analogy: there Francis Walker argued that immigration reduced the natural fertility of the indigenous population, substituting 'ready-made' adults from across the seas for the averted births.[36] The high Irish fertility of that period is nowadays often equated with 'backwardness': perhaps a fuller view, which considers children as pleasant but costly objects, would regard the high fertility, from a welfare standpoint, as one of the benefits of emigration. In the newspeak of economics the psychic pleasure to the parents and society of bearing the children, knowing full well that they were destined to emigrate, may be approximated by the cost of their upbringing minus emigrant remittances. Alternatively, as Mokyr and I have explained elsewhere, that cost may be equated with the foregone earnings of the emigrants in Ireland.[37]

The size of this boon will have depended not only on the volume but on the age structure of the emigration. Earlier attempts to put it at 1–2 per cent of national income in the immediate pre-Famine years, and at 1–3 per cent in the 1950s and 1960s. In the latter period a big dent is made in it by emigrant remittances and emigrant tourism.

In one sense this sum may be regarded as an economic loss to Ireland from emigration. This is how the analogous gain to United States has been interpreted by Uselding and others.[38] However, one can equally admit that 'the great psychological satisfaction in rearing children normally compensates for such monetary sacrifice as is involved'.[39] In the Irish case, then, emigration allowed the luxuries of both impartible inheritance and large families. The inheritance system is endogenised, partly at least.

4. Wills and dowries

Thus far we have focused exclusively on the implications of inheritance practice for the male issue. And, of course, wills were mostly male affairs. Land mostly passed from male to male, largely in front of male witnesses. Yet they can also tell us some-thng about women's economic status. Farmers' widows regularly featured as legatees when no son was old enough to take over; when a son got the farm, usually the mother's interests were taken care of. But more interesting is the provision made for daughters. Testators typically made provision for their unmarried daughters.

The dowry or 'fortune' was part of a custom called the 'match', the arranged marriage so well analysed by Kenneth Connell. The following account from County Longford captures its most important features.[40]

What usually happened was that the boy or his parents sent some person to the girl's parents first to sound them out about the match and get their opinion. If the parents were satisfied, then the boy and the girl, and the parents, fathers anyway of the boy and girl respectively, would meet, and the man who started the negotiations would be there too. They'd meet in some pub in the town.

The discussion then took place about how much money the girl had and what land, stock, etc., the boy had. The boy's parents and brothers and sisters would be discussed also, whether they expected any of the fortune or not . . . Fifty years ago from £70 to £100 was a good dowry. The dowry was paid on the morning of the marriage, before the ceremony took place. The bridegroom called to the bride's house, before the ceremony.

The costs of the match in terms of romantic bliss are often highlighted. To mention a well known source, Sissy O'Brien of the famous farm by Lougu Gur could remember only one marriage 'for love or by the lovers' own choice' in her part of east Limerick. For the rest 'in those days young girls had nothing to look forward to but a loveless marriage, hard work, poverty, a large family and often a husband who drank'.[41]

In the Longford example just quoted and in many other descriptions the fathers are part of the haggling associated with the match. But what if they died? In that event the sum set aside in wills may be regarded as the cost of entry for the farmer's daughter to another holding similar to her own in size. Considerations such as the prestige of having a priest in the family or the farming skills of the prospective partners played a part. Hence 'is fearr bean ná spré' ('the woman is worth more than the dowry'). Family size also played a role: an only daughter stood a better chance than one of five or six. In the end, though, 'the son of a small farmer would only get a small fortune, and the daughter of a small farmer would only have a small fortune to get'.[42] Or in Arensberg's words, 'fortune and farm must be roughly equivalent'.[43] Indeed, the fortune received by the 'favoured' son was often seen as dowry for one of his sisters.

Were the sums set aside for fortunes rising over time? Much of the recent literature on the condition of women in post-Famine Ireland suggests that they should have been. The decline in domestic industry, the shift in farming from tillage to pasture and the decline in the ranks of farm labourers are all seen as injurious to women's bargaining power; the high and rising share of women in the emigrant outflow from the rural areas was the result.[44] Why should change in ratio tell us anything? Imagine a world of farmers, half of whom have only sons, the other half daughters. Those with daughters are 'unlucky' in the sense that they must give their daughters dowries, say £100 each, in order to marry a farmer's son. Suppose this continues until, suddenly, there is a demand for female workers abroad. Some daughters leave, and farmers with sons musta ccept those who remain as marriage partners for dowries less than £100. A drop in the value of the dowry may therefore be regarded as a sign of improved times for women. On the other hand, a reduction in the demand for female labour would induce farmers to pay their daughters bigger dowries relative to the value of their properties as a marriage-ticket. Table 47 therefore analyses the proportion dowries bore to the probate value of wills in samples drawn from c. 1860–78 and c. 1900–20.

TABLE 47 *The trend in dowry shares (number of observations in parentheses)*

Probate value (£)	Share c. 1870	Share c. 1910
0–100	2·065 (16)	1·535 (41)
101–200	0·641 (23)	0·785 (40)
201–300	0·583 (23)	0·431 (36)
301–450	0·524 (19)	0·353 (23)
451–600	0·468 (31)	0·399 (11)
601–1,000	0·283 (16)	0·265 (12)
Over 1,000	0·275 (27)	0·162 (12)
Total	0·631 (155)	0·729 (175)

Note. In the first period the exact probate value is rarely given. Descriptions such as 'under £100', 'under £200', 'under £450', etc., are used instead. In tabulating we used the mean of the appropriate interval.

The samples were taken from the will books of Waterford, Cork, Limerick and Tuam registration districts.[45] Bequests to married women were excluded: when two or more daughters were given different amounts the largest sum mentioned was used.

Given the small number of observations, perhaps not too much should be made of the results. Nevertheless the tendency for the share of dowries to decline with an increase in probate value is clear enough. Second, the increase in the mean share over time seems to be due to more smallholders making wills. Most important, the tendency for the will/probate share to fall over time holds across size of probate.

Table 48 tells the story in another way, by using simple regression analysis to explain the variation in dowry provision by size of probate. The evidence here is that the provision made for daughters dropped relative to probate value in the few decades before the Great War. Women who stayed at home thus seem to

TABLE 48 Regression predictions

Probate	1870s	1910s
50	115	77
100	126	89
200	148	113
500	211	159
750	262	193
1,000	311	217
3,000	638	368
RSQ	0·44	0·28
N	155	175

Note. A quadratic was used for the first regression, a cubic term was added for the second.

have bettered their bargaining position. Is this all that surprising? After all, in the late nineteenth century emigrant women seem to have been improving their lot relative to men: why shouldn't their stay-at-home sisters have done likewise?

A final comment. The two main inferences drawn from the wills—those of intra-familial 'fairness' and a fall in dowry share—may seem to add some cheer to the standard view of post-Famine rural life. Still, I hope that they are not read as evidence of a 'harmony' or idyllic view of those times. If living standards were rising, there is still evidence aplenty against such a view in the simmering tensions between labourer and farmer and in the very uneven division of the spoils of the Land War. But those issues are best discussed elsewhere.

Appendix 7 Irish marital fertility after the Famine

This appendix is an attempt at providing a rough indication of the course of marital fertility after mid-century. Table 50 presents my estimate of a standard measure of marital fertility, I_g, for the thirty-two counties. The results, while resting on shaky foundations, are not implausible.

Irish marital fertility trends after the Famine are something of a puzzle. Estimation from censal data is bedevilled by under-recording; information of infant mortality is lacking, and, more generally, there are no adequate civil registration data. However, both infant mortality and under-registration declined in time. Using the number of children under one year or up to four years to calculate the trend in fertility will therefore produce an upward bias. The following procedure has been adopted here. The basis of the numerator in the calculation is the number of recorded children aged up to four years; corrections for infant mortality and under-recording yield Ig. A drop in infant mortality from about 225 thousand in 1841 (250 in Connacht and Munster, 200 in Ulster and Leinster) to 150 (165 and 135) in 1881 and 100 (110 and 90) in 1911 has been assumed. A drop in child under-registration from 10 per cent in 1841 to 7 per cent in 1881 and 5 per cent in 1911 has been supposed. The Hutterite weights have been used, with interpolation where necessary. The 1841 and 1851 data are the most problematic. There are some obvious anomalies, and the 1851 data in many counties probably reflect the effects of the Famine (as might be expected from our discussion in chapter 3). The data indicate no change or even a slight rise in fertility between 1841 and 1881 and a drop generally thereafter. The results for the early years are not used in our calculations here: those for 1881 and 1911, used in the regressions, are not implausible. The Hutterite weights used were the following:

	1841		1851 and later
Under 17	0·550	17–24	0·550
17–25	0·550	25–34	0·475
26–35	0·475	35–44	0·320
36–45	0·300	45–54	0·035
46–54	0·020		

TABLE 49 Calculated I_gs, 1841-1911

	1841	1851	1881	1911
Carlow	772	718	798	735
Louth	697	725	782	721
Dublin	578	573	605	582
Kildare	791	796	816	681
Kilkenny	764	755	830	757
King's	772	764	800	743
Longford	752	751	833	768
Meath	767	800	856	724
Queen's	817	748	822	752
Westmeath	782	750	830	708
Wexford	782	772	808	741
Wicklow	824	818	809	676
Clare	773	697	935	848
Cork	743	693	839	734
Kerry	726	690	932	911
Limerick	796	707	850	786
Tipperary	775	748	868	783
Waterford	887	693	812	725
Antrim	731	722	728	598
Armagh	752	728	753	598
Cavan	764	776	818	792
Donegal	796	790	844	881
Down	769	754	777	649
Fermanagh	794	751	806	778
Derry	778	774	794	725
Monaghan	739	713	816	760
Tyrone	786	791	807	730
Galway	495	684	870	909
Leitrim	925	781	887	886
Mayo	750	682	886	917
Roscommon	758	750	904	840
Sligo	771	752	870	896

Appendix 8 How the data were collected

The two lists on the following pages give the flavour of the data on which the analysis is based. The terms of the wills are as transcribed in the will books deposited in the Public Record Office, and the probate values as in the testamentary index for the relevant year. The first set (1–30) is taken from the Cavan Registration District and the second (1–48) from the Cork registration District.

1. Lavey, 1895 (probate value £35). Farm to wife for Thos. Patrick (eldest) executor.
2. Loughtee, 1883 (probate value £201). Part of house and £20 to wife. Farm to John. Any money in bank to be divided equally between ten children.
3. Drumeel, 1891 (probate value £73). Farm to Wm. £100 ea. to Hannah and Marianne, £5 p.a. to Margrate as long as she remains in house, 1s to Thos. If Wm. doesn't come home, farm to Marianne, £200 to Hannah.
4. Cornamuckla, 1892 (probate value £84). £75 to Rose, farm to Jas. if he returns home; otherwise to testator's brother.
5. Ardagh, 1893 (probate value £267). One farm to Mary, other to Lizzy (no sons, girls minors).
6. Abbeylara, 1894 (probate value £113). Farm to Thos. £60 ea. to Mary and Bridget if they leave home, 1s ea. to Patk, Ml, Cath. (in America) 'in case they at any time return back they can never give any annoyance to the family here who remained by me till death'.
7. Shercock, 1982 (probate value £68). Farm to Jas., but some fields to Kate.
8. Enniskeen, 1886. Farm (ten acres) to wife for Patrick, £20 ea. to Bridget and Rose.
9. Cavan, 1984 (probate value £230). Farm to Frederick; if he dies, to George.
10. Glasdrummond, 1890 (probate value £131). Farm to wife and Josiah for jt. use, £70 to Margaret (subject to her marrying with consent of rector), £20 to John Jas.
11. Knockbride, 1892 (probate value £177). Farm to wife 'to give a share to each according to her means'.
12. Urcher, 1894 (probate value £484). Farms equally divided between Hugh and Jas., 'including the land recently purchased from my son Patrick'. Support for wife. £30 for Mary (married) in New York, £3 to Patrick.
13. Commas, 1892 (probate value £306). Farm to David, to support wife and Ann.
14. Killelandrick, 1896 (probate value £27). Farm to Francis, £12 to Patk., £10 to Rose.
15. Ballintemple, 1896 (probate value £233). Farm to Wm., £160 to Edw., £50 to Patk. after five years (in US).
16. Doreagh, 1896 (probate value £235). Farm to wife for son (in Africa), part of bequest to El. Jane.
17. Drumgoon, 1891 (probate value £35). Farm to Jas., subject to 1s. ea. to Robt., John, Mgt. Ann; £3 to Eliza Jane, £5 to Wm., £5 to David,

£20 plus calf to Matilda.

18. Dring, 1894 (probate value £77). Farm (fourteen acres) to Eugene, 1s. ea. to seven others.

19. Gowlan (probate value £896). 'four parts to be made of everything I may die possessed of'; one to Moses, others to wife for daughters.

20. Rathmore, 1891 (probate value £289). Farm to wife in trust for John subject to ten ea. to twelve others.

21. Drumlish, 1895 (probate value £96). Farm (twenty acres— to Patk., £40 to Francis, £70 to Mary, three acres plus board for wife.

22. Denn, 1896 (probate value £218). £70 to John (eldest), farm to Hugh, £70 to Patk., £1 to Owen. Farm to Patk., if Hugh doesn't hold it, and £70 then to Hugh.

23. Ballymahon, 1896. Farm to Francis subject to £100 to Peter, £10 to Michael, £595 to others (priests, gdch.), residue to Michael.

24. Mullagh, 1894 (probate value £88). Fourteen acres to Mary as marriage settlement, fifty acres to Francis (subject to £12 2s 6d p.a. to Irish Land Commission), £10 plus site to Cath. if she returns from America.

25. Castlerahan, 1896 (probate value £183). Farm to wife for Mary.

26. Tullyboy (probate value £205). Farm to Thos., £70 to Leander, £30 to John (in America) 'if should ask it'.

27. Kldrumsheridan, 1895 (probate value £130). Farm to Robt., £40 to Wm., £20 to Elizabeth, care for wife.

28. Urcher, 1855 (probate value £98). Farm to wife; but is she marries, 2s 6d to her, £7 to Jas. (eldest) 'providing he emigrates to America or Australia', byt 'on no account' is he to get farm. farm to Thos., otherwise Laurence, bound 'to assist in settling their younger sisters'.

29. Cloone, 1894 (probate value £325). Farm to Ml., subject to £150 to Patk., £100 ea. to Mgt., Mary Anne, Eliza.

30. Kilnaleck, 1896 (probate value £79). Farm to John support to wife, £10 to Ml., 1s each to four daughters.

1. Drimoleague, 1896 (probate value £218). Farm to Patk., £100 to Daniel, £100 to Mary.

2. Carrigeen, 1897 (probate value £37). Farm to youngest son, £70 to Mgt.

3. Lisgoold, 1897 (probate value £839). £400 to eldest son, rest to second son subject to care and his marriage portion to wife.

4. Clonfert, 1897 (probate value £189?). Farm ea. to Benjamin and Jerh., both to look after wife (turf, potatoes, etc.).

5. Bridgemount, 1885 (probate value £569). Farm to eldest son, room for Patk. (executor), £250 for Cath.

6. Dooneens, 1895 (probate value £298). Farm held in trust by wife for David till he marries, when he pays Peter £300 and mother £10 p.a. plus keep.

7. Glounamuckla, 1894 (probate value £500). Divided between Dennis and Thos., latter getting specified land plus fifteen cows, horse and car, proper house; former to pay mother £12 p.a. plus care, £200 ea. to Hannah and Barth., £100 in eleven years time) to Danl.

8. Ballinoriskig, 1895 (probate value £184). Farm to Patk., £60 to Annie.

9. Newcestown, 1894 (probate value £242). Farm, etc., to parents, £200 to 'beloved wife'.

10. Gurranegoppel (probate value £409). Farm to Batt., £160 to Mary.

11. Gurteen, 1896. £200 plus two sheep to Cath., £40 plus yearling colt to Dennis 'but it is my further will and desire that said Dennis will have more sense in future', remainder to Patk.

12. Killinadrish, 1891 (probate value £200). Farm to Patk., £100 to Ellen, care plus £5 p.a. for wife.

13. Drumnim, 1894 (probate value £155). Farm to Daniel (aged eighteen), £50 plus care for mother, £55 between two younger sisters when twenty-one, £20 to Ellen and £20 ea. to 'Norah and Julia now in America in case they demand it on return from America'.

14. Ballyclough, 1894 (probate value £726). Farm to Arthur, £100 ea. to Thos., Wm., and Edw., care plus £5 p.a. for wife.

15. Coolgreen, 1898 (probate value £177). Farm, etc., to two sons, 'conjointly and in equal shares', £200 to Mgt. 'whenever a suitable opportunity offers for her marriage'.

16. Carriganimid, 1897. Pub and farm to wife to leave to Cornelius, £8 ea. to Danl. and Patk.

17. Coolbane, 1898 (probate value £402). Farm, etc., to Thos., £300 between Mary and Ellen, young colt and donkey and the grass of two yearlings to John 'until he comes of age'.

18. Dunmanway, 1898 (probate value £479). Divided equally between Danl. and Timothy.

19. Lismire, 1883 (probate value £151). Farm to Dennis, £250 plus beds to Honora.

20. Corbally, 1898 (probate value £709). Farm to brother, £340 to wife, £200 to child 'if my wife Julia have issue by me'.

21. Lislee, 1897 (probate value £133). Farm to Jas., £36 to Danl., £80 to Cath., support for wife.

22. Lisquinlan, 1895 (probate value £889). 'Old farm' to Timothy, 'middle farm' plus some other land equally divided between Jas. and Ml.; stock, crops shared equally between the three, £200 plus keep for Margaret and Anne, paid by sons.

23. Garryvoe, 1897 (probate value £135). Farm to wife 'for the benefit of my beloved sons, John, Timothy and Maurice'.

24. Ballymakeigh, 1897 (probate value £667). Farm to eldest son, Pierce, who is to maintain uncle, £200 to Maurice, £200 to Mary Ellen.

25. Clonard, 1895 (probate value £445). £120 to Danl., £120 to Mgt., £80 to Ellen, £40 to Richd., rest to Wm.

26. Ballinagone, 1898 (probate value £349). Farm to Maurice, £200 plus keep for Ellen, £50 plus keep for mother.

27. Dripsey, 1898 (probate value £854). Farm to wife for 'one of my sons Timothy or Denis', eldest son Barth. housed and clothed and always fed at the same table; 'who gets my farm and place shall do as best he can for his sisters and brothers and mother'.

28. Lisaniskey, 1897 (probate value £213). Farm to wife for Ml., £50 to Jas., £30 to Wm.

29. Liscahane, 1898 (provate value £7,254). Farm to my wife to be 'divided between my children as it shall seem fit and proper to my wife'.

30. Ahilnane, 1897 (probate value £282). Farm to elder son Denis at age thirty-one, subject to fiar provision of executor for other son John and Johanna. Wife to be 'properly dieted and cared for'.

31. Knockroe, 1898 (probate value £376). Farm to John, £40 for Sarah, keep for wife (plus £50 if John marries), keep for Anne and Richd. 'as long as they wish to reside', £50 for Richd., £50 for Anne, £30 for Ellen, £10 for Elizabeth (married).

32. Ballymacshoneen, 1886 (probate value £215). Farm to wife and Daniel, share and share alike, subject to £5 ea. to Norah and Kate. 'It is my express will and wish that no part of my property should be given to any of my children who have emigrated or left my house to fend for themselves.'

33. Dromtariffe, 1878. Farm at Islandohill to Patk., £200 to Ellen plus £10 p.a. Another son Terry co-executor.

34. Liscubba, 1890 (probate value £440). Choice of two farms (£30 and £40 rent, held from Reginald Bence-Jones) to John; other to Jas. Stock, etc., in equal shares. £170 to Alice, £20 to Mary (married); 'such sums of money to be paid to my younger sons Cornelius, Edward and Richard . . . as . . . will be equitable and proper for their advancement in life having regard to the value of said farms'. Brothers John and Cornelius to be looked after whoever chooses the better farm; other duties fall on both farms equally.

35. Clonakilty, 1898 (probate value £80). Farm to wife for Con., and to daughter Ellen Casey if Con. dies without issue. Should daughter Nellie Daly return from America, a room and a quarter of manured land provided her husband does not reside with her.

36. Derrileagh, 1883 (probate value £624). Farm with house to Patk., other to Garrett, stock shared equally. Wm. to get £30 chargeable on Garrett. Patk. to keep John.

37. Castlemaine, 1898 (probate value £290). Farm tow ife for Wm., who is to marry within three yrs. Then £120 to Lucy. Otherwise wife does as she thinks proper.

38. Coneybeg, 1898 (probate value £71). 'To be divided equally between my said three children.'

39. Cahirkirky, 1882 (probate value £150). Twenty-five acres of lease-hold land to Richd. plus four cows, a horse, two calves, four sheep, and 'what pigs I have'. To John and Jerh. the house plus six acres, a cow, two sheep, a calf, and use of Richd.'s implements and horse.

40. Killinardrish, 1897 (probate value £261). Farm to John, keep plus £6 p.a. for 'dear dear wife', £160 plus keep to Danl. while unmarried, £40 to Honora.

41. Aglish, 1898 (probate value £301). Farm to Michl., £200 plus £8 p.a. to Timothy (provided T. works on farm), £250 to Nora, keep for wife.

42. Donoughmore, 1897 (probate value £423). Farm to Timothy, £200 to Lizzie plus room and support, £100 to Jerh. plus £5 yearly for assistance on farm. Timothy to pay debts and 'keep old servant man Michael

Callaghan during his life'.

43. Roscarbery, 1897 (probate value £298). To wife to provide for 'all my children'; 'should she hand over the farms to any of my sons the said son do give her two hundred pounds as a help towards settling down the other members of my family'.

44. Ballyrichard, 1897 (probate value £368). home farm (fifty-two acres) plus cattle to Thos., eighteen acres plus mare, ten sheep, three heifers to Con., £50 to 'my child Ellen', £200 to Maggie. Thos. to support mother.

45. Pruntus, 1893 (probate value £823). Farm to Mathew, subject to maintenance of testator's sister, and £200 ea. to Johanna, Bridget, Mary.

46. Kilnamartyra, 1898 (probate value £262). Farm to Danl., £250 to Hannah, £12 p.a. plus keep for wife. Danl. to pay executors £250 in lieu of farm when he marries. Shilling clause.

47. Clondrohid, 1899 (probate value £264). Farm to wife 'to provide for herself and my children in such manner as she and my son John think most prudent'.

48. Lactify, 1895 (probate value £254). Farm to Patk. nine years from testator's death; £100 to Mgt.; £100 ea. to Michael and Julia if they work the place for nine years.

Notes

1 E. Le Roy Ladurie, 'Family structures and inheritance customs in sixteenth-century France', in J. Goody *et al.*, *Family and Inheritance: Rural Society in Western Europe 1200-1800* (Cambridge, 1976), pp. 37-70.

2 Le Roy Ladurie, 'Family structures'; A. Hermalin and E. van de Walle, 'The civil code and nuptiality: empirical investigation of a hypothesis', in R. D. Lee (ed.), *Population Patterns in the Past* (New York, 1977), pp. 71-112; L. Berkner, 'Inheritance, land tenure and peasant family structures', in Goody *et al.*, pp. 71-95; *id.*, 'Peasant household organization and demographic change in Lower Saxony (1689-1766), in Lee (ed.), *Population Patterns*, pp. 53-70; J. W. Cole and E. R. Wolf, *The Hidden Frontier: Ecology and Ethnicity in an Alpine Valley* (New York, 1974); J. Goy, 'Permanences et changements: les baronies pyrenéennes aux 18e et 19e siècles', in L. M. Cullen and T. C. Smout (eds,), *Irlande et France, XVIIe-XXe siècles: pour une histoire rurale comparée* (Paris, 1981), pp. 139-48; Lee Alston and M. O. Schapiro, 'Inheritance laws across colonies: causes and consequences', *Journal of Economic History*, XLIV (1984), 277-87.

3 Cf. Devon Commission, Part I, Appendix 14; P. O'Flanagan, 'Rural change south of the river Bride in Counties Cork and Waterford: the surveyors' evidence, 1716-1851', *Irish Geography*, XV (1982), 51-69; J. H. Andrews, *A Paper Landscape: the Ordnance Survey in Nineteenth Century Ireland* (Oxford, 1975).

4 Kenneth H. Connell, 'Marriage in Ireland after the Famine: the diffusion of the match', *Journal of theStatistical and Social Inquiry Society of Ireland*, XIX (1956), 82-103.

5 T. C. Murray, *The Pipe in the Field and Birthright* (Dublin, 1928).

6 S. Ó Fáoláin, *A Nest of Simple Folk* (London, 1925).

7 Patrick Kavanagh, *The Great Hunger* (London, 1944).

8 Hugh Brody, *Inishkillane: Change and Decline in the West of Ireland* (London, 1973).

9 R. D. Lee, introduction to Lee (ed.), *Population Patterns*, p. 4.

10 Goy, 'Permanences et changements'. P. Bourdieu, 'Célibat et condition paysanne', *Etudes Rurales* (1962), Nos. 5-6; 'Les stratégies matrimoniales dans le système

de reproduction', *Annales E.S.C.*, July 1972.

11 Berkner, 'Peasant household organization . . . in Lower Saxony'. For an analysis of the effects of birth order in an Irish urban setting see B. M. Walsh, 'Marital status and birth order in a sample of Dublin males', *Journal of Biosocial Science*, 5 (2) (1973), 187–93.

12 K. H. Connell, 'Marriage in Ireland'; *id.*, 'Peasant marriage in Ireland after the great Famine', *Past and Present*, No. 12 (1957); *id.*, 'Peasant marriage in Ireland: its structure and development after the Famine', *Economic History Review*, ser. 2, XIV (1962), 76–91; *id.*, 'Catholicism and marriage in the century following the Famine', in *Irish Peasant Society* (Oxford, 1968), pp. 113–62; K. Arensberg and S. Kimball, *Family and Community in Ireland*, 2nd ed. (Cambridge, 1968); K. Arensberg, *The Irish Countryman* (London, 1937), chapter 3.

13 J. C. W. Wylie, *Irish Land Law* (Dublin, 1975), chapters 14–15.

14 See D. Fitzpatrick, 'Class, family and rural unrest in nineteenth-century Ireland', in P. J. Drudy (ed.), *Ireland: Land, Politics and People* (Cambridge, 1982), pp. 37–76.

15 David Thompson and M. McGusty (eds.), *The Irish Journals of Elizabeth Smith* (Oxford, 1980), pp. 120–2.

16 All the wills and probate material consulted are held in the Public Record Office, Dublin. They are identified by name, county, and year of probate. Many of the wills analysed date from before tenant purchase. It may seem curious to find neither lawyer nor landlord objecting to farmers' bequeathing property which, strictly speaking, was not theirs to bequeath–but that is another story.

17 Maurice McGuire, 'Rural inheritance in nineteenth-century Ireland', *Dal gCais* (1984).

18 Compare Ó Gráda, 'Primogeniture and ultimogeniture in rural Ireland', *Journal of Interdisciplinary History*, X (1980), 491–7.

19 Will of Patrick McDonagh, Galway, 1911.

20 Will of Luke Lee, Longford, 1915.

21 Compare from O'Faoláin: 'Will Leo portion off the girls? What will happen Phil? How can your daughters ever marry if they're depending on this encumbered bit of land? James will never be able to think of marrying. They will all be impoverished for life. It's a most unusual will. Your husband will never agree to it.' (*A Nest*, p. 62.)

22 Lee, 'Introduction', in Lee (ed.), *Population Patterns*, p. 4.

23 Saorstát Éireann, *1926 Census* (Dublin, 1930), vol. 5, Part 2, pp. 60–5.

24 The 'English Canadian system of inheritance' described by David Gagan for Peel County, Ontario, closely parallels the custom explained here. The Canadian system was a solution to 'the problem of attempting to reconcile the legitimate claims of most, if not all . . . heirs, with [farmers'] unwillingness to liquidate the capital investment represented by real property, their principal form of wealth, in order to provide settlements for their heirs equitable both in kind and degree'. A big difference, however, is the role of emigration in the Irish system, as explained below. David Gagan, 'The indivisibility of land: a microanalysis of the system of inheritance in nineteenth-century Ontario', *Journal of Economic History*, 36 (1976), 126–41.

25 Ó Gráda, 'Primogeniture'.

26 R. E. Kennedy, Jr., *The Irish: Emigration, Marriage and Fertility* (Berkeley, Cal., 1973), pp. 203–4.

27 US Bureau of Statistics, *Labor in Europe and America* (Philadelphia, 1875), pp. 359–61, 375, 739–47, 798–9.

28 Paul A. David and P. M. Solar, 'A bicentenary contribution to the history of the cost of living in America', *Research in Economic History*, II (1977), 1–80.

29 J. F. Maguire, *The Irish in America* (London, 1869), pp. 331–2; US Immigration Commission, vol. 2 (Washington, D.C., 1911), p. 427; vol. 37, pp. 273–4. See also Arnold Schrier, *Ireland and the American Migration* (Minneapolis, 1956), chapter 5. The Immigration Commission's estimate may be conservative, in so far as it assumes that the Irish remitted less per head than other United Kingdom

emigrants.
30 Mary E. Daly, 'Social structure of the Dublin working class, 1871–1911', *Irish Historical Studies*, XXIII (1982), 121–33.
31 Compare M. Drake, 'Marriage and population growth in Ireland, 1750–1845', *Economic History Review*, ser. 2, XVI (1963), 301–13.
32 Kingsley Davis, 'The theory of change and response in demographic history', *Population Index*, 29 (1963), 345–66.
33 Jacques Dupâquier, 'De l'animal a l'homme: le mecanisme autorégulateur des populations traditionelles', *Revue de l'Institut de Sociologie*, No. 2 (1972), 177–211; Berkner, 'Peasant household organization'. Also Gary D. Libecap and George Alter, 'Agricultural productivity, partible inheritance, and the demographic response to rural poverty: an examination of the Spanish southwest', *Explorations in Economic History*, 19 (1982), 184–200.
34 I have greatly benefited from discussion with Dr David Fitzpatrick about this issue.
35 M. Livi-Bacci argues that emigration allowed nineteenth-century Italians to maintain high fertility. Knodel's parallel study of Germany suggests that the association between high fertility and emigration is due to both being caused by 'backwardness'. LOWVAL in our regression .i3; (3) attempts to control for such backwardness.
M. Livi-Bacci, *A History of Italian Fertility during the last two Centuries* (Princeton, N.J., 1977), pp. 269, 276; John Knodel, *The Decline of German Fertility* (Princeton, N.J., 1973), p. 222.
36 W. S. Thompson and P. K. Whelpton, *Population Trends in the United States* (New York, 1933).
37 Joel Mokyr and C. Ó Gráda, 'Emigration and poverty in prefamine Ireland', *Explorations in Economic History*, 19 (1982), 360–84.
38 Paul Uselding, 'Conjectural estimates of gross human capital inflow to the American economy, 1790–1860', *Explorations in Economic History*, XI (1971), 49–61; Larry Neal and Paul Uselding, 'Immigration, a neglected source of American economic growth, 1790–1912', *Oxford Economic Papers*, XXIV (1972), 68–88.
39 Commission on Emigration and other Population Problems, *Report* (Dublin, 1956), p. 140.
40 Connell, 'Peasant marriage'; Coimisiún Béaloideasa Éireann (Irish Folklore Commission), 1480/472-3.
41 Mary Carbery, *The Farm by Lough Gur* (London, 1937), p. 47. Still, one must not make too much of such earnest claims. As my colleague Brendan Walsh points out, all but the first outcome would have ensued from even the most romantic marriages!
42 C.B.E., 1481/146.
43 Arensberg, *The Irish Countryman*, p. 77.
44 Joseph Lee, 'Women and the Church since the Famine', in Margaret McCurtain and Donnchadh Ó Corráin (eds.), *Women in Irish Society: the Historical Dimension* (Dublin, 1979), pp. 37–8; Hasia Diner, *Erin's Daughters in America* (Baltimore, Md., 1983), chapter 1; Robert E. Kennedy, *The Irish*, p. 84. Between 1851 and 1881 County Clare, for example, lost slightly more males than females, but between 1881 and 1911 it lost 66·6 per cent of its fifteen-to-twenty-four-year-old males and 69·6 per cent of its females. In Mayo in the latter period the percentages were 65·9 and 71.
45 The sample is based on a exhaustive search of the will books. Waterford contributed only to the first period, Tuam only to the second. Cork and Limerick produced data for both periods. The greater preponderance of small wills in the later period is due in large part to Tuam.

INDEX

Act of Union, 27-8
ageing, 143-5, 151
agricultural implements, 56, 70-3, 142
agricultural output, 47-52, 68-70, 128-30
agriculture, 46-77, 128-51
Allen, Robert C., 61, 76
Ambirajan, S., 79
Aran Islands, 118-22
Arensberg, Conrad, 156

banks, 28-30
Barker, Francis, and John Cheyne, 4
Belfast, 27, 30
Bentinck, Lord George, 78, 117
Berkner, Lutz, 155, 163
Bianconi, Charles, 31
Bicheno, John, 16, 46, 53, 138
Black, R. D. C., 110-11
Boate, Gerard, 65, 129
Bourke, P. M. A., 45, 48-9, 51, 53, 70, 80-1
Boyle, Phelim P., 40, 83, 84
'brain drain', 144-5
Brody, Hugh, 155
Bulfin, Liam, 136

canals, 30
child mortality, 15, 37-8
Chorley, Patrick, 62
Congested Districts Board, 118, 143, 146
Connell, Kenneth H., 1-2, 156, 163, 165
cottage industry, 26
cottiers, 83
Cousens, S. H., 75, 83

Crafts, N. F. R., 59
crop yields, 53, 60-2
Crotty, 50, 118, 129, 130, 131, 143
Cullen, L. M., 40, 45

Daly, Mary E., 81, 116, 117, 176
Daultrey, Stuart, 40
David, Paul A., 161
de Tocqueville, Alexis, 112
Devon Commission, 12, 14
Dickson, David, 40
domestic industry, 21, 23, 26-7
Donnelly, James S., 81, 114, 117
dowries, 165-8
Doyle, Martin, 10
Dublin Society Surveys, 11, 60, 61, 65
Dubourdieu, John, 65
Dutton, Hely, 65

Edgeworth, Maria, 10, 113
Edwards, Robin D., and T. D. Williams, 79, 80, 116, 126
efficiency wage, 55-6, 75, 116
emigration, 144-5, 163-5
evictions, 115, 131-2
excess mortality, 2-4, 82-8
external economies, 27, 131

famine, 3, 6, 67-70, 78-127
famine relief, 113-18
farming, 59-67, 135-43
Ferguson, Samuel, 118, 119
fertility, marital, 168-9
Fitzpatrick, David, 163
Floud, Roderick, 17
food entitlements, 106-10
Fraser, Robert, 65

Galbraith, John K., 39
'genocide', 81, 122
Ginnell, Lawrence, 144
gombeenmen, 88, 124
Goubert, Pierre, 83
Goy, Joseph, 155, 163
grain yields, 60-4
Great Famine, Ch. 3 *passim*
Green, E. R. R., 27, 80
Gregory clause, 87, 109-10

Hall, Mr and Mrs S. C., 44, 76
Hickey, Patrick, 81, 114, 123, 126, 127
Hoffman, Elizabeth, and Joel Mokyr, 40
Hymer, Stephen, and Stephen Resnick, 33

ideology, 110-16
'indolence', 56, 132, 135-8
industry, 25-8
Inglis, H. D., 12-13
inheritance, 153-68, 170-4
Irish Agricultural Organisation Society, 118, 146
Irish Poor Inquiry, 2-3, 14, 22-3, 75

Kane, Robert, 16
Kavanagh, Patrick, 137, 151, 155
Kennedy, Liam, 75
Kennedy, Robert E., 161
Kravis, Irving, 40
Kuznets, Simon, 33

labour productivity, 51-4, 129-31
land-labour ratio, 52-3
landlord and tenant, 34, 131-5, 148-9
Lee, Joseph J., 143
Lee, Ronald D., 155, 160, 163
Le Roy Ladurie, 153
Lewis, Samuel, 59, 71-3, 76
life expectancy, 15
literacy, 18-20
livestock, 57, 70-3, 128-9, 146-7
living standards, 22-5, 110, 129-31,

161-2
Longfield, Mountifort, 10
Lyons, F. S. L., 80

McCloskey, Donald N., and John Nash, 90, 106
MacDonagh, Oliver, 9
McLysaght, Edward, 136
Maddison, Angus, 40
Malthus, Thomas Robert, 1-2, 6, 24, 25, 39, 118, 153
Martineau, Harriet, 67
Marx, Karl, 83
Mitchel, John, 79, 81
Mokyr, Joel, 6, 8, 9, 13, 17, 83, 117, 165
Murray, T. C., 153, 154

natural grasses, 65
Newenham, Thomas, 4, 38
Nicholls, George, 115

O'Brien, George, 3, 27, 28, 39, 46
Ó Callanáin, Peatsaí, 1
O'Connell, 31, 35, 111, 117
old age pension, 144
O'Neill, Timothy P., 4-5, 39, 126
O'Rourke, John, 81, 86
Ó Súileabháin, Amhlaoimh, 2, 9, 14, 51
overpopulation, 1-3, 24-5, 153

Phytophthora infestans, 3, 35, 82, 118, 119
Pim, Jonathan, 1
Plunkett, Horace, 136
Poor Law, 87, 109, 111-2, 114
Post, John D., 4
potatoes, 8-12
potato prices, 88-106
potato varieties, 1, 11, 90-106, 140-1
probate records, 156-61, 170-4

Rashid, Salim, 89
Ravaillon, Martin, 90
regional differences, 19-21, 70-3, 86-7, 132-5

rent, 34, 115, 131-2
Ricardo, David, 13, 34, 57
Russell, Lord John, 111, 115, 124

Sandberg, Lars, 13
Sen, Amartya K., 79, 82, 106-10
Senior, Nassau William, 67, 111,
    112-13, 125, 138
Slicher van Bath, B., 60
Smith, Adam, 16, 88
soil quality, 53-4, 74-5
Solar, Peter M., 44, 62, 70, 161
Solow, Barbara L., 129, 130, 140,
    149
soup kitchens, 114, 116
subjective impoverishment index,
    22-4

Thackeray, William Makepeace, 2,
    12, 27
transport, 30-1
Trevelyan, Charles E., 10, 67, 111,
    116, 125
Turner, Michael, 149

ultimogeniture, 157-8
Uselding, Paul, 165

Vaughan, William E., 129, 131

wages, 14, 161-2
Wakefield, Edward G., 12, 53, 62,
    64
weeding, 60, 61, 138-9
Wilde, William, 3, 37, 78, 79, 87,
    121
Williams, Charles Wye, 30
wills, 156-68
Woodham-Smith, Cecil, 80, 82,
    122, 125

Young, Arthur, 8, 16, 46, 47, 53,
    60, 76, 77